A JUMP FOR LIFE

A JUMP FOR LIFE

A Survivor's Journal
from Nazi-Occupied Poland

RUTH ALTBEKER CYPRYS

EDITED BY
ELAINE POTTER

WITH A FOREWORD BY
MARTIN GILBERT

LONDON   NEW YORK   SYDNEY   TORONTO

CONTENTS

CONTENTS

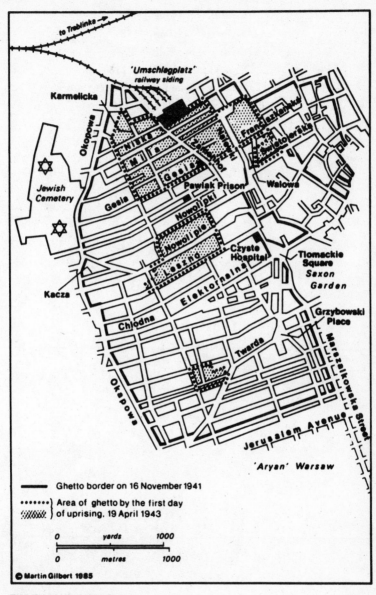

to Treblinka →

'Umschlagplatz'
railway siding

Karmelicka

Okopowa

Mila

Gesia

Jewish
Cemetery

Gesia

Zamenhofa

Pawiak Prison

Nowolipki

Nowolipie

Nowolna

Leszno

Czyste
Hospital

Kacza

Elektoralna

Chłodna

Okopowa

Twarda

Franciszkanska

Świetojerska

Walowa

Tlomackie
Square
Saxon
Garden

Grzybowski
Place

Marszalkowska Street

Jerusalem Avenue

'Aryan' Warsaw

——— Ghetto border on 16 November 1941

•••••• } Area of ghetto by the first day
░░░░░ } of uprising, 19 April 1943

| 0 | yards | 1000 |
| 0 | metres | 1000 |

© Martin Gilbert 1985

THE WARSAW GHETTO

FOREWORD

by MARTIN GILBERT

In the quest for new evidence about the course and nature of the Holocaust, this book shows how important it is to comb every attic and search (as in this case) every chest of drawers. The result of this particular search was the journal of a Jewish woman, Ruth Altbeker, who was born in Warsaw before the First World War, and who survived the Second World War in the most extraordinary circumstances, together with her child, Eva.

When one considers that Warsaw had, before the war, the largest Jewish population after New York, and that this great, dynamic, vibrant society (with its writers, artists, poets, rabbis, philosophers, lawyers, journalists, doctors – the whole panorama of civilised life) was all but wiped out, a document like this is a true treasure.

Ruth Altbeker tells us a great deal about life and death in the Warsaw ghetto, about the terrifying deportations that began in the summer of 1942, about her own incredible escape with her child from a deportation train, and about their subsequent struggle to hide and to be unnoticed as Jews, with the help of Christian Poles. Ruth Altbeker was a witness of the Warsaw ghetto revolt of 1943 from outside the ghetto walls, and of the drama of the Polish uprising of 1944. Her account – fraught with drama to the moment of liberation in 1945 – is extraordinarily moving, gripping the reader with its clarity and its intensity.

Very few Warsaw Jews survived starvation in the ghetto, deportation to the death camp at Treblinka, the crushing of the ghetto revolt, and hiding. If only as a chronicle of survival this book is important. It is more than that. It is a testimony to the human spirit when confronted with adversity and torments that few of us, fortunately, will ever have to face.

Martin Gilbert

EDITOR'S NOTE

No one knows who translated Ruth's story from the Polish into English. What is known and testified to by Ruth's sister, is that it was translated immediately after she had written it in 1946 by a Polish speaking woman. The English version is a very literal translation from the Polish and in many instances too literal. In preparing the book for publication I ironed out some of the gaucheries resulting from the translation, while doing everything possible to keep the sound and sense of Ruth intact. I was very strict in intervening only when sense or syntax dictated. Some of the chapter headings were Ruth's but others I have added to ease the flow and structure of the narrative. I am glad to say that both Eva Panas and Annabelle Boal, Ruth's two daughters, feel that in the journal their mother's voice remains loud and clear.

ACKNOWLEDGEMENTS

I would like to thank Bella Shapiro and Gil Polonsky who brought Eva and me together and whose persistence and friendship ensured that Ruth's story would be heard. Thanks too to Sir Martin Gilbert, who found time in his busy and prolific life to write a foreword to the book, and for giving us permission to reproduce his excellent map of the Warsaw ghetto. And a thank you to our very special publisher, whose editorial director Carol O'Brien saw the power of the book. Finally I would like to thank Eva for finding the courage to face her own story and allowing it to be told.

Elaine Potter

Beginnings

Iᴛ ᴡᴀꜱ ᴀ ɢʀᴇʏ London day, just a few days after her mother's death on 30 March 1979. The grand Edwardian house in Heath Drive, Hampstead, was filled with complex memories. She went into her mother's study touching things which had been hers, idly opening cupboards, glancing randomly at whatever presented itself. Opening one chest of drawers, Annabelle Boal, a twenty-nine-year-old London solicitor, found a pair of bulky, faded, brown envelopes, folded over: inside were sheet upon sheet of closely typed foolscap pages, old-fashioned carbon copies on thin, semi-transparent paper. One envelope contained a document written in Polish, the other in English, clearly a translation. With a sense of foreboding she began to read the English script, and it gradually came to her what she had found. She went to telephone her sister Eva,* ten years older than herself, and intimately involved in what was about to be revealed, to tell her of the find.

Eva Panas, married and with three children of her own, was thirty-nine that spring of 1979 when her mother died. She had long harboured a suspicion that such a document existed but had never sought to find it. On learning that her suspicions had been confirmed, she was overwhelmed with a sense of trepidation and

---

* Her Polish name was Ewa but she adopted the English form of the name after leaving Poland.

misery. It took many weeks before she would even touch it, let alone look at it. 'Every time I would sit down this terrible sick feeling would come over me,' Eva explains, and when she eventually forced herself to deal with it, she could do so only in instalments, each time at great emotional cost. It was a story which had divided the sisters throughout their lives: Eva for having lived it, Annabelle for not being part of it. It would take Eva another fourteen years before she was really willing or able to confront what was revealed in the document, which was her mother's extraordinary account of their lives together in wartime Warsaw, first in the Jewish ghetto and later in Gentile Warsaw. The journal had been written at war's end by Eva's and Annabelle's mother Ruth,* and then hidden away for the rest of her life.

Ruth Altbeker was a lawyer in Warsaw in the 1930s and, as her journal reveals, a quite remarkable survivor. Born in 1910, she was the third of four children from a prosperous and strictly observant Jewish family. Few were as successful as the Altbekers and Ruth was one of only a handful of women to be admitted to the Bar in Warsaw. Ruth's father was an educated man who became a successful jeweller and travelled frequently throughout Europe on business. He regularly spoke German to his children and brought them up to respect and admire German literature and culture, though the family spoke Polish among themselves. Many members of the Jewish community spoke Yiddish at home but the Altbekers' decision to immerse their children in both German and Polish gave Ruth a fluency and an unaccented mastery of the Polish language which was to help save her life. By the time the children were born, the Altbekers could afford maids and nannies and to have their two eldest children, both sons, educated at home by a resident tutor. Ruth and her younger sister Esther went to kindergarten and then to a Gymnasium or senior school, where Ruth excelled and established herself as the family member with the greatest aptitude for learning.

In 1929 Ruth enrolled at Warsaw University to study law, though she was permitted to do so only on condition that she abide by certain rules imposed by her very orthodox father. Thus on

---

* Her Polish name was Ruta but over the years she came to be called Ruth, the name we have used for her throughout this book.

Saturdays, the Jewish sabbath, she had to walk to lessons if there were any, her books had to be covered in newspaper so as to give the appearance of being prayer books and she would have to be on time for Saturday lunch. In other ways too they were a strict and obedient family, where the will of the parents was wholly respected and embraced. In 1936 Esther, the younger daughter, regarded as the rebel of the family because of her Zionism, returned to Warsaw from Palestine expressly to ask permission of her parents to have children. Such permission had to be obtained if a younger sister considered having a child before an older sister, regardless of other considerations: in this case, Esther had been married for two years and had been living far from home for more than half a decade.

Ruth was an outstanding student, conscientious, clever, and very disciplined. She was often applauded by the tutors and cited as an example of excellence to fellow students. One among them was George Joshua Cyprys,* a large, handsome, dark-haired man from Sierpc, a small village outside Warsaw. His family was also Jewish, though as the only Jews in their village they were not very rigid in their observance. George had a more cavalier attitude to his studies than Ruth and was altogether less interested in law than she was, but the two students were drawn to each other and two years after graduating from Warsaw University, on Christmas Day in 1934, they married. By then both George and Ruth had completed their articles – George at the Warsaw District Council, Ruth at a well-established law firm in Warsaw, specializing in criminal law. The young couple set up home at 6 Przechodnia Street, where they also set up in legal practice together.

Warsaw in the thirties was the metropolitan centre of Poland and the largest Jewish centre in Europe. Ruth often dressed up in her furs and expensive jewellery for a night out at the theatre or the cinema. In the winter she and George went to the mountains, they walked and they skied. They travelled to Italy and elsewhere in Europe, to Prague and to other centres which rivalled Warsaw as watering-holes of the affluent. Ruth would always tell her children about how lively a town Warsaw had been, with its superabundance of pastry and fashion shops and its magnetic

* His Polish forenames were Jerzy Jozue, but after leaving Poland he adopted the anglicized version of his name used in this book.

appeal to the intelligentsia, and how secure she and her friends had felt in the city which was home.

But on 1 September 1939 that all came to a sudden and devastating end as German tanks rolled into Poland and later in the week enemy bombs lambasted Warsaw, thrusting the world into war. Ruth was twenty-nine years old and pregnant with her first child. Ruth's journal begins with the German invasion and the call-up of her husband George into the Polish army. There is surprisingly little about George in the journal, which is written very much as the story of a woman alone. She saw him only once more before the war ended and he would not meet their as yet unborn daughter Eva until she was six years old. What is known of George's war and how he too survived is described in the epilogue to the journal.

As soon as they heard of the German march into Poland, Ruth's parents packed a small bag each, which included valuable caches of diamonds, and left Warsaw with the thousands of young people heading for Vilna (Vilnius), the capital of neighbouring Lithuania. At first they went by coach and horse and later by train. They were just two of the quarter million Polish Jews who fled eastwards to cross into the Soviet zone while the borders remained open, which was the case until early December. Thereafter Soviet soldiers began sealing off the borders, as Ruth herself experienced. The Altbekers set up temporary home in Vilna 'living like students', as they wrote to Esther in Palestine. She was very well placed to obtain permits for her parents to enter Palestine, an immensely valuable capability at a time when refuges for Jews had largely closed down. Even then it took most of a year to achieve: not only did Esther have to obtain certificates from the British who held Palestine under a mandate, but her brother Isadore in South Africa had to pay a £1000 guarantee to facilitate his parents' departure from Europe. The problem of getting out of Lithuania still remained. Their valuable store of diamonds, hidden under Mrs Altbeker's wig – worn by all very orthodox Jewish women – and in the hollow heels of her shoes on their journey to Vilna, was kept on the balcony of their flat once there. When the time came to leave they needed to crack open the ice encasing the diamonds to pay their way out of Soviet-held Lithuania. Many months slipped by as they waited for the costly emigration papers from Moscow. As soon as they had been obtained the Altbekers departed, which meant travelling on a Saturday, something they had never done in their lives before. They journeyed across Eastern Europe and all the way through China to Shanghai, where the Jewish community fed and cared for them; they continued for months on an immense detour to Odessa, where they took a boat to Constantinople. From there they travelled to Syria and finally to Palestine where they spent the rest of their lives. Ruth's brother Isadore had gone to South Africa in 1936 where, using his father's contacts, he set up a jewellery business in Johannesburg, and never saw the war. Of her immediate family, only her eldest brother Jozef, did not survive. It was partly because of a promise she made to Jozef, as she explains in her journal, that Ruth herself did not escape war-torn Europe.

Instead she was to live through the most harrowing times, to see the ghetto grow up around her, to move from the comfort of her own home to the crowded and cramped floor of a fur factory where twelve-hour work shifts seven days a week, hiding a small unwelcome child amidst the constant threat and terror of 'round-ups' became her way of life. And then, after an extraordinary escape from a train on its way to Treblinka and certain death, she adopted a new identity as a result of a great kindness shown to her by a stranger on another train, and moved into Gentile Warsaw. The once glamorous Warsaw advocate donned down-at-heel shoes, a drab coat and headscarf and became governess to a succession of young Polish children. In four days she learned the Catholic catechism by heart so that she could teach it to her young charges. For reasons which emerge in Ruth's journal, she separated from Eva, who was moved from one family to another. One of Ruth's more tormented moments occurred after Eva had been moved through the Polish underground to a location known only to one woman. As she tells in her journal, shortly after Eva's placement the woman was arrested and remained in jail for more than three months. Time and again she made difficult decisions and took risks which each time could have meant the end of her and Eva's lives but without which neither she nor her child would have survived.

It was while sitting at the elegant dinner table of one of her families that she first learned of the uprising in the ghetto. Later, in the spring of 1943, she watched the final destruction of the ghetto

and its tragic inmates from the top deck of a tram as she rode back
and forth. She tells of one of her last tram journeys past the ghetto
when she saw a girl in a burning dress leap from a window: 'That
ghastly torch flashed briefly then vanished behind the wall, while
the tram rolled peacefully on. The scum of society stood by the
ghetto walls. Some were tempted by the possibility of looting
Jewish property, others lurked for easy prey – a Jew who might try
to creep over to the Aryan side through a crevice or chink in the
wall.' After the final destruction of the ghetto Ruth could not resist
stealing back into the quarter to see for herself what had happened
there. She described 'the empty space which had once been a part
of Warsaw, inhabited by hundreds of thousands of people. In such
a short time not a single stone or a burned or demolished house
remained, not a ruin, only a vast empty stretch of scorched earth, a
desert.' Later, during the Warsaw uprising in the autumn of 1944,
Ruth was buried under the rubble of a seven-storey building which
had taken a direct hit from a German bomb. She survived that too.
And in January 1945, when she was again rounded up by the
Germans and held for deportation to Germany, she engineered
another courageous escape.

Ruth's account of events was of necessity written from the
viewpoint of an isolated individual witnessing, experiencing and
coping with the horrors around her. The broader context of Poland
in the 1930s was of a largely agricultural country with only a
quarter of its population living in towns. Warsaw, the Polish
capital, was by far the largest town and at the start of the war its
400,000 Jews made up nearly a third of its population. Only one
city in the world was home to more Jews than Warsaw, and that
was New York. Nearly a quarter of a million lived in the predomi-
nantly Jewish district of the capital, while the remaining 150,000
were scattered throughout the city. From the moment the Nazis
entered Warsaw at the end of the first week of the war, Jewish life
was threatened. Polish Jewry was familiar with anti-Semitism but
until the German invasion there was at least the protection of some
of its well-established institutions, including representatives in the
Polish parliament. Thereafter, week after week, new burdens and
deprivations were imposed on Warsaw's Jews. From November
1939 Jews were forbidden to buy or sell to 'Aryans', to bake bread
or to travel by train. After January 1940 Jews were placed under

curfew and forbidden to be in the streets after nine o'clock in the evening and before five in the morning.

On 3 October 1940, at the start of the Jewish New Year, the German governor of Warsaw announced that all Jews living outside the Jewish area would have to leave their homes and move into the Jewish quarter. A month later, on 16 November, the much reduced Jewish quarter, with its narrow streets and with all the parks and gardens carefully zoned out, was sealed. The misery that was the ghetto – a word with medieval overtones whose use was forbidden by the Nazis, who preferred 'Jewish residential district' – came into being as a six-foot wall topped by barbed wire to imprison the community. Each day new rules were invented to make life more difficult for those sealed into the ghetto, as Jews from all over Poland were forced to squeeze into the already grotesquely over-crowded Jewish quarter. Jews were forced to wear identifying armbands, they were forbidden to use public libraries or to travel on trains. They were executed for illegally being on the Gentile side of Warsaw. In 1941, in the middle of a freezing winter, the Germans forbade the Jews to use fuel or any other form of heating and at the same time issued an order that all Jews should give up their furs to the Germans. Failure to comply was punishable by death. Once the ghetto 'closed' the Germans allowed food rations of just 184 calories per person a day into the ghetto compared with the 699 calories allowed for Poles and 2613 for the Germans. The death toll from starvation approached 50,000 in the ghetto in 1941,* but it would have been very much higher without the large-scale illegal smuggling of food, which itself carried the death penalty. Those who did not starve or freeze to death, or die of the diseases which were rampant in these terrible conditions, might be murdered or brutally rounded up for forced labour.

The launch of the German invasion of the Soviet Union in June 1941, known as Operation Barbarossa, marked the turning-point in German policy towards the Jews. While terror, starvation and random killings had become commonplace, for the first time the comprehensive and systematic destruction of whole Jewish communities now began. It would be another year before the Jews of Warsaw would experience the full horror of the mass deportations.

* Figures taken from Martin Gilbert, *The Holocaust* (London, 1986), p. 294.

For during the murderous course of 1942, the gravel pits near the rural railway station of Treblinka, forty miles north-east of Warsaw, were being transformed from a labour camp into a death camp for the Jews of central Poland, including the 350,000 Jews still alive in the Warsaw ghetto. It was to be the fourth death camp created by the Nazis after Chelmno, Belzec and Sobibor. In July 1942 a directive went out to the head of the police forces in the General Government, the administrative area under which Warsaw fell, that the 'resettlement' of Warsaw Jewry – a misnomer for removal to the gas chambers – was to be completed by the end of the year. Thus on 22 July, as Ruth recounts so vividly, the round-ups and deportations began in earnest and on 23 July the Treblinka gas ovens became operational with the first consignment of unfortunate men, women and children who were herded like cattle to their deaths. The terrifying round-ups continued without pause until 12 September. Each day more than 4000 Jews were taken from their homes or seized in the streets and were murdered. On a single day in 1942, 4 August, 13,000 Jews were rounded up in Warsaw and gassed at Treblinka.

All in all across German-occupied Europe more than 400,000 Jews were murdered that August. In those first seven weeks of the 'resettlement to the East', a total of 265,000 Warsaw Jews were sent in the trains to Treblinka where they met their deaths in the three gas chambers.* It was the largest slaughter of a single community in the Second World War. It is estimated that fewer than 100 people survived Treblinka, but in September 1942, one of those survivors returned to Warsaw to give his account of where the trains went and what happened on arrival. This knowledge and what she did about it marked Ruth out as the extraordinary survivor that she proved to be and led directly to her escape from the death train, as she records in her journal.

By the end of September 1942 there were no more than 55,000 Jews left in the ghetto. The survivors tended to be those the Germans wanted to keep in the ghetto at productive work and who had been issued with 'Ausweis' or employment cards. But even those with such cards, as Ruth describes, could not escape the Nazis' need to fill their quotas for the death ovens, and were simply

* Ibid., p. 197.

rounded up. After the completion of the big deportations at the end of September, ghetto residents were not allowed into the streets during work hours; communication between one factory and another and the housing-blocks alongside them were almost completely severed. Ruth and her daughter survived against the odds as by the end of 1942 very few women and almost no children remained in the ghetto.* Nearly four months went by without any deportations, then on 18 January 1943 the Germans marched into the frozen, starving ghetto, alternately killing and rounding up the tragic remains of the ghetto community. Six hundred Jews were thought to have been murdered in the streets that day and 5000 were rounded up. Two days later Ruth's and Eva's turn finally came and they made the last of their several journeys to the Umschlagplatz, the bleak railway siding which was the final round-up point for the Jews transported to Treblinka.

· Like all those who survived long enough to testify to the terrible fate of the Jews, she witnessed great horror, great pain and great courage. She describes the terrible cruelty of round-ups and selections and how differently people responded to them:

There were ghastly scenes when parents were separated from their children. I saw mothers prostrate at the Germans' feet, pleading for the life of their children; I saw mothers from whom neither the German fist nor the heavy hand of a militia man could tear their babies away from them. In such cases the Germans would make use of a precious bullet and the mother would die hugging her child until her last breath. And I saw other young mothers who at the moment of selection abandoned their children, tore away the little hands clutching at their skirts; on her own she might have had a chance, but with a child her death was a certainty. Then, standing with the group of the released and facing her child in the condemned crowd, she would cover her eyes so as not to see it, she would plug her ears not to hear her little one crying ... All God's rules, humane instincts, all those precepts and commandments inculcated in us since time immemorial, lay in the dust on the Umschlagplatz.

* This is reported in Yisrael Gutman, *The Jews of Warsaw, 1939–1943*, translated by Ina Friedman (Brighton, 1982).

She describes her own first journey to the Umschlagplatz and how thereafter she always took her small daughter to the factory to try and ensure that the child was not taken while she was away at work. In that first stifling summer amidst the clouds of dust and fur particles Eva fell ill with whooping cough and later dysentery. Still Ruth kept the forbidden and largely silent child hidden under vests on her lap while sewing without a break for twelve-hour stretches.

She tells too of a workman she saw who had tied his child around his waist to smuggle under an overcoat and of the German who slit the ropes with a dagger. 'It did not matter to him,' she wrote, 'that he mortally wounded the child and stained the poor father with his child's blood.' And the story of an elderly couple who argued about who should keep the single 'life number' they had between them, which on that day meant escape from a selection. Standing next to the couple were a father and his young son, also with only one life number between them. The old woman went to the little boy and handing the life number to him said 'You are young, you will survive' and with that gave him her last 500 zloty. Then both husband and wife swallowed some white powder and a moment later were dead. 'Nobody moved to save them', Ruth observed. 'On the contrary, everybody envied them.'

The brutal murder of an old and paralyzed woman, brought out in an armchair into the snow was a vision she would never dispel. When the woman failed to obey an order to stand up she was shot through the eye. Alive, but still unable to obey the order to stand up, she was shot through her remaining eye. 'Terrible bloody tears began to trickle from her eye sockets down her shabby clothes and onto the soft white snow', Ruth wrote of this scene she had witnessed. Another of her most heart-rending stories concerned a letter delivered to the ghetto by a Polish policeman, so moved by its contents that he brought it himself. The letter was from a young girl rounded up with a group of children while separated from their parents. Written on the train to Treblinka, the child wrote 'I do not know exactly where we are going but I guess we are going to our death . . . I remember now that I did not kiss you good morning today, as I will not be able to kiss you any more.' She tells her mother not to be sad, that she is keeping the other children occupied and that she has explained to them that some day all people must die and that there is nothing wrong in dying soon.

Ruth was witness to many, many acts of unimaginable cruelty. When in 1944 the Polish resistance stepped up its activities, the Germans let it be known that for every German killed, ten Poles would be murdered. In preparation, they rode round Warsaw picking up hostages. In their last moments before execution some would sing the Polish anthem which seemed to make the death of the hostage easier. One morning Ruth watched as the hostages were shaved and their mouths filed with a mixture of plaster and cement to prevent them uttering a sound. 'In the busiest streets of Warsaw the Poles would now be executed naked from their waists and die mute under the executioners' bullets,' she wrote.

The journal provides a moving account of the terrible cold winter day on which Ruth and Eva were finally rounded up and marched over dead bodies through what remained of the ghetto and led to the Umschlagplatz. There the frozen human herds were loaded into excrement-covered cattle trains by Nazis wielding whips. While the trains waited, the men and women crowded into Ruth's carriage began singing the mournful prayer for the dead, soon joined by the voices of those locked into other carriages, waiting to journey to their deaths. Her extraordinary account of her and Eva's escape from the death train, and of those who helped her and those who refused to, of how she escaped back to Warsaw, spending the first night in a dog's kennel, and how she survived again and again, brings home just how difficult it was to stay alive.

The journal is distinctly divided between Ruth's time in the Warsaw ghetto, where she lived in ever more gruelling circumstances until January 1943, and her time in Gentile Warsaw after her escape from the Treblinka-bound train. Despite the prevalence of anti-Semitism in Poland and the certain death penalty which awaited those who helped Jews, there were Poles who displayed huge courage and humanity and Ruth was fortunate enough to find a number of such protectors. Sometime after arriving in Gentile Warsaw she learned that a friend and her son were in hiding, and were being put up at the home of a prostitute. Even while she clearly understood that survival was all, Ruth's values were such that she expressed considerable shock at the conditions under which the friend was in hiding. She reported that she 'even used to sleep with her landlady on one couch and was compelled to listen to the stories and anecdotes of a streetwalker. I wondered how my friend could stand the company of such a woman.' The prostitute is commemorated as a 'righteous Gentile' at the Yad Vashem memorial in Jerusalem.

Despite the anguish and pain of these stories and experiences, Ruth's journal is an uplifting account of a remarkable survivor. Because so few witnesses outlived the holocaust, the accounts of those who did are enormously precious. Each will have seen and experienced things no other survivor will have done. Luck most certainly played its part but so did the many decisions Ruth made, the many risks she took, each one of which could have resulted in death but was indeed a chance for life. Her strength of character and courage undoubtedly helped but her appearance was probably just as important: many times her blond hair and blue eyes protected her while others with more Semitic features were sent to their deaths. Thus she was also able to move relatively freely around Gentile Warsaw – though never without fear – once she moved out of the ghetto. No one will ever quite know why Ruth chose first to write her story and then to hide it, but it provides a fascinating insight into just how one individual survived.

Elaine Potter

THE JOURNAL

· 1 ·

The Invasion

IT WAS SUNDAY 3 September 1939 when my husband was called to the colours. A pervasive air of excitement gripped the city as I accompanied him to Warsaw Central, the main railway station. Repeatedly the loudspeakers spilled out the happy news: England and France are at war with the Huns. Military operations have begun.

Strangers in the streets embraced and kissed one another. The people of Warsaw were filled with hope. This optimism was reflected all over the city as people declared 'Now with such powerful Allies we shall certainly win the war quickly. Germany's strength, that's bluff! A country with no butter, no fuel, with people who wear ersatz clothes, cannot win the war. We have Great Britain on our side and Britain has never lost any war.' Enthusiastic Warsovians were convinced that war would last no more than a few weeks, with the English and French striking from the west, we from the east. We would meet in Berlin within days. At the station, smiles on the faces of those peering through the windows of the carriages matched the fine day and mirrored the smiles of relatives and friends who saw the soldiers off with the promise 'see you soon'. The Polish anthem, sung alongside the French and British anthems, was the first manifestation of Brotherhood in Arms.

'Attention! Attention! Warsaw, Cracow, Katowice and all Polish

Radio Stations. Tonight Berlin was attacked by 300 Polish bombers which resulted in many fires. All our planes returned safely.' Despite these encouraging radio reports, by the next day a great state of nervousness was felt in Warsaw. Whispers that one ministry and government office after another was being evacuated, rumours that important military documents were being sent away, spread through Warsaw and the better-off, particularly those who owned cars, started to slip out of the capital. Long queues could be seen at grocery shops as people feverishly tried to build up reserves. A complete black-out was to be observed at night, and now and then frightening announcements were broadcast through the loudspeakers. 'Attention! Attention! Warsaw under alert.' And after a while 'Attention! Attention! Closing down!' was followed by some mysterious names and numbers.

Front-line guns could be heard more and more distinctly, yet broadcast political news was full of hope: the situation at the front was good and very good, the English and the French armies had crossed the German border and our own forces were resisting bravely in the east. Then came the unforgettable night of 5 September. An order was broadcast to the male population to leave the city eastwards, following the retreat of our forces. A panic ensued. People packed their rucksacks and hurriedly took leave of their families. My father, who was over sixty, joined the young people leaving Warsaw accompanied by my mother. 'I do not want to see the Germans', my father said. Taking some money, his briefcase and his umbrella, he left.

That night I spent many hours in the street. The traffic was heavier than during the day, everybody moving in the direction of Prague. There were no motorcars. People on foot, in carts, on bikes and wheelbarrows rushed in confusion towards the Vistula, desperate to reach the other side of the river, further from the front. The Polish Radio kept on explaining that while the enemy was approaching Warsaw, the political situation was improving and that it was our very strategy to draw the Germans deep inside the country in order to cut them off from their supplies and munitions depots, to lure them on to our bad roads. Once inside our country, it was argued we would destroy them easily.

The terrible siege of Warsaw began with its constant bombing, alerts without respite, fires and famine. Dr Stefan Starzynski, the mayor of the city, went on encouraging us. He called for order and calm, appealed to the population to open the shops, to clean the streets and help the hungry and wounded. In those trying days all the inhabitants of Warsaw loved their mayor and when one day he broadcast a call for 300 young volunteers to fulfil a dangerous mission which could result in their deaths, thousands gathered at the appointed place within hours.

'Hallo, hallo, the Westerplatte garrison is holding on.' Westerplatte, the furthest Polish stronghold on the west still held on. 'Hallo, hallo, we are resisting but the enemy is attacking and we haven't any more ammunition', until Westerplatte grew deadly silent.

During one of the heavy shellings of the capital my brother and his nine-year-old daughter were seriously wounded. From a synagogue in Ptasia Street, where a first-aid point was established, some good people carried him to the Holy Spirit Hospital in Elektoralna Street. A big red cross was painted on the roof but the Germans continually bombed the hospital so that the wounded had to be evacuated. Many of them found death when the hospital caught fire after the repeated dropping of incendiaries. Luckily we had carried my brother away before the hospital burned down.

In those days of such horror, we were filled with a sense of brotherliness. People helped each other, every bit of food was shared, wounds were dressed and many blocks established aid points. Soldiers returning from the front were given fresh underwear, fed and helped. Their worn faces betrayed defeat. Now the mayor called only for calm and perseverance. Responding to his call, I brought some bed linen to one of the newly formed hospitals, where within a few hours generous Warsovians had piled up mountains of bed clothes and goods of all kinds. Then the voice of Polish Radio faded out and we heard our mayor no more. Although pregnant at the time I was always busy, breaking through barricades and trying to reach wherever help was needed.

More and more bombing and shelling from heavy guns, and air raids with no respite, left the town with big fires and no water, gas, electricity, telephones or radio and with disease spreading. We felt terribly hungry. The carcass of a horse or dog killed in the streets would immediately attract hungry inhabitants who, regardless of their safety, would cut off pieces of carrion. In no time only bones remained. This was the way we were fed by the Germans. The dead were buried in nearby squares and any empty space might be turned into a graveyard. Complete defeat seemed inevitable as many were at the end of their endurance, some already looking forward to the coming of the Germans. 'What can they do to us, we are a civil population', oppressed Warsovians believed.

The ill-fated capital surrendered and the conditions of the capitulation were pasted over the walls. It was the last time mayor Starzynski was to sign an appeal in which he asked the population to preserve calm and dignity and to observe the conditions of the surrender. Mr Starzynski himself was taken hostage, put into a concentration camp and eventually murdered.

Autumn of that year was exceptionally fine, as if laughing at us in our utmost distress. On a sunny beautiful morning a few days after the capitulation, German troops entered the town. Haughty, happy, formidably equipped, the victors marched into the devastated capital. Regiment after regiment, tank after tank paraded through empty streets where fires had not yet been extinguished, and human and animal corpses not buried.

The western part of Poland was incorporated into the Reich. The east was taken by Russia, and the rest formed the so-called General Government,* with the River Bug as the eastern frontier.† At the outset the German presence was little felt. It was a period of expectancy. The tormented people slowly began to organize their private lives. Less damaged flats were patched up, windowpanes replaced with plywood, and rubble cleared away. The most restless were the Jews. 'What will the Germans do with us?', they fearfully asked. 'It won't be so bad', the optimists answered. 'In an occupied territory they won't behave as they do in their fatherland and besides there are so many millions of Jews in Poland.' In spite of this optimism more and more groups of Jews stole across the River Bug to Russia. They were mainly young men who feared forced labour and concentration camps. The older people stayed on. 'What could even the cruellest of occupiers do to an old man, woman or child?', we asked. The better-off reckoned that even if

---

* The General Government was an administrative area covering central Poland, which included Warsaw, set up under the governorship of Hans Frank.
† Poland was partitioned at the end of September, with the Soviet forces occupying many of the eastern Polish cities along a prearranged line to the east of Warsaw.

the Germans did not allow them to earn a living, they had enough ready money for quite a few years. So it seemed wiser to wait peacefully in one's own home than to move to Soviet Russia and an uncertain future.

My brother's wounds were healing slowly when one of our acquaintances brought us news about our parents, whom we had believed killed by a bomb on their flight. They were alive and with my husband, living somewhere in the eastern territory. Capitulation of the Polish forces posed particular dangers for Jewish soldiers and before the end of September George was on the run. He fled east to Lvov (Lemberg) already occupied by the Soviet forces. Soon after this news had reached me, I packed some of my parents' and husband's clothes and with a suitcase I set out. Before my journey I had to take an oath on our parents' health to return as soon as I could to my sick brother. This oath was to prove nearly fatal to me.

A small group of women and I travelled on a rickety peasant wagon to Szepietowka, a small town already on the Russian side. On the journey we discovered that each of us was carrying jewellery or money and, having the most Aryan appearance of my fellow travellers, I was entrusted with concealing all the rings, armbands and watches. This proved to be the right thing to do for, when we reached the Russian border three days later, all my companions were stripped naked and had to undergo a very thorough search by Russian gendarmes. I was not searched at all. My blue eyes and straight nose proved useful for the first time.

At that time Russian border towns were a strange sight. The streets were hugely overcrowded, filled with gathering young refugees. They could be seen with rucksacks on their backs in the squares and in the market-places, discussing what to do. In an unbelievably full train – the railways were free at that time – I reached Bialystok, then a capital and haven for tens of thousands of Jewish refugees. Every flat housed some of them. They crowded even the smallest cafés or restaurants and could be distinguished by their worn-out, dusty clothes and rucksacks.

I learned from an acquaintance of my parents that my husband had visited him a few hours earlier, telling him that he was leaving for Vilna to join my parents there. Overjoyed, I started asking about my husband all over the town but this proved fruitless.

Eventually I went to the railway station, where vast hordes of people had already been waiting for hours. In a manner more suited to a circus performer, I climbed into a carriage through the window. After a journey of fifteen hours I reached Vilna to discover that my husband had been travelling on the same train!

We found my parents in the best of health. Of course they would not hear of my returning to Warsaw, but I had given an oath to my brother and decided to leave the following day. The next morning I was on my way to Bialystok and from there to the border town, only to discover that the Russian guards had barred the way. The border was closed. A colleague of mine, barrister Jozef R., and I tried to cross. He told me that he could not stand the separation from his daughter any longer and had to go back to her but the Russians would not let him pass either. The unhappy father pleaded that he did not want to go to the 'Jerries', that it was only for the sake of joining his small gold-haired child, as he begged the gendarmes in Russian, and breaking down, burst into tears. The Russians were moved and let him pass. Unfortunately he was not to enjoy the company of his daughter for long. After a few weeks he was arrested and murdered by the Germans.

I stayed near the border for a few days but, seeing the futility of this, I went back to Vilna. Meanwhile the situation in Vilna had worsened. The Russians had left the town to the Lithuanians; the Polish currency had lost its value and the Lithuanian one was not to be had. At the beginning of November 1939 Vilna was full of hungry, restless, frightened people and rumours about the anti-Semitic feeling of the Lithuanians abounded.

The oath given to my brother weighed heavily on my mind so, as soon as I heard people whispering about better chances of crossing the border, I set out again. There were quite a number of us. People longing for their families, wanting to enjoy their homes again and just to rest after their trials. Mainly it was the women going back. After all, what harm could Germans do to a woman? She could not be conscripted and she was not fit for hard labour – or so it was thought.

After many experiences I reached Warsaw on 11 November 1939. At that time the first refugees from the incorporated parts of Poland began to flow into the capital. These provinces were to be 'Judenrein' (cleansed of Jews) and the Germans had expelled all the Jewish population,* including my parents-in-law. In most cases the Jews were not allowed to take their belongings and left without even a handbag or briefcase. Those Jews, poor, barefoot, naked and broken, converged from all parts to inhabit the Jewish quarters in Warsaw. They filled all kinds of night lodgings and shelters erected especially for refugees.

* At a conference in Berlin on 21 September 1939, headed by Reinhard Heydrich, the Chief of the Reich Central Security Office, the policy was promulgated to clear extensive areas of Poland of Jews and to concentrate them in the larger cities.

The German
Grip Tightens

THE FIRST BIG German 'achievements' were the so-called 'Kott and Wawer cases'. In January 1940 the Germans had arrested Andrzej Kott, the leader of a young resistance group. Kott's parents had converted to Catholicism but were in origin Jewish, which provided the Germans with an excuse to arrest 255 Jews, including large numbers of the intelligentsia among whom were doctors, barristers, engineers, teachers, musicians and industrialists. They were taken to the Palmiry woods outside Warsaw where they were shot. And in Wawer, a small town near Warsaw, two German policemen were found dead. As a reprisal several hundred men of the local population were first ordered to dig ditches and then hanged.

Capturing Jews on the streets became a daily routine. From these manhunts, completely unprepared people were taken for several days' labour. However, there were as yet no overt anti-Jewish decrees. Only here and there a Jew was expelled from his or her flat in a fashionable quarter, or a smart Jewish shop was simply 'taken'. The first serious act was the requirement that all Jews should wear 'Judenbinde'. The order, signed by the Governor General, was posted up in all public places, and stated that Jews of both sexes over the age of twelve had to wear a band on their right arm. The band with a blue Star of David on a white background, conforming to given measurements, was a strict requirement. A

Jew seen on the street without an armband or with one not complying with the rules was liable to imprisonment and a fine. The so-called 'armband tragedies' began. I knew of people who after the publication of this order would not leave their homes for months, so as not to be compelled to wear this humiliating badge. Apart from this, we simply could not get used to this new part of our garment and often went out without it. Such forgetfulness would often result in a Jew being severely beaten by gendarmes and could end with imprisonment or deportation to unknown destinations, or both.

The armband industry was born. At first, white linen bands with the blue star painted on were manufactured. However, this proved impractical, so next came the band with the star made of blue fabric or ribbon sewn on. Ingenious Jews went further, flooding the market with celluloid bands, ultimately producing the peak of smartness – an easy to clean rubber armband, fitted to another. The Star of David was to be exhibited on all Jewish shops and businesses, and even included trams in which Jews were allowed to ride. Alas, were it not so tragic, it could have been ridiculous. For instance a two-wagon tram, travelling through Marszalkowska Street or some other fashionable street, would have the first coach 'for Aryans' and the next for Jews. The trailer would carry the big sign of David in place of its destination number. I think that nowhere, not even in Palestine, were so many David's symbols to be seen as in Warsaw during the German occupation.

Jews were still allowed to live where they liked and when later on this was restricted to certain streets, they could still walk everywhere until seven o'clock in the evening. At night they had to be enclosed in the 'Jewish quarters', the official term for areas where Jews were allowed to live. A severe punishment was inflicted for the use of the word 'ghetto' in either speech or in writing. Our overlords did not like words smelling of the Middle Ages, reminding them of backwardness.

I admit that at first I did not put on the armband. I felt pleasure in cheating Germans and considered it a good sport. But then a pretty woman, young and strong, appeared in the streets and she terrorized all young Jewesses not wearing the star. I will never know whether she was a madwoman, as some maintained, or just a German, or as some others suggested, a Pole who hated Jewesses.

As soon as she would see a young Jewess she would let out a
furious cry of 'Jude' and would assault and beat the unhappy
victim to the accompaniment of wild screaming. I remember that
one day, at the beginning of January 1940, I was walking along
Marszalkowska Street with an elderly lady chatting peacefully.
Suddenly I heard the well-known shrill cry and some twenty metres
ahead of me spotted that dangerous woman running towards me.
There were not many people in the street at that time and my very
advanced pregnancy slowed me down. I tried to scuttle away, but
the distance between us was getting smaller. At my wits' end, I
jumped on the pavement, certain that she would get me. I could
not expect any help from the few passers-by who feared she might
be a German. Helpless and desperate, I thought that there was no
rescue for me. All at once the driver of a passing tram, having seen
what was going on, stopped the tram next to me. He shouted to
me to jump in quickly and with all my strength I pulled myself on
to the platform and the tram started, leaving behind the horrible
woman, gesticulating wildly. These were glimpses of life in Warsaw
of that time.

The Germans had good reason to single out Jewish shops with
the Jewish star. The scum understood how to avail themselves of
such an opportunity. A German or a 'Volksdeutsch'* would enter
a Jewish shop pretending to be a customer and would ask for some
merchandise. After getting it, he would either not pay at all, or pay
his own price. The Jew could not complain, could ask no one for
help and very often thanked God that he had received no beating
on such an occasion. That was the reason why from the beginning
of the German invasion, the shops were seemingly without merchandise. Goods were sold only to people who inspired confidence.
Because of my appearance, I was sometimes refused service and
had to prove my Jewish origin. The scum would soon throw out a
marked Jew waiting in a queue at Wedel's – where chocolate was
sold at government prices – or some other shop and thus get his
'better' place.

At the same time many Aryan shop entrances started displaying
small white rectangular signs with the typed inscription 'Für Juden

---

* The Volksdeutsch or ethnic Germans were descendants of eighteenth-century German
settlers and usually spoke German.

Eintritt verboten' (Entry for Jews forbidden). These signs were being sold by the Hitler youth – little boys of twelve, in brown uniforms, foster-children of the German youth organization. The cakes at Gajewski's and Ziemianska looked so good, but both entrances were 'decorated' with those signs. Yet the majority of those cards had the inscription turned inside the shops, leaving the blank white facing the street. Once in the summer of 1940 when I stopped at Gajewski's shop window, I was approached by a shop assistant and cordially invited to enter. 'You know that this is a German order, not ours. Please do always come, and repeat this invitation to all your acquaintances.' The same happened at Gogolewski's and Ziemianska and it became a rule to shop in spite of those placards. We treated this rather like a game of making fun of the Germans. But only a small number of Jews derived profit from this 'blessing'. The majority did not leave the Jewish quarter at all.

More and more frequently, fashionable flats belonging to Jews were expropriated in the space of a few minutes, and Jewish shopkeepers were obliged to abandon their shops, leaving all their goods behind. The flat or the shop would be taken over by a German or a newly created Volksdeutsch. On the whole these Volksdeutsche became the greatest pests. A German could be recognized by his pronunciation, but a Volksdeutsch was really a Pole who had signed the Volksdeutsch list because it was convenient at the time. He received German rations and was exempted from labour. What is more, such a fellow could seize any beautiful flat or store, or become a 'Treuhandler'* (trustee) in a Jewish apartment house or Jewish business. A Volksdeutsch in many cases had a typical Polish surname with a 'ski' ending, as in Zawadzki or Nowicki, and often could not even speak German. In order to be put on the 'Volksliste' it sufficed to write on the application that one's grandmother or great-grandmother had been born in Germany, or had simply had a German-sounding name such as Vogel or Richter. People would dig up some long-forgotten parentage in order to become a member of the 'Herrenvolk'. Naturally this was done only by a certain sort of person, eager to catch fish

---

* No Jews were allowed to manage a business or an apartment block and instead they were obliged to appoint a Treuhänder or trustee (usually German and Volksdeutsch, though at the beginning sometimes Polish).

in troubled waters. Nevertheless there were many Gentiles in Warsaw, well known for their German origins, who did not admit this, considered themselves Polish and would not sign the Volksliste.

Besides legal pilfering, and depriving Jews of their flats, the normal procedure was to take some particular objects from them. For example, a young woman accompanied by a German in uniform, or a Polish cad, would enter a flat. Introducing themselves as Germans, they would open the cupboards and wardrobes, choose whatever they liked and force the owner of the flat to wrap his own things neatly and to carry the bundle to the waiting car. 'Requisitioning' of better furniture and personal belongings took place and the proprietor served as porter in carrying the furniture downstairs. The local mob usually guided the Germans to the rich Jewish houses and stores. With the deepest shame I must admit that there were some Jews among the scum. The fact that a Mojsze Zylberszejn had hidden some cloth, gold or jewels was usually known to another Jew, either his friend or relation. Prompted by greed or vindictiveness they would betray the person to a German who then robbed the victim of everything. Such things were done not only by a professional 'Muser' (blackmailer) but, unfortunately, also by an embittered wife or mistress, a quarrelling business partner, dissatisfied employee or competitor in trade.

A 'poem' was even composed to this effect:

> Mummy, Daddy, listen do
> With a German the Gestapo came two by two
> What shame, what a disgrace
> The first was a Pole, the second a Jew!
> Mummy, Daddy, listen do
> Here come the Gestapo, do you know who?
> What a shame, the worst disgrace
> The first is a Jew, and the second is too!

Well-to-do people began to hide more valuable objects at the homes of their Gentile friends and if they had none, at some poor Jew's dingy and squalid rooms. No German molested the poor because they supposed nothing worth their while could be found there. These German visits (including 'polite calls' of senior Wehrmacht officers in uniforms) to Jewish houses became the plague of the Jewish quarter. The tenants of the house where I lived were well organized: the moment the Germans appeared on the ground floor, I was informed by means of some signals, in spite of living on the fifth floor. Then we would turn our homes upside down, producing an awful disorder on purpose to make our house look dirty and poor. What could a German look for in a poor Jewish flat? It was even better to lie in bed because the Germans were frightfully scared of epidemics and left such an 'infected' house in a hurry.

I remember one such day in February 1940. On the signal 'Germans in the house', I threw the whole contents out of my dirty-linen closet on the floor of my dining-room and emptied the rubbish can on my beautifully polished floor. The Germans just looked in and left without a word. The second time on such an occasion my sister-in-law undressed quickly and lay down in bed, putting a basin full of water near it and arranging some bottles of medicine on the night table. After a second, two smart lieutenants appeared, small suitcases in their hands. They behaved very politely towards me and noticing my pregnancy they asked me not to get excited and commiserated with me on account of my husband's unknown fate. The 'gentlemen' offered to write to the Red Cross in Berlin asking for information about him. So we three sat down at the desk in my study and one of them started writing a letter. The door leading to the bedroom stood wide open and my presumably ill sister-in-law kept on coughing and sneezing. 'Diese ist schwer Lungenkrank' (She has a serious lung disease), I told my guests, and no one dared to explore that room. I concluded that my wardrobe with my clothes was safe. Among other things on the desk there was my fountain pen. Suddenly one of my visitors picked it up, looked at it carefully and noticing the Parker trademark, put the pen in his pocket. I pretended to see nothing and continued our friendly talk. After a while the other German took my beautiful marble paper-weight, examined it and put it into his suitcase. And again I seemed to notice nothing. The letter completed, both Germans took their leave according to the best manners of Herren-volk officers. What a charming and edifying picture this was. Could this have happened in any other Officer Corps? I later had the honour of receiving more visits of this kind, always preceded by preparations such as lying in bed, dirtying everything, but the visit described was memorable because those callers had been polite and well-behaved German officers. A suitcase became a necessary item of German uniform, sometimes complemented by a strong-looking whip.

In mid-February 1940 my brother Jozef left Warsaw and crossed the River Bug, his destination being the town of Vilna where my parents were still staying. This period of searches, requisitioning, manhunting and other new 'Judengesetze' (Jewish laws) lasted until the birth of my child, on 4 March 1940. By then I already knew that my husband had been arrested and was somewhere in a Russian prison. I had nobody to consult about my child's name so I called her Eva in memory of the first woman on earth. After a difficult birth, I returned home to find anti-Jewish riots raging. Through my window I could see the mob breaking into Jewish shops, smashing shop windows and stealing goods. I saw this mob accosting Jewish passers-by and beating them. At first the Germans stood by laughing. Later I saw two of them approaching an injured Jew, and pretending to protect him against the lifted fist of a Pole. But this 'noble act of defence' was in fact being photographed by another German as a propaganda 'play', otherwise the Pole would surely have taken to his heels. It was all the same to the Jews, whoever had been beating them, or why. Many were wounded and many shops robbed of goods.

In April 1940 the official requisitioning of immovable Jewish property began. A decree was issued to the effect that no Jew could manage his property, let flats or accept rents. Custodians of Jewish property were created. An order followed that Jews had to declare all their property, both immovable and movable valuables, even fur coats, jewellery and cash. No Jew could possess more than 2000 zloty, including clothes and jewels – the rest must be put in banks under the special 'Sperrkonto' (frozen assets) system. Everybody declared the immovable property but concealed the other things. We already knew too well that one must elude the German regulations in order to survive.

The most painful order was that of compulsory Jewish labour imposed on men and women under a certain age. The Jewish Council* was obliged to prepare lists of workers and supply them

* Warsaw's Jewish Council, which had been set up under Nazi order to help control the

accordingly. These men were used for clearing away the debris and shovelling the snow. At first they were given some ridiculously small wage and a plate of soup. Of course such a labourer returned home bruised and bleeding according to the German maxim 'Arbeit macht das Leben süss' (Work makes life sweet). New refugees came to Warsaw, the Jews expelled from Cracow and its vicinity. Cracow, as the capital of the General Government and residence of the Governor Dr Hans Frank, could not shelter many Jews. So the majority were expelled, with only those employed in German factories left behind. At that time I let two rooms in my flat to two refugees from Cracow. They were two charming young girls from Leipzig who had been driven to Cracow, then to Warsaw. We could not complain of monotony. More new decrees and orders were issued, often impossible to execute, as for example, forbidding the baking of bread for the free market, or prohibiting the sale of sugar: this carried the death penalty.

Misery and hunger spread mainly among the refugees who came to Warsaw, naked and barefoot. The stubborn optimists kept saying: 'me wet im iberleben' (we will survive him). German armies were victorious on all fronts in Europe and Africa, yet Jews were still optimistic. They would say, 'It's all right, let Hitler occupy even more countries, let him swell and he shall burst.' Those who busied themselves with politics were wealthy people with time to spare and they would end their discussions with an unchangeable 'sy git' (it's quite all right). The greater the success of the German army, the shorter the war, they would say. People sitting in small cafés on Nalewki and Leszno streets and sipping the ersatz and unsweetened coffee would tell one another stories about hunger riots in Berlin, women revolting, demanding their husbands' return from the fronts. They said the situation was the same as in 1918 and thus the war would soon come to an end. Some witty people called this 'IWA' – Idn wiln azoj' (Jews' wishful thinking). The joke was good, the stories untrue, but they played an important part in people's lives because they helped them to survive and to put up with poverty and hunger.

---

movement of Jews, offered to organize a daily quota of Jewish workers in exchange for an agreement that the random abduction of Jews seized in the streets for forced labour would cease.

· 3 ·

Closing the Ghetto

At the end of October 1940 a decree was published regarding the formation of the Jewish quarter – the ghetto – and giving a list of streets where Jews were allowed to live. From 1 November all Jews had to abandon flats situated outside the prescribed boundary and settle in the ghetto. Failure to comply called for the death penalty. Polish caretakers of the houses in the ghetto had to move out, Jewish ones had to take their place. I exchanged my flat with an Aryan for a much smaller and worse one at 29 Elektoralna Street. Jews always lost in these exchanges. As a rule a contract was signed stressing the temporary nature of the exchange for the duration of the war and providing for the eventual reinstatement of the lawful owner.

Optimists again comforted themselves with the thought that it was virtually impossible to close particular streets of a big city. When the morning of 1 November arrived, German gendarmerie and Polish policemen appeared at the boundary line and forbade any Jew to cross to the Aryan quarter. We understood that we were definitely confined to the ghetto and cut off from the world. This date of 1 November 1940 was memorable in the history of the Warsaw ghetto. It was a decisive step towards the complete extermination of Jews. I understood it immediately. I was a barrister and at my office I had many cases pending and documents belonging to my Aryan clients. I summoned them before 1 November and returned all their legal papers which were in my possession. Also before that date I wrote a farewell letter to my parents in Vilna, made my will and gave all the important documents into the keeping of my Aryan colleague.

Immediately after the sealing up of the ghetto we started a new life. It was a state within a state. A Jewish Post Office was established, Jewish police organized and the Jewish Council grew to very large dimensions with many and various departments. Speaking about the Jewish police, who played a big and tragic part in the later liquidation of the ghetto, I must emphasize that the organization and composition of it was left to the discretion of the Council. The enlistment was voluntary; any healthy man could become a policeman, and there were more applicants than vacancies. It was simply a remunerative position, officers being mostly professional men, among them many of my colleagues from the Bar. The policemen got special caps and leather belts and with an air of self-importance they appeared in the Jewish streets. The Jewish Post Office was situated on Gesia Street and accepted only postcards, refusing letters and telegrams. The positive thing was that a couple of Jews got jobs there; the ridiculous thing was that a postcard in the ghetto cost much more than it did outside because of the many additional payments imposed by the Jewish Council. The Jewish Council, with its many departments and clerks, was very powerful; it was in charge of conscripting Jews for compulsory labour and was allowed to use force if necessary.

After the closing of the ghetto, boundary walls were erected. They were high, made of brick and topped with splinters of glass and barbed wire. That was the so-called 'bigger ghetto', extending from Elektoralna Street, across Leszno to Nalewki and Gesia with their lanes. Then there was the 'smaller ghetto', including Twarda and Panska with their side-streets. Between these two stretched the Aryan quarter. The Jewish part of Zielna Street was the only passage from one ghetto to the other with a German gendarme controlling the traffic. The Jewish ghetto was a tragic small state with its own churches, one in the bigger and another in the smaller ghetto. Christians who were considered Jews according to the Nuremberg Law worshipped there. The congregation in the church on Leszno Street wore armlets with the Star of David and prayed to Jesus Christ. I was invited to a wedding in this church. The bridegroom was a young man, born a Christian son of converted parents. The bride, an Aryan from generations, who fell in love with a 'Nuremberg Jew', agreed to enter the ghetto and become a Jewess by this marriage.

A beggar woman on the church steps, a rosary in her hand and prayers on her lips, also had a Jewish armband because her grandmother had been a Jewess. Such was the law of our masters. We Jews were persecuted and suffered much in this Jewish Reservation, but we knew the reason: our Jewishness. The other people who often had no idea about their Jewish ancestors, for whom the Jewish milieu was strange, who knew neither the Jewish language nor customs, suffered even more in the ghetto. Many personal tragedies were lived out among them. For instance, when such a Nuremberg Jew had an Aryan wife it was no wonder that such a spouse refused to enter the ghetto and chose to remain in the Gentile quarter. Our masters were very considerate in such cases. It was sufficient if this pure-blooded spouse declared his or her intent to divorce the Jewish life-partner. Then he or she became a reinstated Aryan with full rights to live on the Aryan side. If the couple had children, they were treated as 'Mischlingen' (half-castes) and were tolerated in the Gentile quarter. The Nuremberg Jews had even more troubles from us. The scum made fun of them on their leaving the church. During their lifetimes such Nuremberg Jews were forbidden to step out of the ghetto, but they became free after death; a hearse would come to convey the body to the Christian cemetery. Only two or three mourners of the family were allowed into the car bearing a painted cross and not the Jewish star, still worn by the mourners on their arms.

Slowly we grew accustomed to sights of that kind. They ceased to strike us and often we did not even notice the anomalies of the Warsaw ghetto. Our deep concern was for one thing only – how to live on, how to put up with all this misery.

The question which came to dominate our lives was 'Are they catching in the street or not?' People became so cunning, walked the streets with such care, that it was difficult for the Germans to catch even the smallest number of people. A young man coming out of his house would simply ask passers-by, 'My chapt, cy my chapt nyszt?' (Are they catching or not?) and upon learning that everything was safe, he would venture out. Such a procedure was repeated at every street corner and in case of danger, the man would take cover.

Gradually the Germans reduced the size of the ghetto, excluding street after street, or even parts of them. The habitable space decreased while the population swelled as Jews expelled from other towns were forced into the ghetto. Even then it was obvious that the Germans aimed to concentrate the largest number of Jews in Warsaw. The constant changes in the size of the ghetto were annoying because a flat had become more than a place in which to live. In fact, everybody had hiding places for their more valuable possessions in case of searches and requisitioning. Some people buried them, others walled them in; kitchen stoves, ovens, floors and walls were hiding-places for these precious little savings, things intended for sale in order to survive. So abandoning a flat was always a calamity. It was often necessary to tear out floor boards because of hidden silver cutlery or even merchandise, to take off the tiles from such newly invented safes as kitchen stoves and ovens. Scarcity of housing space grew acute – people had to live in a smaller area. The Jewish Council opened a Housing Department which kept a list of all the flats in the ghetto and the number of tenants in each of them. A 'density of population' was prescribed as four to five people per room, depending upon its size; one family in the broadest meaning of this word was allowed to have only one room, even if this meant ten people in it.

After the definite closing of the ghetto, life took shape accordingly. Slowly people adjusted to these new conditions and even tried to make life pleasant. I stopped worrying about my new shabby flat and took to making it habitable and cosy. Armed with a brush and paint, I painted my room pink, polished the doors and windows to a mirror finish and even hung up pink Venetian blinds. My greatest luxury was a kind of a bathroom installed in the kitchen. At home I tried to forget the ghetto. I was reminded of it by a small note pinned to my door and written by myself: 'Don't forget to put your armband on.' Such warnings could be seen on many a door in the ghetto.

From some points of view certain things were better in this closed area than they had been before; constant German and Volksdeutsch visitors stopped calling and with that robberies ceased. The ghetto was locked up and admission passes had to be produced by callers. They were issued to Polish policemen, tax collectors, gas and electricity meter readers and bailiffs.

In this small area the social contrasts were increasingly striking. There were fashionable streets like, for instance, Sienna, Elektoralna, Orla and Leszno, inhabited by wealthy people, with cafés, pastry shops, revue theatres and cabarets. It may seem strange, but in this horrible, overcrowded ghetto there were restaurants in which the most sought-after delicacies could be obtained, cafés with bands and artistic revues and dance floors. Certain people were well off, making a lot of money by trading in foreign currency and gold, while others made money from trading with the Germans and the Gentile quarter. Money was being spent by everyone, even by those who for years had scraped pennies to put them away for rainy days. We were people with no future, so why save up, why hide it and count? Who knew whether the end would come soon? So rather spend and enjoy it and get the best. Extremes of luxury and poverty were to be seen. A smartly dressed woman walked alongside a man in rags. A restaurant in Leszno Street displayed a roasted goose and at its door a boy was starving. People leaving a theatre in Leszno Street passed a poor, emaciated child shivering from cold and begging in the doorway.

I remember such a small boy whose beat was in Leszno Street near Solna Street. He was apparently from a better-off family, for when I first saw him, he was cleanly and neatly clad. He was standing on the pavement ceaselessly reciting 'W piwnicznej izbie' and 'Powrót Taty'.* I saw this boy over a period of two years. As the months passed, his rosy cheeks became pale and showed signs of road dust and poverty. The boy would not be standing, but would sit on shop steps. He still recited his poems. Still later he was lying in dust and mud, yet his child's voice sounded on and the lines of 'In a Basement' could be heard distinctly, however faintly. Several times I tried to make him talk but he would never tell me anything about himself and the bread I gave him was always put away. 'That's for later on', he tried to explain. He looked wretched, his clothes more and more decayed and his voice growing hoarse. Some time afterwards, I passed his usual place. I saw his small corpse covered with newspaper. From a still strong beggar standing

---

* 'In a Basement' and 'Father's Return', two well-known Polish poems.

nearby I learned that he had been the child of a wealthy family from Lodz. The whole family lived in a shelter, both parents were ill and unable to make a living. Nobody had ever seen the child eat anything. He had taken everything home to feed his family.

I remember another boy who also stood in Leszno Street. This boy, a refugee from Berlin, would constantly recite 'Lorelei' in German. But this child survived. Luckily he had no family and what he begged he could eat.

When someone died of exhaustion on the streets, passers-by would cover the corpse with newspapers, lay some stones on it and life rolled on. Some laughed, others cried. Ghastly scenes lost the power to move us, to impress themselves upon us. Then the so-called 'chapers' (snatchers) appeared on the streets of the ghetto. A chaper was usually a strong and ragged beggar who assaulted people carrying a loaf of bread or a parcel containing food. The chaper took his victim unawares, snatching whatever he was carrying. The unfortunate victim would have no hope of chasing the beggar and recovering the loss, for the booty was usually consumed during his flight.

I remember once going with my two-year-old daughter to a pastry shop in Leszno and buying her a tea cake. The child was sitting near the entrance when the door burst open, and before I could grasp the situation, the cake was snatched from her and the chaper gone. My little daughter did not even cry; she understood that it was the snatcher and the cake was lost. The chapers grew so skilful that they were never mistaken about the contents of a parcel, and so swift that catching them was practically impossible. Their skill and cheek made them snatch even from people riding in rickshaws.

Rickshaws were a product of the ghetto – they later found their way to the Aryan quarter. The lack of trams or cars and the high cost of maintaining a cabhorse begot a new means of transportation: a three-wheeled bicycle with a front bench for two, even three people. The fare was low – there was no need to feed a horse, only a weary human being. Ingenious rickshaw drivers striving to win customers outdid one another in the elegance of their vehicles. They painted them various colours and made the front seats comfortable. A provident rickshaw-man would not leave it at having one or two passengers but, while pedalling, would call: 'Whoever wants

Twarda or Leszno, please get in, please have a seat', and for a
lower fare would accept more passengers. They would do anything
to earn a bit more, because at home hungry mouths were waiting.

There were still lines of communication with the Aryan quarter;
we could telephone and therefore shops with telephones were
literally besieged. There was also another 'window on the world' in
the ghetto, the building of the Lower Court at Leszno, whose huge
premises were finished a few months before the war. The building
had one gate from Leszno Street, the second from Ogrodowa Street.
The entrance from Leszno, which belonged to the ghetto, was
guarded by a gendarme and Polish and Jewish policemen who took
care that only Jews could pass through this gate. To get into the
building, of course, an explanation was required, but even an old
summons to the Court, or Income Tax Department (which was
also in the same building) proved sufficient. Inside the Court
building Jews met non-Jews, busying themselves with all kinds of
affairs and bargaining. There was, at that time, a considerable
difference between the prices charged in the ghetto and those in the
Gentile quarter. Food was cheaper on the Aryan side, whereas
workmanship and various goods were much less expensive in the
ghetto. Therefore parcels and bundles changed hands inside the
building and certain elegant Aryan women accustomed to their old
dressmakers and tailors made appointments just there. An obliging
usher let the back rooms be used for trying on overcoats and
dresses, top-boots, girdles and brassières in exchange for a few
zloty. I even remember a case when a dental assistant, an acquaintance of mine, within the walls of this building, fixed a beautiful
denture in the mouth of his Gentile client. In those times human
ingenuity was so great.

Hundreds of kilograms of foodstuffs and other goods passed
through the Law Court building daily. It was clear that after some
time the Germans had naturally been examining the parcels of the
Court's clients, thus reducing this quaint import and export business to a large extent. The Court ushers, however, continued to co-
operate. Girdles and brassières were still tried on in cosy surroundings of Court side-chambers. Those dissatisfied with the daily fresh
cakes from the Jewish pastry shop Studnia Bros. could have them
from Gajewski's or Gogolewski's – but at a certain time. In spite of
ever stricter controls, the Court gates were still the easiest way of

getting to the Gentile side. A Jew with non-Jewish features could simply enter the Court premises by the Leszno gate, remove his armlet in a quiet corner, step out as an Aryan by the Ogrodowa gate, and all was over. Smuggling through the Court building was, however, like a drop in the ocean. Besides, it was only for amateurs and people with a few friends. One should not forget that the Warsaw ghetto comprised 400,000 souls, and the Germans allowed only rationed goods, 'couponed' food to be sent. Everything else had to be brought in illegally in order to prevent mass hunger, starvation and death.

There were several kinds of smuggling: the first was large-scale business. It was organized by wealthy wholesalers who had their associates on the Gentile side and a squad of 'Szmalcowniki', who bribed the gendarmes and Polish and Jewish militiamen, who in turn monitored the goods carried in wagons through the main gates of the ghetto – mostly at night. Smuggling on a minor scale was carried out by grocers and outsiders who lugged their contraband through the cellars of some houses connected with those in the ghetto, through all sorts of secret passages and dug subways. Children played a big role in smuggling. The walls encircling the ghetto were built of brick. Where the wall crossed a roadway there remained an opening some two bricks in diameter above the gutters through which water from the Jewish gutter flowed into the Aryan one. A small Jewish child could wriggle onto the other side through such a hole, carry back small quantities of victuals even several times in one night. Such a child was often the only supporter of a large family, an expert in goods and a reliable expert in working out bills and accounts.

I knew a Jewish family who before the war had a big shop with pottery and glassware. Unfortunately it stood in Zimma Street and was cut off from the ghetto. Impoverished as they were, their relatives, also formerly well-off merchants expelled from Lodz, soon joined them. Two boys from this family breached the gutter several times a night; they co-operated with some boys from the Gentile side – the suppliers. I wondered whether such a small goy would not take the money and beat or give away his Jewish associate, and was really surprised at the downright denial from Josek or Srulek. It never happened. There was a great decency in dealings among those little merchants, one did not cheat the other, and if Nojtek said that the parcel contained half a kilogram of butter or sausage, the weight was true and the merchandise of good quality. The children carried on their hard work without grumbling, although they well knew that when caught they would, at best, get away with a severe beating.

For a long time I got our milk supply from a woman whose child, a beautiful eight-year-old blond boy, used to crawl through a hole at night to contact his mother's former maid, in order to get milk. The boy could get through the small opening but the milk cans were too big; so a tinsmith in the ghetto had made a special long, narrow container to enable the boy to perform his nightly task. When one day the milk was not brought I went to enquire and found the little smuggler in bed. It had happened that Zosia, the Aryan maid, had bought him a toy. Precious night hours had been spent playing with this marvellous novelty. The boy had been returning with his loads of milk at dawn. On the other side of the wall time dragged for the restlessly waiting mother, who knew nothing about the plaything. At last she heard Srulek's whistle; she answered with a sigh of relief. The first can appeared, then the second – priority was always given for goods – and then little Srulek forced his little hands and head through. His mother was already holding his feeble hips when a shot rang out. In the daylight a German soldier had spotted the small feet of the big criminal who had no right to live; he shot and hit one of the child's legs. His mother pulled the boy out and a doctor dressed his wound but the bone was shattered into small pieces and so the leg had to be amputated. After a few weeks, however, the milk appeared again. Little Srulek took up his neglected duties. 'Oh, I am quite all right', he answered cheerfully when I enquired after his health, 'and it doesn't matter at all. I can make it even without the crutch, because I can hop very well. And, besides, our Zosia lives not far from the wall.' Yes, the poor child had to carry on, for his mother and sister were too 'fat' for this job! The ghetto loved its little self-sacrificing sustainers and appreciated the jobs they performed. The little smuggler was immortalized in a beautiful and moving ballad: '. . . Through holes, through walls, a little boy crawls . . .'

Ghetto life dragged on. Another month, another year, the war must surely come to an end. We were locked in a prison surrounded by thick walls, and yet we lived on. People loved, married, had children, and some even got rich and danced. Yet the poverty increased daily and in all the world there was no bigger mortality rate than in those days in Warsaw. I must admit that the welfare institutions did their best, the so-called 'Check-in Welfare' endeavoured to admit everyone, giving out a few meals, but it was difficult to cope with the number of refugees from all over Poland. The misery was too great for some of the better-off citizens to be of any real help. Just the same, the people in the ghetto got used to the thought of death: 'You today, me tomorrow', one would say at the sight of a corpse covered up with newspapers.

In the midst of all this bustled the Jewish Gestapo men, well fed, well dressed, wearing officers' top-boots. These were the notorious 'Thirteen', a sort of militia which should not, however, be confused with the militia of the Jewish Council. Collaborators of the worst kind, they wore caps edged with green and derived their name from the address of their headquarters at 13 Leszno Street. 'You had better look out', could often be heard. 'No talk of politics. Here stands one of "The Thirteen". Take care that nobody sees the textiles in your room because your neighbour works at "The Thirteen"', was advice given by those who knew. In short, we were very much afraid of 'The Thirteen'.

Spring 1941

WITH THE SPRING of 1941 came new hope that our circumstances would certainly change for the better. There was no regular newspaper, for obviously no printing was allowed in the ghetto, and it was more and more difficult to obtain a Polish newspaper. On the Gentile side there was a newspaper published in Polish: *Nowy Kurier Warszawski (New Warsaw Courier)*. This was in fact a German paper published in the Polish language. In the beginning it could be obtained in the ghetto but then the sale of any newspaper was prohibited. 'Verboten', said an order, and one had to comply. In consequence this rag was now and again smuggled in, its price 200 per cent higher than on 'the other side' only a few yards away. The news was depressing; forward, ever forward the German armies were advancing. Incessantly and eagerly we anticipated a war between Russia and Germany. The headlines, however, proclaimed that never was the friendship between those two countries so deep and true than in this spring of 1941. That in spite of British endeavours the friendly relations of those great powers were everlasting due to their mutual ideology: the fight against British capitalism and imperialism; there was a great personal friendship between Hitler and Stalin. The trash of German propaganda was well directed.

At last came 22 June 1941. The half-dead ghetto revived: WAR with RUSSIA! Now everything would certainly end soon, as the

Germans had to lose. The first Russian planes over Warsaw, the planes which we had dreamed of hearing, were enthusiastically welcomed. But they proved to be only reconnaissance squadrons, and after dropping no bombs they flew away. Feeling in the ghetto was running high, as if a new spirit permeated the people, and although the first communiqués already reported the routing of the Russian armies and further German territorial gains, these successes would not depress the Jews. 'It is just as it was meant to be', maintained the optimists, 'the Russians should drag them as deep as they can into their frozen country. Besides, everybody knows how bad their roads are, and this is where the German tanks and guns will founder! And they have no oil, and oil rules the world. The history of Napoleon will repeat itself, and their defeat will be equal to his in 1812!' So people talked about Napoleon everywhere and the poor illiterate shopkeeper of a grocery in the ghetto would mention his name trembling with emotion, not knowing who he really was. 'I wish Napoleon would come at last, may God help him.' I did not have the heart to put the poor unhappy creature straight. On this score, perhaps she and others breathed easier with this illusion and hope about Napoleon. Hope was a big thing in the ghetto, which even at the price of truth should not be denied anyone. Meanwhile the Germans made further gains in Russia, and we in the ghetto were worse and worse off.*

At the end of the summer of 1941 the Jews were ordered to surrender all their furs within two days. This applied not only to complete fur coats but to all fur collars and trimmings down to the smallest pieces, including children's fur slippers or quilts. On pain of death these had to be deposited at the premises of the Jewish Council in Grzybowska Street. All this was required for the success of the German campaign in frosty Russia. We were desperate; already we had no fuel for the winter and now we were to remain with no warm overcoats. There were people who had nothing but their old mouldy fur coats to put on. But nobody could help us and we had to comply. A few hours after the publication of this order we obediently formed long queues, in front of the building of the

---

* The end of the German–Soviet alliance marked the beginning of the sytematic and comprehensive annihilation of the Jews; the full brunt of this new destructive force did not befall Warsaw until a year later.

Jewish Council to rid ourselves of this duty as quickly as possible. Owners of beautiful broadtails and Persian lamb coats offered their furs as if doing a favour. We could only wonder what use a soldier at the German front would make of a fluffy silver fox or any other elegant piece of fur, definitely unsuited to form part of a soldier's uniform. But this will probably remain the secret of the Herrenvolk. Next to an elegant female with her expensive fox you would see a poorly dressed woman giving away her worn-out sheepskin and her children's miserable pelts. 'Ale glach, ale glach, urem, rach' (All equal, all equal, rich and poor) cried the philosopher of the Warsaw ghetto, a ragged, half-mad stripling whom everyone in the ghetto knew well. Of course, the optimists were not put out of countenance. 'All's not rosy with Hitler', they would say. 'If he cannot clothe his troops for the severe Russian winter our furs won't help him, he must lose the war! We will outlast him.'

The Council officials worked hard until late at night in order to admit and issue receipts for all their furs. These vouchers were carefully kept as proof because after the prescribed deadline, houses were to be searched. I shall never forget the last day of that order. It was Sunday and a couple of dealers succeeded somehow in entering the ghetto through the Chlodna–Elektoralna gate. It paid to give a princely bribe to the sentries, for the bargains to be had were quite exceptional. For a few cents one could get sealskin or Persian lamb, broadtails or foxes. Women who had never in their lives worn furs were fussy about buying Persian lambs because thin broadtails were more elegant! And a woman stall-keeper would frown at a silver fox which was not fluffy enough and would eventually take it for one or two kilograms of butter. These buyers exploited the Jews most shamelessly. They knew well that in another hour or two the furs had to be surrendered – free. On the other hand, no decent Gentile came at that time to the ghetto. It was only the rabble who would always take advantage of circumstances for profit. I decided not to give my furs away. I didn't give a damn if they denounced me – no criminals were going to have my furs! I concealed the furs belonging to myself and my mother in hermetically sealed cans in the attic of the house where I had a flat. Since I had to have some vouchers, I gave up some old and ragged pieces.

In December 1941 the Germans were at the gates of Moscow and Stalingrad. The Warsaw Jews were cold without coal or wood, yet their spirits were high. When the Germans deprived the Jews of the use of electricity, the people rigged up small gas lamps, and when this too was forbidden, carbide and candles were used. Then the electric and gas meters were tampered with, and in spite of the order, the electric lights burned on. Anyway, a constant ransom was paid to the electricity collectors who were clearly well aware of our tinkering.

In those times every apartment house in the Warsaw ghetto formed a unit, the inhabitants being organized into House Committees. Heading the Committee was a Chairman with one or more deputies, depending on the size of an apartment house (there were blocks with more than 1000 souls) and a few members of the board. These included a financial committee, auditors, a treasurer and a culture and education department. The most important person was considered the 'Hausmeister' (caretaker), usually a former merchant or a professional man. In our block he was a medical student. The Chairman and other members of the Committee were elected at a general meeting of all inhabitants. Important resolutions could be decided only after such meetings. One should understand that the home owners, even if they lived on the premises, had, at that time, no links with their property because no rents were collected or paid. Responsibility for the maintenance of a block, for order, clearing of garbage, mending of installations, employing an administrative executive or a caretaker was therefore laid upon the House Committee. The main task of the Committee, however, was the welfare of the poor tenants of the apartment house. If a few poor families lived in a relatively 'rich' block, they suffered no hunger. Ordered by the Committee, those better off gave some provisions to the destitute, fed poor children at their tables and contributed money or clothes for collecting.

The inhabitants of each block formed what amounted to one big family. After curfew hours we would gather at one of the tenants where the topic was always politics. On summer evenings the courtyard of a block was a kind of social club. One would exchange all sorts of news and gossip. In digging up money for their poor, the members of the Committee showed great ingenuity. They created 'entertainment commissions' who arranged all kinds of tea parties and dances, even with bands and artistic shows, and who made the most of the human passion for gambling and organized small card clubs. Naturally all the profits went to the poor of the block.

Now and again the Germans reduced the area of the ghetto. I knew people who within one year had to move four or five times. Of course, each change was for the worse. In each flat something had been left behind, belongings grew scarcer and scarcer, and each time a smaller van was required for the transport. We in fact needed less. At first one would worry about pictures and carpets, crystal and pottery; but after a fifth or sixth move, when instead of a flat one had to be content with a cubicle, the most primitive furniture was more than enough. I was lucky that the flat into which I had moved remained in the ghetto area until the end and when my Court appearances ceased, I busied myself entirely with the education of my daughter. My nicely brought-up child was rosy with health. In our district there was no park or even a small garden, so I had to take her for walks in overcrowded streets. Twice, as I was standing with the pram on a small square in front of the synagogue at Tlomackie Street, I witnessed scenes of Germans jumping down from passing lorries to beat a crowd of women into dispersing. At the close of 1941 the misery in Warsaw seemed to reach its peak. We received less and less on our ration cards and therefore more and more people died of hunger. In the streets ragged women and children sang ghetto hits about ration cards.

Sometimes at twelve o'clock on a frosty night, although the curfew hour was fixed at seven, one could hear a plaintive cry of a homeless, hungry creature who had once been a human being: 'Drop me a piece of bread, a few crusts, a little piece of old, stale bread.' Curfew breaking was punishable by death but what could frighten a poor beggar for whom death from a bullet was easier than life? My windows faced Elektoralna Street, the other side of which, fenced off, belonged to the Gentile quarter. On quiet evenings when traffic had died down, sitting on the windowsill, I could hear the noises of the big city – of Gentile Warsaw. Car horns, tram bells, and often radio music. Over there, behind the walls, people lived their normal lives. They moved freely about while we were imprisoned, in fact, condemned. Against a background of the vibrating sounds of big Warsaw the song of a wretched Jew, 'Drop a piece of bread', echoed strangely in the night.

Sometimes we could hear the whistle of a train, so somewhere beyond these walls there was a world still. How strange it seemed that there were people who were able to travel. We knew we were helplessly lost. The ghetto streets chanted songs which encapsulated our thoughts: Where should I go, all roads are closed. Where should I go, I am asked day and night. Where should I go, where's a road, where's a shore. Where should I go, they don't allow me to proceed. You are pushed back because you are a Jew.

But the wretched, doomed ghetto had its romanticism too. Apart from those sad songs one could sometimes even hear a Neapolitan ditty; however odd it might sound in these surroundings, this had its merit in making people forget their lot for a while. I remember a young singer with an extremely pleasant voice who for her repertoire had chosen just such non-ghetto songs; another one with a beautiful alto, which grew hoarse, used to sing: 'O Moreno, gidenkst du dajn nacht in Toledo. Es war ja so szejn' (Oh, Moreno, do you remember that night in Toledo, it was so beautiful).

· 5 ·

Joining the Workforce: The Expulsions Begin

LARGE GERMAN FACTORIES employing Jewish labour sprang up in the ghetto area, the so-called 'shops' in which, at first, only poor Jews worked. The job was hard and the wages a pittance. One of the biggest was Schultz & Co. at 51 Nowolipie Street, a furrier who worked exclusively for the Wehrmacht. It belonged to an old German named Schultz who, at the beginning, employed a Jewish manager. My two subtenants, both German Jewesses, started working in this shop as simple workwomen, later on becoming forewomen of some sections. The spring of 1942 brought rumours that some new restrictions against the Jews were in preparation, that from now on every Jew, regardless of sex, would have to work somewhere. So as early as April 1942 my subtenants enlisted me as a workwoman at Schultz & Co. and I began working as a furrier-outfitter on twelve-hour alternate shifts, one week at night, another in the daytime. Since I did not care for the poor wages, I went to work every second day in order to be on the payroll and have proper identity papers.

On 1 July 1942 news about the expulsion of the Jews from Lublin caused a panic. How much truth was in it nobody knew, but the general apprehension reached its climax when on the night of 16 July several Jewish doctors were arrested. There followed the suicide of Mr Czerniakow, Chairman of the Jewish Council, who swallowed potassium cyanide because he did not want to sign certain German orders against the Jews.* By now, in any case, I was going to work regularly.

On 21 July I went to the shop as usual, quietly sewed on buttons and made loops and knots. All of a sudden there was a great stir and confusion arose; something had happened but nobody knew exactly what. Someone cried out 'Expulsion. We have to be expelled. No, no, not all of us, only those who don't work.' Moments later there were new cries: 'They have already swept this and that street.' The name of the street where I was living was mentioned, among others. My blood froze. My baby had been in the care of my old and helpless aunt there in the flat. Frantic to save the child, I rushed to the door, but at the shop exit a German 'Werkschutz' (workshop guard) stood firm and let nobody out. Tormented by the thought that my baby was in danger I had to sew on, sew on, quickly. At about two o'clock Mr Schultz came to us in person and solemnly let us know that an order was published evicting all Jews from the Warsaw area except those who were employed in the factories. The spouse, parents and children of a worker were considered as 'protected'. Steps to issue suitable papers were undertaken immediately. As soon as I received such a document I implored the German to let me go home to the baby. Schultz himself granted me leave and I ran home. With a sigh of relief I found all of them safe, though in two neighbouring blocks the eviction had started: all Jews had been expelled and the houses totally emptied.

Thus a little reassured on my personal score I could read the notorious order dealing with the liquidation of the Warsaw ghetto. This order, dated 21 July 1942,† proclaimed that because of overcrowding in the Warsaw ghetto all Jews, regardless of sex and age, must be resettled in the newly conquered eastern territories. The Jews would be employed in the east; experts would practise their trades. One was allowed to take along household utensils, some clothes, linen and money, but not jewellery and foreign

---

* Adam Czerniakow was Chairman of the Jewish Council from its inception in 1939 until 1942 and in this role was responsible for supplying many thousands of Jews for forced labour. When the deportations began and Czerniakow gradually realized what he was being called upon to do, he committed suicide.

† This order marked the beginning of a seven-week purge of Warsaw Jews, with a quarter of a million people being sent to their deaths in the gas ovens of Treblinka.

currency. Applicants would receive free transport and board until their arrival at the new destination. Those employed by German businesses and institutions, Jewish Council workers, Jewish policemen, block executives, administration clerks and shop owners selling rationed goods, were allowed to remain in Warsaw. These were the contents of the order, practically a death sentence, which was passed on 400,000 Jews living in the Warsaw ghetto. At first, however, a considerable number of Jews could remain in Warsaw.

Optimists consoled themselves that the order applied only to the unemployed and to poor refugees, enabling all others to move about freely. The day following the publication of the order a great many refugees went voluntarily to the rallying centre, the Umschlagplatz. Warsaw was indeed overcrowded, and the possibility of earning a living, especially for refugees, was negligible. 'Perhaps over there, in the east, somewhere near Smolensk, we shall find some work and they will give us, however poor, some food and lodgings', reasoned those trusting people. 'Besides, fortunes of war are changing, the Russians may regain their lost territory and then we shall be in Russia, far from the Germans. Who knows?', asserted others.

Since working in a 'shop' could protect one from expulsion, people began feverishly to look for a job in a factory. Huge sums were paid to foremen, charge hands or men responsible for even small sections, simply to get a job and the required papers. But there were too few workshops to shelter all those eager to work, so artificial 'shops' had to be created. The way this was effected was rather simple. Jews who had some dealings with Germans would establish a new workshop under a German name. Of course, it would cost enormous sums in gold and foreign currency, but the main thing was that it could provide people with papers. Several new tailors, furriers and saddlery workshops were then established and existed for a few months; the majority of these new undertakings, however, were based on fraud, extracting money out of those wretched people. The Germans did not respect the new identity papers, and those who carried them were mercilessly expelled.

Many Jews dreamed about getting a job at one of the biggest factories, Schultz & Co. No wonder that this enterprise grew far beyond its initial tasks – the furriery – with departments such as tailors, shoemakers, carpenters, fitters and saddlers. Yet the furriery, because of its basic value to the war effort against Russia, retained the highest esteem and was overburdened with orders for the troops. Thanks to my good fortune I belonged to the 'aristocracy' of shops and was envied by all my acquaintances. 'What extraordinary luck to be employed by Schultz!', my friends would say. And so, lucky me – I would sit for twelve hours a day bent over some vests, in a hot, stuffy, crammed room with the eternal worry that at home, at Elektoralna Street, everything was in order, hoping that the identity papers which should protect my child would prove effective.

Immediately after the publication of the 'Resettlement Order' the manhunts started. Ordinary large carts, accompanied by a few Jewish policemen, appeared in the streets. All those with inadequate documents, or with none, were forcibly pushed on to the carriages. These 'razias' were, at first, restricted to street catching and evictions of Jews inhabiting lodging-houses, known as the 'housing'. These horse-driven carts pulled up at dawn and the militia loaded them full with all the tenants, even the old and sick, and onward to the Umschlagplatz they would roll. The same happened to all the inmates of the Jewish jail.

I witnessed the expulsion of the Korczak Orphanage. The famous Korczak Orphanage had formerly occupied premises in Krochmalna Street but when this part of Krochmalna was attached to the Gentile quarter, Mr Korczak moved his orphanage to Sliska Street, the building of a former Jewish school. All that time the orphanage was directed in an exemplary manner by its founder and headmaster, Mr Janusz Korczak, a well-known writer, pedagogue and teacher. Thanks to his superhuman efforts, his children were well off. On the day that they left the ghetto they made a strange procession as they walked along Sliska Street led by an elderly, dignified man, and accompanied only by a few policemen. The orphans, dressed in their finery, marched in twos, the younger ones followed by the older. With them were the teachers and all the orphanage staff. Were it not for the expression of stony peace and overbearing sadness on the face of the elderly gentleman, it could have been taken for a children's excursion or a peaceful stroll. But he knew where he was leading his children, this man whose supreme love was for his little homeless wards. The Germans had given him permission to remain in Warsaw. He had refused. In the Umschlagplatz he was again offered the chance to return to the city, but Mr Korczak would not leave his children. And I learned, later, that he gave the same answer to his Aryan friends when they tried several times to take him to the Aryan quarter.

In the first weeks after the expulsion order the Germans did not show up in the ghetto. Jews themselves, as for example the Jewish militia, were entrusted with the job. They carried out the checking of identity papers in the streets and even on the Umschlagplatz where the Germans were present; the loading and forcing of Jews into the railway carriages was left to the militia men. After all 'points' and other places of collective Jewish misery had been cleared out, street catching was carried out ceaselessly. People without a work ticket, the so-called 'Ausweis', did not leave their homes. However, the number of people caught was still insufficient for the Germans. 'We need more', cried the Germans, and the number of people who were to be delivered by the militia to the Umschlagplatz increased daily. The German Moloch* digested at first 6000 people daily, gradually increasing its demands.

The institution of the blockades carried out by the Jewish militia became a daily routine. During a blockade, which as a rule took place in the early hours of the morning, a strong detachment of militia men would cordon off a whole street or a part of a big road, and begin sweeping the blocks. There would be a shrill whistle and shouts of 'All down, all to the courtyard' which would announce the beginning of a blockade. After a while the militia men would enter the flats, chasing the inhabitants out. They were very efficient in their searches, even too meticulous, for they looked into the night tables and drawers, they climbed into the attics and descended to the cellars. The courtyards were swarming with militia men and when all the tenants were gathered, an officer would begin the checking. The lucky owners of good Ausweis passes were placed on one side of the yard, all the others on the other side. They were then chased out into the street and loaded into the waiting carts. A blockade would of course be accompanied by tears, shouts, pleas

---

* Moloch meaning king, is a biblical reference to the god to whose shrine human sacrifices were made (Kings and Jeremiah).

and even strong resistance, but all such incidents would be terminated by a cuff or club of a gallant officer.

The house I lived in was blockaded many times. The shrill whistle followed by the yell 'blockade' would tear me away from my bed, in which I had lain down exhausted, only minutes after my return from the all-night shift. I would quickly dress my child and myself and go down into the courtyard. The procedure of searching the house and checking the documents always took several hours, and one could only return to one's flat after everything had been finished. But long afterwards we could hear the sobs and weeping of those whose dearest ones had been taken away. These blockades were repeated with greater frequency for Ausweis cards were acknowledged by the Germans, and in spite of the conscientious militia, a few people always managed to escape their lot by hiding successfully. People not liable to expulsion diminished daily, eventually leaving only those employed in the shops and a part of the administration of the Jewish Council. After clearing out the major part of the ghetto and deporting the majority of its inhabitants, the Germans themselves came into action, still with the eager and efficient help of the Jewish militia.

During the early days of August 1942 notices posted in all shops ordered all workmen to leave their flats and to move into the workshop premises. The factory area usually comprised several adjoining blocks and could be inhabited only by workmen of the particular workshop. We were allotted a part of Nowolipie Street, from the Narmelicka corner to the Smocza corner. This area was closed by a temporarily erected wall across the roadway, at the entrance of which stood a guard of two militia men and one German gendarme both day and night. Sadly we had to move to our new places. We had to go through all our belongings and take only necessities with us. We were now living in small room so the greater part of our furniture and cradle bedding, even my little daughter's clothes, had to be abandoned in our flat. I took leave of the remaining furniture and other household trifles as if they were living creatures: each pot or piece of crystal had its own history and reminded me of some anniversary or birthday, or . . . simply yesterday.

I moved into 49a Nowolipie Street on 3 August 1942 together with my sister-in-law and her little daughter. My previous subtenants, the two girls from Leipzig, moved into another room in the same flat which consisted of four rooms each occupied by one family – all workers of Schultz & Co. We started our life in the workshop area. Our new world from 3 August was confined to a stretch of 150 yards from the corner of Karmelicka to the corner of Smocza Street. Yet I dreamed I might be given the grace of moving freely about this small place until the end of the war.

On about 5 August all 'workshop territories' were hermetically closed and Germans and Ukrainians started a ruthless expulsion of anyone found outside these areas – always with the efficient help of the Jewish militia. Wherever a German or a Ukrainian did not venture the militia men would gladly fish out as many as possible of those still hidden in cellars and vaults, only to oblige the Germans.

Our place was quiet for the time being but we could hear the almost incessant sounds of evictions, shouts and cries and shooting. From our windows we could see crowds of wretches driven to the Umschlagplatz. We were not allowed to leave our confinement even to call on a mother or brother working in a nearby shop. 'Strictly prohibited. Death penalty', proclaimed the placards pasted all over the walls. We were assured that since our factory was 'Kriegswichtig' (essential for war) and belonged to the war industry we were directly subject to the authority of the Wehrmacht and we were not to be moved without their consent. They provided us with very important-looking new cards bearing official German stamps, stating our identity and that the holder was subject to the Wehrmacht as a workman of the 'outfitting industry'. Living as we did in this small street under the protective arm of a German factory and possessing a document valid until January 1943, we felt somehow safe. What did it matter that our communication with Jews from other shops had ceased to exist, that any connection with the Gentile quarter was cut off and terrible famine was spreading? Of what importance was the lack of bread and the diminishing provisions of our 'black' baker! The dollar fell at that time to the value of 10 zloty and a loaf of bread cost 120 zloty. Hardly anybody would accept dollars for bread, but one could easily get it in exchange for butter, sugar or similar foodstuff which could be consumed without cooking, for there were days one could not cook at all. 'My dear, of what use is gold?', a happy owner of a few loaves of bread would ask, 'if you can't bite into it?' We were deprived of gas and electricity but we did not care. We worked in the factory very conscientiously from six o'clock in the morning until six at night. We clung to the workshop fiercely for it had promised to save our lives.

· 6 ·

My First Round-up

On 6 August I was resting at home after my night shift when I suddenly heard a terrible noise in the street, loud cries, shots and shouts of 'Alles runter' (all downstairs). I knew what this meant. The street was already full of Germans, Ukrainians and Jewish militia. A normal blockade had started. We all had to go out into the street guarded by Germans, Ukrainians and Shaulis (Lithuanians), while the militia searched the rooms and hideouts, forever dragging somebody out. I was in despair because my sister-in-law was out and her twelve-year-old daughter had been left in my care. During this blockade I had two children; my own who I held in my arms, and this girl with no documents. Yet I still had blind confidence in my identity card with all the stamps, eagles and 'Hakenkreuzen' (swastikas).

Alas, they checked no papers. Only the families of the milita men were released on the spot. The rest, formed in fives, were hurried to the Umschlagplatz. The way was strewn with horrific sights. Along dead, deserted streets of the big empty ghetto we were driven stumbling over scattered bundles, haversacks and all kinds of clothes – every few steps a corpse. By a doorway in Gesia Street the body of a dead woman lay face-down on the pavement. From underneath the corpse, the live feet of a little baby struggled in vain to emerge, the baby crying desperately, half asphyxiated by the body of his dead mother. The woman carrying her baby had been shot and had pressed it down with her weight during the fall. This picture will remain in my memory for ever.

The Germans hurried us along with shouts of 'Laufen, schnell laufen' (Run, run quickly), and we had to run quickly to keep pace with the guard, who was comfortably reclining in a rickshaw pushed by our rickshaw-man. They rode and we had to catch up with the greatest speed that the tired feet of the poor rickshaw-man could muster. It did not matter that among the captured his mother or sister could be running. It did not matter that an aged woman would stumble and fall; the Ukrainian shot the woman and the son pedalled on . . . 'Schnell, schnell, laufen, laufen!'

At the entrance to the Umschlagplatz two corpses lay entwined in a last embrace. We jumped over them and for the first time I was faced with the notorious place; it was a big square behind hospital buildings and enclosed by high walls topped with barbed wire entanglements. Into this place, apart from our group, were herded great numbers of Jews from various districts of the ghetto. Several goods trains with their engines steaming gave proof that we would soon be loaded on to them and transported out. I then lost the last glimmer of hope. It happened that due to the lack of carriages people were kept waiting for as long as two days. In the meanwhile the relatives could get in touch with the policemen guarding the place, bribe them, and get the victim out of the Umschlagplatz. In this way one of my cousins had bought himself off three times, but a woman with two children was lost. Patiently I awaited my turn to cross the barrier, to walk over into the station.

I will never forget the behaviour of an officer of the militia – a barrister and a personal acquaintance of mine whose zeal in serving the Germans was already well known. When I simply asked him whether any documents were being checked, he turned his back on me without a word and went away to carry on his noble mission. Utterly dejected I hugged my baby closer to me, gave half of my money to my niece and waited. At the barrier leading to the coaches stood two Special Duty officers making final selections of victims. I saw that they never looked at a single document and directed people to one side or another according to whim. As if driven by some inner force I turned to the German whose face bore traces of some remaining humanity and begged him: 'Bitte, lassen Sie mich', (Please, spare me). Even before I had finished the sentence this

German had pushed me so viciously against a group that had it not
been for the human wall I should have fallen with the children.
'Quick, hide the children', I heard my comrades say, and before
anybody could see, the children were concealed. So I was saved! I
had been pushed to the group of strong young people fit for work.
Nobody could understand why the German had released a woman
with children, and I myself do not know how I found the courage
to appeal that way to the feelings of a man who belonged to the
Vernichtungskommando (the extermination squad).

When I had recovered a little I took a closer look at those two
Germans who had the power of deciding between life and death.
The one to whom I had appealed directed people here and there
but seemed somehow quieter and did not ill-treat anybody. The
second, a fat chap, beat and kicked his victims and slapped any
woman begging for mercy. I saw a couple passing the barrier with
their twelve-year-old son. The fat German sent the strong, healthy
husband to the group of the released, directing the wife and boy
for deportation. The husband implored the German to let him go
with his family, knelt in despair before him, wanted to kiss his
boot, but the German kicked him in the face and the militia led the
bleeding victim away – to those who were saved. 'You are still
healthy', yelled the fat, ruddy German after him. 'You must still
work for us.'

A woman implored the German to allow her to say a last
goodbye her husband. 'Gut', said the German and ordered the
husband to be brought over to the condemned group and – did not
let him go back. The despair of the wife who had herself condemned
her husband was beyond words, but the German only laughed.
This cruel beast mocked his victims by releasing those who
entreated to be deported with their families. There were ghastly
scenes when parents were separated from their children. I saw
mothers prostrate at the German's feet, pleading for the life of their
children; I saw mothers from whom neither the German fist nor the
heavy hand of a militia man could tear their babies away from
them. In such cases the German would make use of a precious
bullet and the mother would die hugging her child until her last
breath. And I saw other young mothers who at the moment of
selection abandoned their children, tore way the little hands
clutching at their skirts; on her own she might have had a chance,

but with a child her death was a certainty. Then, standing with the group of the released and facing her child in the condemned crowd, she would cover her eyes so as not to see it, she would plug her ears not to hear her little one crying. And when, sometimes, the motherly feeling defeating the last instinct of life the mother ran to her child, the fat German would not let her go. All God's rules, humane instincts, all those precepts and commandments inculcated in us since time immemorial, lay in the dust on the Umschlagplatz.

After witnessing another incident I then understood why I had been so brutally pushed by the other German. It must have happened when the fat one had his back turned, for if he had seen me I would have been lost. I noticed a woman already released by the first German when the fat villain saw her and with a shout of 'Hans, mach doch kein Schwein' (Hans, don't be a pig) kicked the woman towards the condemned group. The torture of looking at all this took over an hour, we were so numerous. During all this time the Jewish militia loaded the freight wagons with struggling people, sealed them in, while new trains pulled in to the station and were filled with the old and sick, some on stretchers, people who had not passed the selection barrier. They were shoved into the wagons straightaway and the stretchers taken back to the carts. If a flicker of hope existed that people from the Umschlagplatz were being deported to some place of work, it now vanished. In that place I understood for the first time that 'Umschlagplatz' meant only death. At long last the selection of human cattle came to an end. Amidst constant cries and shots, the death wagons left the station. The Germans went. There remained only a few corpses and those of us who had been released. The militia men formed groups of inhabitants of ghetto districts before leading us away home. Without waiting for the order 'Laufen', we ran. We wanted to be as far as possible from the nightmare of the Umschlagplatz.

Those at home thought we had been deported. It is difficult to describe how my sister-in-law welcomed us. In the factory we were told that the selection and blockade had been aimed at getting rid of all those 'undesirables' who were living in the workshop area and were not employed by the factory. We were provided with new documents and again reassured that those working conscientiously should not fear deportation. Nevertheless, after my experience on the Umschlagplatz, I became very cautious and always took my child with me to the shop. I knew of mothers who did not find their children on returning home from work, although their guardians possessed the best and safest documents available. So I used to take my little Eva with me in spite of all the difficulties that this entailed.

The furriers' outfitting department in which I was employed was situated on the fourth floor just under the roof. The hall was low and comparatively small for the number of women working there; we were not allowed to open the windows. It was summer 1942 and we were still quite a crowd, so we had to sit tightly crammed one against the other. The air was close and stifling and from the vests, made of badly tanned hides, rose clouds of dust and fur particles. In the midst of this I kept my baby with me, even when she was sick with whooping cough. But there was no other way. It was clear that children on factory premises were strictly prohibited, therefore I had to smuggle her in every morning so that the 'Werkschutz' would not spot her. I would keep the coughing child on my lap all the time while sewing the vests without a break. The foreman of our department – a Jew – threatened to chase me and the baby out several times but seeing my stubbornness eventually gave in and pretended not to see her at all.

We were often visited by dignitaries from the Wehrmacht or SS – the masters of life and death. Five or six of them, medalled officers, would enter the hall, slowly pass the benches, look at the work, make remarks and give advice. My heart would seem to stop beating because on some occasions I had my Eva on my lap. Bent over my work I would conceal her golden hair under a vest and quickly flash my needle. I knew that our lives depended upon a single word of a German. On top of all this Eva got dysentery. Confined to the hot, sticky room, fed on the dreadful factory soup made of rotten turnips and cabbage, ill with whooping cough and then dysentery, the child seemed unlikely to survive. But she was a tough war-child and she always had a healthy appetite, did not cry and gave no trouble in the workshop. August of that year was exceptionally hot. For the first time in my life I cursed the sun blazing through the closed windows of our hall. 'Schnell, schnell arbeiten!', our German and Jewish superiors would shout, threatening the slowest workers with the withdrawal of their documents.

We had lived some twelve days in comparative peace when the

morning of 18 August resounded with the familiar whistles and noises. One glance out of the window confirmed it – a blockade! The street was already full of detachments of strong Germans, Ukrainians and Lithuanians. At the shout 'Alles runter' I snatched the child and ran out into the street. I wanted to get to the factory at all costs, but the soldiers barred my way.

Aligned in rows of fives we had to stand and wait. I still tried to get nearer the factory building and surreptitiously, step by step, I stole through the rows. Tugging my sister-in-law and my niece, I slowly wormed my way ahead. Another pace, a half pace, and I saw the factory gate a block away. But the gate was closed. In deathly fear we stood and waited. Suddenly the gate opened, letting out Schultz and Klimanek, the German manager. A few old workmen cried out 'Herr Schultz, Herr Klimanek, it's me, I have been working in the factory for two years'. The almighty Schultz came nearer and drew out some of the old-timers known to him, letting them into the factory yard.

An indescribable tumult ensued with everybody fighting to get closer to the rescuers, but I could not even dream of it – I was still too far away. Seeing this uproar the Germans and Ukrainians rushed in, mercilessly beating people on the head with their whips and beating people back from the gate. Many Jews fell under the knotted whips, dripping with blood. Others escaped. There were a few more openings in the ranks and I edged nearer the lifesaving gate, my sister-in-law and her daughter following. What did whips matter when the factory meant life? Still I was too far away when Schultz and Klimanek let a few workmen in again. This created a new bustle and Germans began to shoot at the crowd. A deafening shot rang out next to me and, for a moment, I thought I was hit – my sister-in-law tore her hand away from mine and I lost sight of her – but as if in a miracle, people fled from the gate emptying the space around me. Taking advantage of this confusion I leaped to the gate and Klimanek, who remembered me, let me in. Still running I reached the furriers' department and concealed the child under the vests. How wonderful that terrible room then seemed, how good I felt once inside, with what relief I breathed the stifling air! It appeared that neither my child nor I was hurt, only for a couple of hours I could not hear too well.

There were many casualties that day. A few were killed, many

wounded and a great number of workmen were driven away to the
Umschlagplatz. People were taken there from our flat, but my
sister-in-law and niece were saved by a militia man who knew them
and had successfully pleaded with a German for their lives. A great
sorrow befell us as people grieved for their wives and children,
husbands and parents. We entirely lost our willingness to work for
we knew that the factory could no longer ensure our lives.
Klimanek would come in encouraging, pleading with us to go on
with our work; he assured us that the purpose of this blockade had
been to rid the area of people who did not work. He added that the
management of the factory would in future vouch for the safety of
all strong and healthy bearers of the factory documents. Children
and elderly people must, however, disappear from the factory as
they were unproductive elements.

Again life rolled on. Wounds healed surprisingly fast. A few days
later there was no more talk about those who had been taken
away. We again started singing while we worked and went back to
cracking jokes. The food situation improved considerably, provisions were cheaper and several things could be obtained at reason-
able prices. Fruit and dainties appeared, smuggled through
unknown ways from the Gentile side. In our block, in a private flat,
a grocery was set up in which even butter, sausages and sugar were
sold. The instinct of self-preservation is strangely powerful. We
wanted to live at all costs and to live on one had to forget, deceive
oneself that perhaps one would pull through somehow.

In our flat we started some sort of housekeeping and even began
to cook. We learned to chop furniture for firewood. There was
plenty of furniture in our area. In practically every courtyard,
beautiful mahogany or walnut or rosewood furniture lay abandoned. What use could one have for bookcases, sideboards, drawing-room couches? Armchairs and cupboards – to hell with
everything! Every room was used as a bedroom, sometimes for a
score of people. Beds, a rickety table and a few chairs were the only
essentials – the rest was firewood. So we chopped the stylish
furniture, cursing 'Empires' and 'Louises' for their solidity. Human
ingenuity is great, for soon professional choppers appeared – our
factory comrades of course, and in exchange for a few zloty one
could get a kilogram of firewood chopped from one's own
furniture.

Traps and tunnels to the Aryan side were built and once again a daring Gentile woman would steal across to our street and for a little food would buy clothes. This was called the 'ciucha trade' which in Warsaw slang meant dealing in old clothes. Heaps of old clothes, the property of those who had been deported, lay in every flat. A hawker willing to take risks could have it at a ridiculously low price. We were glad to get rid of this as well as of the furniture. Unfortunately no Gentile would buy the furniture for it was simply impossible to get it through a narrow hole in the cellar or wall. Somehow or other we lived on. The time passed and this was important. My baby got over the bout of dysentery but still continued to cough. On a sleepless night when I could hear the distant whistle of a train I would hastily plug my ears; this whistle symbolized a journey of deportation and where could a ghetto Jew now travel if not to his doom? And I would pray not to be forced to travel until the war had ended.

Prepared for the Worst:
Boots and a Hacksaw Blade

IN SEPTEMBER, or maybe at the end of August, we learned for definite where our brethren had been sent. In our area a young man appeared and told us how he, together with his wife and child, had been deported to Treblinka, a small place in the vicinity of Malkinia. How there, under the pretext of having a bath, people were ordered to undress and how they were then gassed to death. He had been employed in sorting out the clothes and loading them on to the trains. He had succeeded in concealing himself under a heap of garments, had thus escaped and had returned to the ghetto.

So then we knew what fate was in store for us, we knew that our chance of survival was next to none, and yet we carried on that curious abnormal life of ours. At this time I made a firm resolution: I would not let myself be taken to Treblinka. I would not let them gas me. When they caught me I would make my escape. I procured a thin and narrow hacksaw blade. I put on a pair of top-boots belonging to a deported man which had been left in our flat and slipped into the boot-leg the precious blade wrapped in cottonwool. From the end of August 1942 I wore the boots continuously, in spite of the heat or the comparative quiet in our street. For hours on end I would practise with the hacksaw blade; on keys, door-knobs, handles and locks. The thin blade would hurt my unpractised fingers but gradually I became accustomed to using it and it did not hurt so much. As time wore on I became quite an expert and all metal parts in our flat bore the signs of my professional achievements; but I used to practise only when I was alone as I feared becoming a laughing-stock. From the moment I had the blade and had learned to make use of it I felt somehow quieter and I knew they would not get me alive to Treblinka.

One night, I think it was 4 or 5 September, we were awakened by a siren alert. A raid on Warsaw. Nobody thought of going down to the shelter in the cellar; a bombing raid seemed the best opportunity of dying a decent death – so I remained in bed. But I did not live alone and when my fellow tenants began to press me I had to get up. We went out on to the staircase and squatting down on the steps we heard the bombs dropped and the barking of the anti-aircraft guns. We prayed to God to make Him drop bombs on our factory and our block and to end our misery. A few bombs did indeed fall in our vicinity and the Court building in Leszno Street was hit. During this bombardment we learned from one of our factory dignitaries that a final purge in the workshop was planned for the next morning and would be followed by the issuing of numbers to each worker. The air raid unfortunately came to an end and I had to think about how to get my child into the shop the next day. It was still dark when I smuggled my little Eva in under my coat.

From that very morning in fact they started distributing the 'life numbers', little green cards stamped with consecutive numbers. A worker had to fix it to his coat by means of a safety-pin and always wear it. I received such a number. One of our foremen was Mr R., a Jew, and a very honest man. He too had a child, and I turned to him begging for help and asking what he had done about his child. He led me to some private flat in the factory building in which I found his wife and child with two other women, the wives of 'Werkführers' with their children. Silently I looked down, holding my breath, for there, downstairs, the blockade had started and the area was being searched thoroughly with militia men on the roofs looking into the chimneys. Suddenly a frightened Mr R. came in and told us that Schultz himself was not sure whether this place was going to be searched and advised us to go down to his private office, which he considered safer. With pounding heart I went down the steps and entered the private study of Mr Schultz on the first floor. There I found two or three women with their children.

All of us sat on the floor in a little corner near the stove, as far away from the window as possible so as not to be seen from the street. For long hours none of us mothers uttered a word, and not a child cried out. The manager, Neumann, entered, the horrible German whom we dreaded so much because he would beat workmen he met in the street. Surprisingly Neumann then behaved quite differently, looked us over and asked if we needed anything. None of us replied, only some heads turned to indicate the negative. 'Don't be afraid, you women, nothing will happen to you here, calm yourselves', he said and left. A little while later in came Schultz. He too calmed us, comforted and assured us that no harm would befall us in his private office which nobody would dare enter.

How slowly time drags by when you are in deadly peril and gaze incessantly at the slow-moving hands of a clock. Suddenly the door burst open and we shrank away in terror – a completely drunk soldier crashed into the study and waving his rifle about howled: 'Runter, alles runter!' (Out, all out!). All our explanations proved useless and he pushed us with his rifle butt, forcing us to leave the safety of the study and go with him. 'We are lost', I thought with sinking heart, yet I went so slowly that I managed to be the last in the row. Seeing that the soldier was prodding those in front of him I had already begun to move back from the half-flight of stairs when a German officer appeared. Not waiting to be spoken to I turned to him complaining about the behaviour of a drunk private who had pushed me out of Mr Schultz's office in which I was waiting for instructions, and asked him for help. 'Come along,' he said, 'I am just going to Mr Schultz's.' After some minutes Schultz entered his study. On seeing only me he wrung his hands.

He was so obviously and truly moved that I could not understand it. 'I wanted to save those children. How did this blackguard enter here? Somebody had certainly left the door open.' Then he started cursing those evil Germans who kept on murdering people in this beastly way. God would punish them and he, Schultz, could not stand it any longer. During his soliloquy, from the wastepaper basket under the desk, first a small black head appeared and then a four-year-old boy crept out. This boy had seen the German soldier burst into the study and had taken advantage of the confusion and hidden in the basket. 'That's the bookkeeper's son', exclaimed

Schultz. He drew out two 'life numbers', pinning one to the boy's and another to my Eva's clothes. He told me to look after the boy whose mother had already been taken away.

It was two p.m. Downstairs the blockade was coming to an end. I heard whistles and loud 'ab', meaning that the victims had been led out. Only then did I dare to approach the window; nobody was in the courtyard. Once more I was saved. I had no courage to think 'Till when, for how long?' Many workers, mainly women, had been carried off in this blockade because there were too few 'life numbers'. In our shop the work lagged behind. There were not so many women at the benches; there were altogether fewer and fewer people.

Our German factory masters solemnly assured us that this had been the last blockade and peace would reign at last. Yet we all understood that 'our Germans', even those German SS officers, like the director Klimanek, had held no sway during a blockade. They did not even know about it in advance. It was clear to us that they really wanted to save us and keep this reduced number of workers in the factory. I do not know whether they were truly touched by our misery or whether they cared only for the maintenance of the factory. At any rate in those awful times our German masters, managers, directors and even the security guards, showed more human feeling and sympathy than I had ever credited them with possessing. And I kept on training in sawing iron.

Some days later, a doctor acquaintance of ours rang up during the night. He was the factory physician and told us that before eight o'clock in the morning, absolutely all Jews must clear out of the street and gather in the Mila quarter where the workers' roll-call would take place. Dr E. also had a child, a little boy whom he was hiding in a cellar. 'Now we shall definitely lose our children', said the desperate Dr E. 'How shall we be able to hide them in a new place?' We talked to each other about things needed for this new move because we knew that we would never return to our homes. During the whole conversation I stood in pitch darkness because the Germans had cut off the gas and electricity to our district.

This new disaster broke me completely. I felt hopeless and unable to fight on. 'Come what may, it's night, and I am going to lie in bed as long as possible.' I went back to my bed, hugged my child

to me, my little girl whom I thought already doomed. Thus I waited
for dawn. Meanwhile the streets grew busy and noisy, with people
rushing madly here and there. Every now and then an acquaintance
would come to us asking what to do, how to act. I did not stir. I
could stay in bed an hour, maybe two, and then . . . the end. There
was nothing to pack because our rucksacks had been prepared
some weeks ago. Besides, I knew where the deportation headed. I
knew that there would be no need for baggage.

It turned out that the new order about clearing our street was a
surprise even to the management of our factory: Schultz and
Klimanek were kept out of our area. It was the great Brandt
himself, the head of the liquidation department who, mistrusting
his own compatriots, had hit upon this devilish way of checking
the factory workers. At seven o'clock in the morning we all left
our homes. On the stairs I met my cousins. These good boys came
to say farewell – who knew whether we would meet again – and
brought me ten beautiful fresh rolls. A baker from Muranowska
Street had made rolls from all his available stock of flour and had
distributed them free among people who probably would not be
alive the next morning. And indeed I had seen my cousins for
the last time. They and their family of fifteen people were taken
to Mila Street. The 'life numbers' of their factory were not
respected.

This march of hopeless, resigned, wandering Jews was terrible to
behold. With bundles, rucksacks, bent down and ill-treated, they
were leaving our little alley, now so precious to everybody. One
can get accustomed to everything and even come to regard it with
affection. The gates of our ghetto stood ajar. For the first time in
many weeks we were allowed to go out. On the pavement of
Smocza Street Jewish militia men were sitting on chairs in order to
prevent any wanderer from going astray and hiding in the deserted
houses of the cleared-out ghetto. The militia men informed us that
the workers from all the shops were to assemble in Mila Street and
Parysow Square, where the Germans would perform a last inspection. There was no way out. Step by step this frightened crowd
moved. 'Forward, get going!', the harsh shouts of the militia men
drove us on. So we went on, nobody knowing whether at the end
of our walk life or death was waiting.

Mila Street and Parysow Square had been cleared of their

inhabitants, and were now full of workers coming from various factories. After a few hours manager Neumann appeared and in the courtyard of one of the blocks delivered a short speech in which he enlightened us thus: 'The Vernichtungskommando (the extermination squad), which was entrusted with carrying out the deportation of Jews, had come to the conclusion that Warsaw had too many Jews, apart from the unemployed who were still in hiding. It was therefore ordered to clear the areas surrounding all factories, gather the workers in one place and, in the mean time, thoroughly search all our streets and houses. The Schultz factory had the right to employ 8000 young, healthy and strong workmen and all those who had numbers would, after checking, be released and returned to their respective workshops. For aged people and children there was no place in the factory areas. That was the effect of the latest order of the Vernichtungskommando SS and SD.'

Heartbroken I went to the place which was in the mean time to house workers from our furriery shop and from other departments of our factory. Among them were a few who had succeeded in concealing their children in attics and cellars. 'What shall we do next?', fathers and mothers asked in despair, because we knew for certain that during a selection the Germans were likely to take children away, often with their parents. So one had to separate from the children, but how, and where was one to leave them? Where could they be hidden, many asked me. For me there was no question. I had nothing to think over. I would go with my child, come what may. I had once experienced going to the Umschlagplatz with a child and had emerged safely.

Dr E., a really decent and honest man, and an exceptionally good father, spoke words which I could never forget: 'I want to live, don't you understand it? I am only thirty and I want to live!' And then as if he were going insane he repeated: 'I want to live, I want to live!' Dr E. concealed his boy and his nurse in a well-hidden cellar in Mila Street and he with his wife luckily passed the selection. My colleague, a woman barrister, had hidden her boy in a cellar that seemed 100 per cent safe; a few others did the same but almost none of them ever saw their children again.

People looked around for hiding-places, searching everywhere. Attics and cellars in Mila Street and Parysow Square were becoming crowded. Caches were feverishly prepared but what could be achieved within a few hours? 'Mother Earth, split yourself,' I prayed, for then I still knew how to pray and had faith. The day was fine, the sun shone as usual, but there was no place on earth for us. No sunshine. Dusk was falling slowly. Everyone stared at the sunset, inwardly wondering whether they would ever see another. The selection was to commence at eight in the morning.

Utterly resigned, I waited for morning. Late in the evening Miss Stark, my former subtenant, ran up to me and with an excited 'Your Eva is saved' made the child drink a cupful of some liquid which she brought with her. The idea was this: a few Jewish foremen from some departments were allowed to return home that very evening. Taking advantage of this, we could put the child – asleep as a result of the drug she had been given – into a rucksack which Miss Stark would carry through to the shop. The plan seemed simple enough to us. Eva drank up the cupful of liquid but did not fall asleep. I dissolved three more powders but the child would not sleep. The entire group of foremen waited for another hour – all in vain – Eva did not fall asleep. A big rucksack lay empty and waiting; the opportunity was exceptional but a little two-and-a-half-year-old child would not let herself be packed into a rucksack. I lost my last hope of salvation. Later – too late – Eva fell into a heavy sleep. I laid her on a table and sat down by it. I was sure that this was to be our last night. In the same room were, among others, my friends Mr N., an engineer, with his wife and two boys, thirteen-year-old Jozio and nine-year-old Jasio. Mr N. was an employee of the Jewish Council, his wife worked in our furrier shop. All night the parents deliberated what to do with the children. All night long the mother cried, calling her younger son 'you, my little dead one'. She wanted her husband to take both boys with him, he argued that with two children they all three would perish. Petrified, I sat and listened, knowing that my position was even worse, a woman with a little child. Apart from Eva nobody slept that night. Not all of us had 'life numbers', besides, there were a few elderly people among us and I knew from experience that even those who were young were not safe at a selection, as the Germans performed this according to whim.

At daybreak we started to prepare ourselves for the march. Oh the irony of Fate. We had to look fine! We could not show the Germans our pale, worn-out faces, we had to look our best lest they considered this Jew sick or weak, unfit for work! The women did their hair in waves and curls, make-up was speedily applied: lips had to be reddened, cheeks made rosy, health had to radiate from each face. Here was something ghastly awaiting this crowd of vividly painted women, adorned with coloured scarves and spangles. Let us only be saved, be allowed to live, thought each one of us. Let us only outlive this day of peril. One of my comrades, a forty-five-year-old woman, put on a white overcoat, a pink shawl, rouged her face heavily and went round asking: 'How young I look, don't I? Please tell me the truth, too young?' I sat motionless, awaiting the turn of events. The child was still sleeping.

We had to form rows of eight, in groups, according to the respective departments of our factory, and the Germans were to pass 1000 of such rows. I did not join the row. I knew I was lost. At the last moment the manager, Neumann, promised to pass some children if an opportunity arose, and allowed me to stay near the gate. The Jewish militia barricaded Mila Street by means of upturned handcarts and dustbins, leaving in the centre a kind of gate. Rows of eight Jews were marched past this gate, having on either side SS men and Vernichtungskommando carefully scrutinizing the rows. Again and again I saw the Germans picking out somebody from the rows, the man showing his 'life number' crying 'But I am young!' and the beastly reply 'Weg du altes Schwein' (To hell with you, you old pig) and the man was thrown aside. 'Fill out the rows', the militia shouted and the newly completed row would tread ahead. The poor creature would still struggle, sometimes asking, imploring, only to be silenced by the slap of a rifle butt on the head.

I saw wives deprived of husbands, husbands whose wives were taken away. How strangely they reacted. Some struggled: 'I want to go with my wife', 'I want to go to my husband', they would cry. Some fought their way through to the condemned group to which their beloved ones had been relegated, for this group was obviously less strongly guarded. But in most cases the saved spouse would head for his or her group without turning back. I saw a strong workman who had tied his child around his waist and had tried to smuggle it under a thick overcoat. The German who noticed it fished him out of the row, proceeding to slit the secure ropes with his dagger. It did not matter that he mortally wounded the child and stained the poor father with his child's blood. 'You are still young, you can work', yelled the German, thrusting the limp child aside to die, and driving the father to join the group of the saved.

Soon the street was covered with the bodies of those who had argued that they were still young, or had resisted, or wanted to join those to be deported. This did not seem to matter. 'Go on, go on', shouted the Germans. 'Fill out the ranks of eight', shouted the militia, and the job went on. I noticed soon that the place where I stood was dangerous. I would certainly be pushed aside if spotted there. I must get out of there, but where to go. I strove in vain. Suddenly I noticed a change of guard among those who were checking us. At that particular moment there were only two of them, our manager Klimanek and one SS man. Without thinking at all I jumped into a passing row whispering to Klimanek: 'Save me.' The German standing nearby had just tried to catch hold of me when Klimanek yelled 'Back', and with all his strength thrust me back. I rolled and heard the second German barking: 'Herr Klimanek, machen Sie doch nich solchen Mist!' (Don't foul things up) but I leaped back as far as I could. The situation worsened meanwhile. There were now four groups of selecting Germans, each thrusting aside victims, even those with 'life numbers'.

It became clear to me that they would not let 8000 workers pass. To stay aside made no sense because I had seen that even Germans from our factory doing their best could not release us. So I looked for the group of women – furriers still awaiting selection – joined their rows and waited. I was considered insane as I was the only one with a child in my arms. Our turn came. Yet another step and the gate – here it is. A big German from our factory who had formerly terrorized us was in charge of the first selection. What to say? 'Um Gotteswillen lassen Sie mich doch!' (For heaven's sake let me stay!). He looked at me and said: 'Meinerseits gehen Sie' (For my part you can go). I went two paces ahead. The second German looked amazed at the child, and then suddenly, wondering at the words which passed my lips, I heard myself saying: 'Das ist ein Kind eines deutschen Offiziers' (It's a child of a German officer). The German glanced at me and said 'Versuchen Sie weiter' (Try further), and I was again two steps ahead. Suddenly: 'Guten Morgen Frau Offizier, hallo', my baby cried out to a German ahead of us and blew him a kiss with her little hand. The German, at first taken aback, burst out laughing but I did not wait and the row went on. The last obstacle: an SS man and our Klimanek. The SS man was astonished to see me with a child. 'Herr Klimanek, ein Kind!' but I readily replied: 'Alle haben Sie durchgelassen!' (All let her through). A moment of hesitation, but I was already running to the group of those who had been released.

My fellow workmen could not understand what had happened. I admit, I do not know myself by what miracle I had passed four control points while most women with children were taken away. Of our group I could now see how that other one had been increased; I noticed that the woman in the white coat and pink shawl had left us. To the Germans she had seemed too old.

The Germans had suddenly had enough of this selection. They said 'Schluss' (Finish) and without checking sent the rest aside. We, the saved, went home under Shaulis and the militia guard. Horrible sights met our gaze. In the streets strewn with dead bodies, scattered garments, suitcases and furniture, our escort and ourselves were the only living creatures. We passed Nalewki Street, once bustling, pulsating with vigour and life – Nalewki, now a haunted desert. On our way we saw a group of militia men surrounded by Shaulis. It seemed that the Germans had ordered the deportation of part of the militia, now of no use. 'The Moor had done his duty, the Moor could go.' Only then did the militia men see that they were Jews like us and nothing more but Jews who could not be saved. We came back home to the factory. Very many of us were missing and the despair of the remaining members of their families was boundless. How were they to save people who were hidden in Mila Street? The SS and Vernichtungskommando searched that district and even our Werkschutz who knew us and were ready to help, could not enter the area. Mothers who had left their children in the hideouts were desperate. But we had to return to our jobs and work hard and conscientiously, for negligence was penalized with the withdrawal of the life ticket. We were told that for the time being the action was finished and the Vernichtungskommando had left Warsaw. Out of their hiding-places crawled a number of people who had no life numbers at all. They had hidden themselves in this very street, having nothing to lose. This had proved the best hideout; the Germans had not searched our street.

The action to rescue those hidden in Mila Street started. About a week after the return a hearse rolled into our street. It was a somewhat unusual incident for people from neighbouring houses to welcome it with cries of joy. But we soon understood their behaviour when the rear door opened and several children aged between seven and twelve jumped out onto the street. A few mothers and fathers joyously hugged their kids; a few went away with bent heads. It appeared that the Jewish Council had obtained permission to clear Mila Street of corpses, and since there were a great many dead bodies, some hearses were sent to do the job. During this operation a small number of children were found and since a passing hearse did not raise the suspicion of any guard, this macabre means of locomotion was used to save them.

My friend Mrs N. got one of her boys back in a way which deserves special mention. Mr N. went with his two boys to the Jewish Council building. The Council gave out life numbers to some though not all of its clerks and Mr N. was given one, and only one, although there were three of them. What were they to do? The older boy did not await his father's decision but left without a word to hide somewhere in the ruins. The father remained with his little Jasio, a beautiful fair-haired boy with blue eyes – but they still had only one number. So they went to stand in the row and waited, unable to do anything. Time was short and a decision had to be taken. Another moment or two, and the check-up would begin. Next to the father and son stood an elderly couple, a husband and wife. He as a Council executive had been given a life number, she had none. And now they stood and argued. He asked her to accept the life ticket, she implored him to retain it; one did not want to live without the other. Finally the old lady went up to little Jasio, handed him her life number and said: 'Here you are, little boy. You are young, you will survive. And here is the picture of my son in Palestine whom I shall never see again, and here, take this too, we part from this world' – and gave him their last 500 zloty. Then they both took some white powder – potassium cyanide – and a moment later they dropped dead. Nobody moved to save them. On the contrary, everybody envied them. A command rang out: 'Fill in the rows' and the group went forward. Only the two bodies of the heroic couple remained on the road. Little Jasio survived the war.

· 8 ·

A Spate of
Peaceful Existence

AFTER THE SELECTION in Mila Street, which took place on 6 September 1942,* a period of peace began. The Vernichtungskommando left Warsaw, the Umschlagplatz stood idle. Optimists considered the liquidation of the ghetto had ended. The Germans in our factory told us that we had the same rights as German workers and would certainly remain alive. Their attitude indeed changed for the better and the food situation improved considerably. We were given special ration cards, honey, sugar, even sweets, and bread was plentiful. Vegetables were brought into our area in large quantities and sold at very cheap prices. The German care for our well-being went so far, that all cellars were requisitioned for the storage of potatoes and cabbage. It was obvious that we were to survive the winter in peace.

Slowly life reshaped itself in our little street. A small factory for making chocolate and sweets was founded, two barbers made permanent waves and dyed hair, a dressmaker was found who accepted orders, but busiest of all were the shoemakers who, by some lucky chance, found material to use. At the same time all of us were working at the Schultz factory. Our little state was named jokingly 'Schulcowizna' – the Schultz Estate. We had everything

*Estimates suggest that at the end of the seven weeks of round-ups, just 55,000 Jews remained in the ghetto and that by the end of November there were only 37,000.

here, but everything, by the will and grace of our almighty Schultz. Mr Schultz was quite almighty – during 'peacetime' – i.e. when the Vernichtungskommando was not at work. And so one day our 'master' ordered all his slaves to surrender their carpets and rugs. The war with Russia was heralded in an announcement on the factory walls. Fabric was needed for waterproof boots for the troops and it was up to us to provide them with it. Gladly I carried my heavy carpet to the factory. In my conscientiousness I even searched each recess and pulled out the smallest piece of rug. We were getting rid of these things light-heartedly. Later, at our shoemakers, I could not find boots made of our local or Persian carpets, but for these little discrepancies or additional profits, nobody bore our master any grudge.

It appeared that an ingenious Jew had succeeded in hiding a cow in an attic, in spite of all blockades. As a great favour I got the 'address' of the cow. One could get a pint of milk, and this only on every second day, but a customer had to bring some fodder besides cash, for the cow had a rebellious nature and would sometimes not give any milk at all. Perhaps she was not satisfied with her pasture in the attic, who knows? However since in our Schulcowizna nothing could happen without the knowledge of our master, Schultz himself soon learned about the cow's existence and official chits for milk were then given out. Thus the welfare of the cow improved considerably now that she received better fodder – legally and officially.

It may seem incredible but in their zest for normal life people went so far as to open shops in our little street. Even cakes were baked. They were pro forma 'Schultz shops', that is, they were administered by workmen of our factory. For instance, the wife stood behind the counter during the day, the husband at night, and both of them worked in the factory. There were shops in which at any hour of the day or night a fresh cheesecake or a dainty piece of roasted goose were served, but the secret of how these things got into our little street was taken by our poor brethren to their graves.

We were still imprisoned, the exits of our area guarded by the gendarmes and Jewish policemen. But in those happy days of 'peace' someone with connections could sometimes leave the area for a brief spell and see the 'world'. The 'world' consisted of a few other factory areas which still existed in Warsaw. The Tobens factory, for example, situated in Prosta Street, had a branch on a small stretch of Leszno Street. Jews worked and lived there under similar conditions to those in our area, its street organization and administration identical with ours. The only difference was that the name of their master was Tobens.

There was Schilling and Doring and a few smaller German factories in which Jews worked, but the biggest were Schultz and Tobens and they lasted till the end. Apart from the factories, there was a pretty big concentration of Jews in the area of the Jewish Council centre with its new premises in Gesia Street. Grzybowska Street, its former headquarters, had been designated on the Gentile side. During this period of relative peace the Council revived its activities. The chairman was, till the end, Mr G. Wielikowski, a barrister who executed his extremely difficult task with devotion and tact. The Council again had several departments and employed a great number of workmen and clerks. The most agile and the busiest were, of course, the food supply and burial sections. A new hospital was organized and people forgot that several offices of the former Council centre, as for example the accommodation, public welfare departments and the previous hospital had been the first to be surrounded suddenly by the Germans and deported. On the contrary, people tried very hard to get a job with the Jewish Council because life was considerably easier there than in the factories. There, on a small stretch of Gesia and Nalewki streets one could walk the streets in daylight. People even talked about entertainments and parties in the Council premises. At any rate, a visit to the Council area was considered a rare pleasure.

Apart from the areas around factories and the Jewish Council, an insignificant number of Jews lived scattered among the blocks of already cleared ghetto. These individuals were called 'outlaws'. They worked nowhere, had no documents or protectors. They were people who managed to survive all blockades in some well-camouflaged shelters or underground bunkers, sometimes in undetectable recesses, who had never seen a selection nor had ever had a life number. In times of danger they had simply taken to their hideouts. Apparently this was the best means of survival – who knows? They were well off, the 'outlaws'; they did not need to toil, had plenty of time to trade. The 'outlaw' was a type of caveman, could very ably sniff out the danger and knew when he should hide. Nevertheless, apart from the Jews at the factory, those of the Jewish Council and a handful of 'outlaws', Warsaw was really cleared of Jews – almost 'Judenrein'.

On the ruins of our former life our present drudgery continued. The cellars of neighbouring blocks in the Aryan quarter were again broken through, smuggling was rife and friendly Werkschutz men on their days off went to the Gentile side to trade our various valuables and deal with mail. A walk to another factory area, of course, bristled with difficulties. One could go only in groups under the guard of German gendarmes and Jewish militia with life numbers visibly displayed. The escorting militia man had to report to the Germans about the direction and scope of his group and obviously the motive always had to be an 'official' one. As our escorts often did not speak German we could sometimes get away with saying anything. Asked by a gendarme about his destination, a certain policeman friend of mine once replied 'To the rabbi for his Saturday tales'. 'That's all right', said the German, giving his fellow policeman a salute, and the group passed. These were our little successes and distractions of that time.

Somehow life went on in our little street and nobody died of hunger although the cost of living was very high. For our labour we received next to nothing from Schultz but a real sense of brotherhood prevailed in our shop. There were now only a few of us and we knew each other well, in our department at least. We toiled for twelve hours a day and had to sew pretty quickly to finish the prescribed minimum of twenty and then thirty vests per day. Slowly we learned to cheat the production executives, and by tricky manipulation we would hand to the receptionists the same vests twice. Yet only a few dared to do it, the rest of us dreading a slip. At the beginning we felt some pangs of remorse, but then we considered that deceiving the Germans was a commendable deed after all.

Our wounds cauterized, singing could even be heard at work. The songs and tales which we told one another brought people back to their lost world, gave us, incorrigible optimists, sweet spells of oblivion. We liked to plunge into an illusion which could turn the nightmare into a different world. Some women had quite pleasant voices. When one of my fellow workers who had lost two children sang 'Eine Nacht in Monte Carlo, will ich tanzen unter'n

Palmen mit dir, O Marie, O Marie', for a while I forgot where I was, and went back to the spring of 1939 when I had really been to Monte Carlo and had danced under the palms. Shyly and secretly I thought that perhaps there would again be Monte Carlo for me. This song grew to the power of a symbol and we chanted it very often. And so we talked about our pleasant experiences of bygone years, about our loved ones, about anything from the past. In contrast to our present life we were drawn to poetry and declaimed German classics from memory. In the hated German language Schiller, Goethe and Heine were recited at the workbenches; to forget, to find oneself in another world for a while at least. How true proved Schiller's verse: 'Schrecklich ist ein Leu zu wecken' (It is terrible to arouse the lion). I do not think that Schiller writing those words had ever guessed at the fury that his compatriots were capable of whipping up. We had seen with our own eyes what the fury of a human being meant, this refined systematic frenzy fortified by scientific developments. However we liked the poetry of the German classics in which a certain Mrs Beit used to excel. She had a son somewhere in England.

Our Werkschutz men made a good team, complaining pretty openly about the war. Their attitude was often more than friendly: they cheered us up, repeating that we would survive the war, they closed their eyes when work slowed down on the night shift, or someone was napping at dawn. One day a new Werkschutz was attached to us. When he entered our halls for the first time I was aghast: I saw the face of Mephistopheles. Acting in accordance with his nickname, which he acquired on the spot, he would always suddenly and ruthlessly spring up from the shadows of our room at night, and with an incomprehensible smile on his thin lips place himself for hours on end at our table. We were terribly afraid of him and never even spoke in his presence. But 'Mephistopheles' disappeared after a short spell. As we learned later, he was also disliked by his German comrades who in order to get rid of him made accusations against him to his superiors.

There had been comparative calm till the end of October as the Day of Atonement approached. Pious Jews in our area endeavoured to persuade Schultz to grant us a day off. He refused and tried to justify this decision by implying that SS men would be coming to check the workers' list on this solemn Jewish holiday. We were, however, to be permitted to pray together. A rabbi lived within our precinct and prayers were held in his house. 'El mole rachamim' (God have mercy on us) had been sung by religious Jews in their 'talles' before they went to work. The next day after the night shift they again prayed at the rabbi's. They all had to leave soon because there was some restlessness in the air. At one o'clock we assembled for prayers because it appeared that the danger had passed. I prayed till evening. The Day of Atonement is a sad holy day in itself, but it was even more so for us, the saddest of all people. My fellow workers prayed ardently and 'Izkor' was sung with moans, groans and tears. Among the congregation there was not one person who had not lost dear ones, family. The last prayer, 'Nilah', had to be finished quickly because nobody dared to be late for the night shift at the factory. Like some of the other women from our workshop I fasted on this day and when we hurried to work in the evening, we took some food for supper. It is a little strange to imagine a Jew fasting on the Day of Atonement sitting at the bench sewing, keeping some scraps of food for supper. The Jew had to sew because such was the order of the German master, the Jew had to wait for supper because such was the German master's wish.

It was soon evident that our anxiety had been justified. At the Tobens factory in Prosta Street the SS men had come on the Day of Atonement, checked the workmen and had carried away scores of people. Among those was my cousin, a pretty girl of nineteen. She had lost everyone but her father. He would never part with his daughter to the extent that he would even work with her at the same bench. He preferred to prick his fingers sewing, although he could have obtained a better and easier job. He wanted only to be near his child at all times. Who knows why the SS men had chosen just this girl, tearing her from her father though she was only nineteen whereas he was over fifty. Desperately he implored the Germans to spare the girl's life, to take him instead, or let them both die. All to no avail. The Germans 'argued' strongly and the beaten, bleeding father was forced to remain at the bench and carry on. After some days I received a letter from him containing a full account of this tragedy and I thought back to that Day of Atonement, of people sunk in their prayers, 'El mole rachamim' and 'Izkor', those two prayers for the dead that were deprived of life by the new angel of death – Adolf Hitler.

Apart from this incident (which we considered relatively unimportant) at the Tobens factory the holiday had passed peacefully in all workshops, at the Jewish Council and among the 'outlaws'. Our conditions were even improved with the restoration of electricity and gas. The worst and most painful trial for these remnants of a Jewish population was loneliness. Imagine a person used to being surrounded by numerous family, parents, husband or wife, children, brothers and sisters, suddenly being completely alone, with terrible thoughts and memories as his or her only companions. Vodka started appearing at that time in our factory. People started drinking in order to forget, to stop thinking, to stop mourning. Marriages of convenience were contracted more and more often, mainly among those mentally crippled people who had to live on and could not bear their loneliness.

On the benches people from totally different walks of life sat side by side. Next to a skilled worker who could hardly read or write were seated those workmen whom necessity had created, formerly well-off merchants, industrialists, doctors, barristers and engineers. Sitting on those same benches, eating the same soup and working for long hours, they took to one another, fraternized and finally loved one another. Common fate and common toil proved a stronger bond than graduation from the same university or emanating from the same social strata. We helped one another as much as we could. The experienced workwomen instructed and guided us in our work and we – the better-off – strove to help the poorer ones with money or food. There, in those ghastly workshops, we became real brethren and I remember till today my poor companions with great affection, those simple but straightforward and decent beings. There were many gentle hearts and souls whom I met among those very simple working people. A society lady could learn a lot from some of those humble girls.

During those long and tiring night shifts we used to talk, sometimes only in soliloquy, in order to keep awake. We picked on any topic, yet conversation always tended to veer towards the past. The present was bad for all of us and it was better not to think about it; the future, we thought, would never be. Even then I felt guilty. What answer could I give a poor little woman who said to me almost reproachfully: 'At least you have had something in your life; you studied, travelled, had a wonderful life. You have had a

husband and baby – you were well-off. But what did I have in my
life? We were six children of poor parents all living in one small
room. I have been working since my childhood, and now that I am
eighteen I must die!' Feeling ashamed both of myself and of the
society to which I belonged, I could find no answer.

My little factory friends, none of you is alive now, there are so
few who survived. Who will remember you? I promise I will never
forget your simplicity, your tender hearts. The Germans put me in
a ghetto but you have always lived there; the Germans forced me
to toil for twelve hours a day with a needle, but you have been
toiling thus all your lives. You were wronged not only by the
Germans, by war, but by your own people and the life you were
forced to lead.

The winter of 1942–3 was exceptionally hard. The factory hall
was so cold that our hands and legs were frozen. Although
surrounded by heaps of furs we were not allowed to cover our
frost-bitten feet. 'Verboten' was the order and we had to put up
with it. 'Schnell, schnell' we were hurried in our work, for at the
front the German troops eagerly awaited our vests. We the frozen
workforce had to ensure the warmth and comfort of 'our' soldiers.
We were given an additional job: fur caps. And we had to make
them at top speed to protect the ears of those who were 'fighting
for us' from cold. The ingenuity of the children of the slums was
striking at this frosty time. I never knew how or from where little
pieces of coal or firewood found their way to our ovens, but the
tireless little friends even thought of a cupful of hot coffee to
warm our chilled bodies. Around the rickety stove they would sit
singing melancholy popular songs and we, in turn, would tell them
about travels and theatres, or review a good book or theatrical
show for hours on end. Only one topic was never touched on: the
possibility of stealing over to the Gentile side. Most of our poor
companions could not speak proper Polish, had no acquaintances
whatsoever on that side; what was more, their features most often
betrayed their Semitic origin. Forced by such circumstances they
had to remain in the factory, so it was wiser not to talk on this
subject.

One desire obsessed me however: to walk once again, even if
only once, in a normal street, to find myself in a big city, see normal
people once again. I learned that one of the neighbouring carpen-

ter's shops sent a group of workers to the Law Court building in Leszno Street every morning to repair damage which had been incurred during the September bombing. They were known to pass by the gate of our little street where it crossed Smocza Street. I decided to join this group and for a couple of hours to breathe different air. One day, after the night shift, I went to the gate and after some pleading made the guard let me out. At the very moment when the group was passing the gate I leaped in and mingled with the crowd. The leader of the carpenters, a decent fellow, did not make a fuss and I went with them.

For the first time in many long months I had left our street to venture onto the Gentile side. The walk from the corner of Nowolipie and Smocza Streets to the Law Court at Leszno would normally take some three minutes, yet we walked for two hours. There was a special march route outlined by the Germans for Jewish labourers to which we had to adhere very strictly, crossing some streets, avoiding others. It did not matter that I was dog-tired after my all-night toil. I walked briskly. I did not care that at some checking post the gendarmes searched us for over an hour. I felt happy to be in a normal street and to see the town. Eventually we reached the Court building, where we were subjected to a last search and then allowed inside.

The men were sent to repair window frames and doors together with their Gentile colleagues and the women were ordered to peel potatoes. I was put in front of a huge basket full of half-rotten potatoes and was told to peel them as fast as I could. And again my indolence came to the fore as I was slower than the others and I was frequently rebuked by the forewoman. How could I tell her that I had been in this Court building quite often, yet had never peeled potatoes? Somehow the time passed and eventually I muddled through to the lunch break. I thought that perhaps during that hour I should get in touch with some of my professional colleagues or at least the Court ushers but it turned out that the part of the building in which we were allowed to move was closed to the public because of the damage sustained during the bombing. I could do nothing about it so from this point of view my excursion failed. When lunch time ended I noticed that the carpenters, too, slowed down with their work, devoting their attention to barter trade. The Jews gave goods, the Aryans food. They showed a keen interest in my boots, my invaluable top-boots which concealed my priceless treasure – the hacksaw blade.

In the evening, highly excited, I returned to the factory and went straight to my work. Naturally all night long I recounted my daytime adventure on the other side – shops, people, cars, cabs, trams, everything seemed so strange, so unusual.

1942 Draws to a Close

THE OFFENSIVE IN Africa filled our hearts with hope, although I had to explain to more than one of my friends that Tobruk was quite a distance from Warsaw and that the distance to Africa was even further than to Lvov. But nonetheless the English could do anything in our eyes and some day, at least, they would march into our factory at 50 Nowolipie Street.

At the end of 1942 we were issued with new documents, valid until 31 December 1943. It was still quiet at the time but clouds were gathering on our horizon. People began putting it about that although there was no danger as far as we were concerned, there were still too many 'outlaws' who benefited from the food supply and did not work at all. I heard such first-hand news from Miss Stark, who was well acquainted with Klimanek and other factory dignitaries. Miss Stark loved my daughter very much and often spoke about her with Klimanek, who showed a great interest in my child and would often bring her sweets and candy.

One day I was summoned to see Klimanek, who bluntly expressed his wish to adopt my little Eva. His wife was barren, he liked the child and Eva would certainly be well treated. He added that he considered such a solution best for both myself and the child. I consented on the spot. In a few days Mrs Klimanek would be coming to settle everything. It is easy to imagine how much this decision cost me. I had to part with the beloved child whom I had saved on so many occasions. But I weighed the situation up rather sensibly; with fewer people around now, another raid would be more dangerous. Until then I had succeeded in saving the child by sheer miracles, miracles which do not often repeat themselves. The thought of giving my child to a German, our biggest foe, the murderer of our brothers, naturally tormented me. I comforted myself however that Klimanek was not like the others. He loved my Eva and would treat her well. She was equally fond of him, often sitting on his lap and calling him 'Uncle Klimanek'. And come what may, let her even be brought up as a German – only let her live. I would rather have her become German than gassed to death at Treblinka. All those thoughts kept flashing through my mind before I could give my consent.

Mrs Klimanek arrived at Christmas. A festive Christmas dinner was prepared by the Gentile wife of a foreman, and Eva went with Miss Stark to meet her future mother. Then something happened which defied any logical explanation. At this decisive moment my little girl refused to approach either him or his wife. All efforts of persuasion, such as offers of sweets or toys, proved futile. Eva simply did not want to shake hands with them and kept on crying and begging to be taken home. Thus she herself determined her fate by choosing to remain with me.

Still I felt uneasy, and decided then and there to take some precautions. I had to cross over to the Aryan side and find a shelter for her there. There was a man who used to supervise work in the Gentile quarter and had a collective pass for several Jews. For 300 zloty he agreed to take me there and back. And so I went. Once in the city, I telephoned my former employer, the barrister M., asking for permission to visit him. I had to ask beforehand, knowing that such a call could endanger an Aryan. From his office I rang Mrs P., my husband's former client, asking her to see me immediately. I knew Mrs P. to be a decent, honest person and I decided to entrust my child to her. She owned a fruit and vegetable farm on the outskirts of Warsaw and I considered that place to be ideal. Our conversation was short. Herself a mother of three children, she was ready for her part to help me and she took Eva's photograph away with her in order to ask for her husband's consent. The reply was to reach me within a few days. I was satisfied at the outcome of my visit. Barrister M., whose advice I had always valued, praised the idea, also voicing his opinion that I should do the same for myself. I spent that day in Warsaw, of course without wearing my armband. It was sheer folly, for I had no documents and any gendarme could arrest me. Yet I could not stop myself. Like a child, I enjoyed my freedom, going from shop to shop, buying unnecessary things for the sheer pleasure of buying, and behaving like a normal human being.

Aimlessly I got on trams, alighting at the following stop. But what a pleasure this was! I scanned the faces of passers-by. I wanted to read people's eyes to find out whether they thought me a normal person; I was constantly sure that my face bore a stigma. I went to see Mr L., a professional barrister colleague, and asked him straight out to judge my appearance impartially. To be doubly sure he called in his wife and both of them scrutinized me, asking me to speak at first slowly, then more quickly, in order to test my mannerisms. The sentence was in my favour. They pronounced me free of any external Semitic marks and vowed that I could pass off easily as a Gentile. Mr L. offered me his help if it was needed. I was very happy as I walked to Nowolipie Street to rejoin the returning group.

Among this group there was a woman who said that she would undertake such excursions every week to visit her Gentile husband, whom she had ostensibly divorced. She could spend only a couple of hours with her beloved spouse, only once a week, and had to pay the smuggler 300 zloty even for that. She was always in dread of possible arrest, yet always eager to see her husband. The day came when her husband waited in vain. His wife was deported to Treblinka.

I came back determined to entrust my child to Mrs P. but to remain at the shop as long as possible. The factory now worked at full speed. The furriers and shoemakers' sections were overloaded with work. In our courtyard thousands of worn-out felt boots lay in piles waiting for repairs and alterations by our shoemakers. The shoemakers' department in our shop consisted of strictly religious Jews, those 'Hasidim', who were followers of a rabbi from Aleksandrow. It was said that Mr H., a pious Hasid himself, paid an exorbitant sum of money from his own pocket in order to secure the shoemakers' section for those Hasidim. Mr H. was a foreman in this department and one had to admit that the shoe workshop was exemplary and appreciated by Schultz himself. The shoemakers formed the best-organized group and prevailed upon the kitchen management to provide them with kosher food prepared strictly according to Jewish religious rites. At appointed hours in the shop kitchen, their representative would ensure that the food was properly prepared. The shoemakers even had special kosher meat and had their meals served on separate plates. All this was, of course, at the personal expense of rich Mr H. Nonetheless the entire group worked very diligently and conscientiously.

Meanwhile certain signs pointed to the growing activity of a Jewish underground organization. The killing of a Jewish Gestapo man, Furst, who worked in the area of the Jewish Council, and of barrister Lejkin, a militia officer directing the deportation of Jews, was an ominous sign. We knew that the death sentence had been passed on them by the Jewish underground organization and we could only regret that this had not been done earlier. Here and there one could hear it voiced that any further German action aimed at the deportation of Jews would now be met with resistance. Jews would not be forced into being slaughtered like sheep. The ghetto began to make clandestine preparations for more self-defence. In our flat I would often meet young men with typically Aryan features who would liaise between the Jewish and Gentile quarters. Help, and especially arms, were to come from the Aryan side. The building of new bunkers and alterations to the existing ones were started. All previous hideouts had been only temporary, meant to shelter Jews only for the duration of a blockade, a few hours, after which they were intended for a different purpose. Overnight a bunker sheltering several people had to be specially constructed to withstand any eventuality. Only those who directly financed their building knew about these vaults. It was thought that it would be better and safer if people were actually to live in such hideouts. The bunkers were built in the strictest secrecy, in tortuous cellars with their access obstructed. The cellars were deepened to make them safer and often under an existing cellar another one was dug. The best ones were built under empty squares, under courtyards of roadsides. The building of a shelter under a roadside was very expensive but I knew of several shelters with electric light (from our own small powerhouses), radio, telephone and well-water. The equipping of such a place with provisions for a long period was not a minor task. It was reckoned to give shelter for a stay lasting months or even a year, until the war ended. There were a small number of soundly built and well-provided shelters but obviously only certain individuals could make use of such sanctuaries. Tales about shelters in the ghetto which I heard later on were much exaggerated. For the time being, however, calm prevailed in all Jewish areas.

The end of 1942 was celebrated boisterously and joyfully. It may appear strange to normal people, but on 31 December 1942 in the Jewish Council area, in all factories and among the 'outlaws', people had a wonderful time, drinking vodka in abundance. 'We have outlived five months of Jewish extermination', people were saying with glasses in their hands, 'we will outlive the war.' 'Tut tut, and the war ends, the Allies march steadily ahead, for the present only in Africa, but it's all right.' All the Allied generals whom we hoped to welcome into Warsaw were soon toasted in wine: people tried in every way they could to make themselves believe that the New Year would bring them freedom.

The beginning of 1943 seemed really peaceful. We grew accustomed to our toil, the Germans supplied us with food, smuggling went on efficiently and hope slowly entered our hearts. 'The Germans need us, our hard, free labour; perhaps we shall survive.' Therefore, despite the fact that Mrs P. had consented to take her, I did not send my Eva away. As long as there was the slightest possibility of keeping her with me, I would not part with her. However we continuously thought of going over to the Aryan quarter. Here and there one came to know that certain people had done so. The first one to know about it was our shop barber and hairdresser, as peroxiding hair became a rule before 'crossing over'. He would make a platinum blonde out of a brunette. The same applied to men who now even let their moustaches grow. My friend Mr M., the dark-haired barrister, gnashed his teeth in vain during such an operation but he wished to have fair hair within a few hours. He was to cross the next day, leaving his wife temporarily in the ghetto. 'The sudden change of colour causes an acute soreness of skin', explained the barber to his client, 'but only the first time', and enlightened the victim about the tricky procedure of touching up the regrowth. 'All right, but what is going to happen to my beard – how can I stop it growing black?', grumbled the poor Jew.

And the peroxiding of hair and growing of moustaches went on for it was thought to be more Aryan-like. On the other hand a rumour was spreading that 'over there' everybody was scrutinized, examined and questioned about all kinds of things; what was more, people were robbed of their money by the most decent Gentiles and handed over to the Gestapo. No wonder that only certain individuals, mainly women, dared to go, the men fearing bodily examination more than anything else. I remember cases where after a few weeks stay in the Aryan quarter women would return to their husbands and families feeling strange among the Gentiles or longing for their dear ones.

The period of comparative calm in the ghetto also resulted in the return of several other people. Not all members of a family had Aryan features or spoke a proper Polish, so mothers would not go without children, children would not leave parents, spouses determined to stick together. In general this idea of not parting cost many lives.

· 10 ·

Into the Cattle Truck

THE APPARENT CALM in the ghetto lasted until 17 January 1943. Then the Vernichtungskommando came to Warsaw again, and the Umschlagplatz was revived. They started with the Jewish hospital, where patients – including those with contagious diseases – and hospital staff were all deported. We were assured by the factory authorities that this new action was against the 'outlaws' only, it had nothing to do with us, German workers with a different status.

Meanwhile the Jews in the ghetto began to resist. Raiding Germans were met with hand grenades and rifle- and machine-gunfire. The very first day there were victims both among Jews and Germans. After a few hours fighting the Germans withdrew. They were not prepared for such open resistance. The next day, 18 January, the Germans, reinforced by Ukrainians and Shaulis and helped by the remnants of the Jewish militia, returned to their job of clearing the Jewish quarter. The Jews bravely resisted. They fired from windows, cellars and roofs. Arms and ammunition being scarce, only individuals put up a fight, and there were more and more Germans armed to the teeth. In these circumstances the liquidation of the ghetto progressed. Still, a person provided with a good hiding-place and some hand grenades could easily survive because the Germans never went down to explore the dark cellars. They stood at the entrance, threw down a grenade and went away. In this way some people were spared.

The 'action' had already lasted some days without respite. The Umschlagplatz was full, goods wagons were filled with people, the murderous operation was in full swing. On 20 January, at daybreak, Karl Bruck, one of the few kind Germans, came into our flat. He was annoyed and upset, ordered me to take my child and go instantly to the factory – our area was to be blockaded. Lieut. Karl Bruck, even without my asking, promised to hide me. He had a plan to conceal me and my child in the barracks. Nobody would search for the Jews there. The idea was really good because the barracks were in the fenced-off part of the factory and no Jew was allowed in. Quietly I put provisions into my bag, some money into my boots, and followed him. Alas! It was too late for any rescue. The factory courtyard was full of soldiers. The kind German wrung his hands. In spite of his good intentions he could do nothing. Surrounded by the terrible soldiers of the Vernichtungskommando we were thrown out into the street and ordered to line up. There we stood for a long time, left in the dark about our future. Every worker had his life number. At last when we had been counted the factory gate swung open and director Klimanek appeared with the representative of the Vernichtungskommando. I stood near the gate and had a very good view of what was happening to my friends.

Line after line of men marched by the gate. Only some people were called and let in by the representative of the Vernichtungskommando, the others were marched away. No woman was allowed in; I knew what this meant. I made up my mind in an instant. I would enter the factory or perish directly on the spot. When my line was passing by I detached myself and at a run tried to steal inside. I heard Klimanek saying: 'She is a skilled furrier'; then a German pushed me off. Still I did not give up and again tried to slip into the courtyard. A soldier hit me with his rifle butt. I shouted 'Kill me rather, you swine, you damned swine!'. A scuffle ensued. I got another blow. Some women took advantage of the confusion and ran quickly into the yard. That was the only result of my revolt. I again hurled abuse at the Germans who did not pay any attention. In normal circumstances I would have been shot on the spot. Utterly spent and subdued, I stood in the line of doomed people. Among them I saw my sister-in-law, my niece, all my women friends. We did not despair although we knew it was the end.

It was impossible to escape, guarded as we were by the Germans, Ukrainians and Shaulis. I was strangely calm and lucid. I comforted my sister-in-law and tried to persuade her that there was yet some hope. Then one of the militia men, an acquaintance, accompanied by a German, came up and pointed at my sister-in-law, as his wife dragged her and her daughter out of the crowd. I managed to shout 'money in the stove' before losing them from my sight. I felt no envy. I felt as if I was in a trance. I stood among the condemned yet I was under the impression that all this had nothing to do with me. I was witnessing these ghastly events not as an actor but as an onlooker. My mind registered everything sharply and clearly. There was no pushing, weeping or shouting as on previous raids. There was no tearing of children away from their mothers, because all the youngsters had been deported long ago. Everything took place in an eerie silence. Very few workers were let through the gate – very many stood in the bitter cold waiting hopelessly.

I searched for our slayers' abnormal, horrible faces. The Vernichtungskommando was not a gendarmerie or army corps. Its members were specially trained murderers, clothed in their own distinct uniforms. Their faces, though they seemed normal, were not human and their dreadful hands could only beat and kill. My attention was drawn to two Shaulis who were carrying out of a house a paralyzed old woman in an armchair, strangely saved till that day. They put her down before a frightful-looking German, saluted and explained the presence of the armchair.

'Stand up!' yelled the German. When the woman did not move, he drew out his revolver and shot her through one eye. The Kommando leader himself then came up, brutally pushed the first German away, aimed carefully and shot the woman through her other eye. The old lady wavered in her chair, the Shaulis supporting her body. Not a cry of pain, not a moan parted her lips, only terrible bloody tears began to trickle from her eye sockets down her shabby clothes and onto the soft white snow. We all stood silent. From nearby houses the Ukrainians then carried out two small children whom no one had claimed and laid them down next to the paralyzed woman. They were dead. The houses were eventually cleared and the action ended but we were still waiting.

Suddenly there was the honking of a horn and a magnificent limousine drew up in front of us. Out of it alighted a bemedalled, beribboned elderly German with a rosy, intelligent face. It was a good-natured face, and an engaging smile flickered on his lips. We immediately noticed that this must be some very important person, for everyone taking part in the blockade stood stiffly to attention. How could this amiable elderly gentleman belong here? Suddenly the leader of the Kommando came up to him and saluted and barked his report: 'Alles in Ordnung' (Everything in order), 'Herr . . .[a whole list of titles followed]. . . Brandt.' I stiffened. So this was the notorious Karl Brandt, in charge of the extermination of Jews in all Poland. The man who put into practice the 'ausrotten' (annihilation) policy and had on his conscience the deaths of millions of Jewish lives. His looks served to illustrate just how deceptive appearances could sometimes be.

The paralyzed woman was placed in a cart near the children and a few sick people, a whistle sounded, a sergeant shouted 'Ab' and we were marched away. The gate of our little street opened, we left the factory area and set out on our journey. All of us knew it was to be the last journey of our lives.

Again the ghastly way through the deserted streets of the Warsaw ghetto, strewn with corpses and decay. Who would believe that a mere six months previously there had been over 400,000 people living here, among shops and factories, the streets throbbing with life, resounding with talk and laughter. These streets were now gaping with desolation as if a terrific hurricane had swept through them. This was the hurricane created not by an angel of death but by Satan himself. 'Laufen, laufen', cried our executioners, hurrying us to the Umschlagplatz. It was all rather different from my previous time there. Apart from our group there were only a few others and a smaller number of policemen. It was apparent that the operation of clearing Warsaw was at an end. We waited for the little group in front of us to reach the carriages. They went in dignified silence and a small boy brought up the rear limping, with only one foot shod, the other red and swollen. I do not know why, but in this little boy closing the procession I saw the personification of the whole tragedy of our people marching to their destruction and I exclaimed involuntarily: 'Lama azawtanu?' (Why did you desert us?). Then the group passed, we waited. A German soldier arrived and handed a piece of paper to the German in charge of the place. A few names were read out, names of those who were to be released. Again we felt a flicker of hope – perhaps, perhaps . . . But only two foremen of some departments of our factory, the wife of our charge-hand – in all a very few people – were released. They left the place under militia guard, to go back to the factory.

At last the splendid limousine drew up and with a cultured smile Brandt calmly reviewed his work. Again a whistle sounded, another shout of 'Ab' and we were marched ahead. Alongside the cattle trucks stood other brutes, apparently the worst ones, their task being the loading of human cattle into carriages by means of a whip or a rifle butt. There were no foot boards or steps to get onto the train but at a stroke of their whip or rifle butt we hardly noticed their absence and slid in with ease.

On two of the railroad tracks, stationary cattle trucks seemed to emit terrible cries, mad laughter and ghastly howling which jangled in our ears. A militia man enlightened us: those wagons loaded with people and sealed up had been standing thus for three days. The laughter and howling came from those who in that time had gone mad. Three days in a packed, stinking wagon, without food or water, in freezing January could be too much even for a Jew. How could one not become insane.

'Schnell, schnell', shouted the German beasts hitting anybody within their reach. They hit not only to compel people to get into the wagons quickly, they did it to make them drop their poor belongings, a bundle, a rucksack or a suitcase. 'Lass' (Leave it), a German or Ukrainian would shout, dealing a fierce blow with his rifle butt, and then he would lift up his victim's bundle dropped in the process. When my turn came, before they could even notice, I had flung my bag into the wagon, handed my child to someone already standing inside and succeeded in climbing in without the help of a whip.

The wagon was packed very closely. 'That is the rule', the militia man told us. 'And besides, you'll feel warmer', he added sympathetically. The heavy doors were slid into place and then we heard dull rhythmic knocks, one, two, one, two. 'They are sealing the wagon', somebody said. The hammer blows ceased; the nails of our coffin were in place. This was the end. I found myself among the shoemakers of our shop, those Hasidim. The only people I knew were Mrs G. and her husband, a very cultured couple. After the hammering had died away the Hasidim exclaimed 'Idyn, myz in tarsztybl' (Jews, we are in a morgue) and pulling out their 'tallis' (prayer shawls) and 'tefillin' (phylactery) stood with little 'sidurs' (prayer books) in hands ready for prayer. 'Iskadal weiskadasz' – they intoned the sad melody of the prayer for the dead and, as if by previous agreement, the other wagons joined in the lugubrious singing. 'El mole rachamim' followed. On the other side of the car two women went to kneel beside the praying Jews. They were two Gentiles. One was an elderly maidservant, who despite the establishment of the ghetto would not leave her Jewish masters and remained with them till the end; the second one was a hawker exchanging some foodstuffs for old clothing. She had had the bad luck of being caught during the last blockade. And now both of them were to share our fate. 'Ktorys cierpial za nas rany, Jezu Chryste ...' (You who suffered wounds for us, O Jesus Christ) mingled with 'El mole rachamim'. And from the other train wild howling, squeaks and laughs of the lunatics chimed in. The cacophony of the doomed.

Petrified I stared at all this. For the first time in my life I thought that there must have been some mistake, something must have gone wrong and all the powers which had governed the world up till then had broken down. Both God and people must have gone mad, leaving the power to rule in Adolf Hitler's hands. Or was it a show in a mad-house? Who rules the world, God or Satan, Truth or Lies, Good or Evil? It was all insane. That cattle truck littered with cattle dung and the excrement of poor devils who had already entered the better world; its new contents, those creatures now locked inside whom their fellow men had first deprived of all human rights and were now doomed to damnation; those prayers to our Lord and Creator who governed such a world. It was all insane, incomprehensible to a normal mind. Perhaps it was all a mistake. Perhaps there was some supreme reason for all this. Who could answer that? The crowd was sunk in prayer. There in that wagon they asked God to forgive their enemies all their wrongs and sins, as they sang Jewish and Christian prayers for absolution. And there outside Satan was continuing his wanton ravages. Horrible German curses accompanied the hiss of whips and shots rang out endlessly.

Suddenly the prayers stopped as if cut short. Outside somebody was heard to shout 'Nojsze Rozenberg, Aaron Zylberberg ...' A pious Jew interrupted his prayer and with all his strength he battered on the closed door. 'That's me, that's me. I am Nojsze Rozenberg!' A few other names were called and some of them were in our wagon. People in their prayer shawls who had been saying prayers for the dead, for themselves, now knocked at the doors and at the walls of their coffin and cried desperately: 'That's me, that's me, open the door, open the doooor!' The beasts outside laughed fit to burst their sides. It was horrible. At last the doors were unbolted and we were all ordered outside. 'It's a miracle', a young Hasid tried to convince us, his side-locks discreetly hidden. 'It's a miracle written in our Holy Books.' The miracle however proved to be much simpler than those written in the Holy Books. Due to the continuing battles in Russia the troops badly needed felt boots during the heavy winter. The management of our factory had persuaded Brandt himself to release a few skilled shoemakers who could go on toiling for the welfare of the Vaterland. Schiemann, one of our kindest Germans, arrived at the station and from our wagon began to call out names from a hurriedly compiled list. About ten men, and several others from the rest, made up about forty people who had won back their freedom. Among them was a man who could not avert his eyes from our group, who would not part with his daughter. 'Father dear, go, please go', she begged. 'No. No, I cannot', he repeated. 'Then I will assault a German soldier, do you hear, and I'll be killed here and now', she warned. The father went away broken, his head bent, weaving like a drunkard. I cherished no illusions. I knew that with a child I would not be released and asked Schiemann for nothing although I knew him well.

Two Gentiles in our wagon tried to explain to the Germans that they did not fit into this society and tried to show their documents. All to no avail. 'Even if you are not a Jew, you are a damned Pole', yelled the German, and, slapping the older woman's face, barked 'Polish swine' and with his rifle butt drove her to the wagon. Depressed and hopeless, we returned to the train. The doors were shut, again we heard the rhythmical hammering which meant the sealing of the wagons and we were definitely locked up. Nobody prayed any more. The tomb-like silence was broken only by the yelling and whining of the lunatics from the next carriage. I sat still and lost in thought. I had not only been deeply religious but also very pious and now I could not even think about God and His grace. I felt only a spiritual barrenness and emptiness. Still my brain was working excellently. With horrible lucidity I took note of every detail of my surroundings and strengthened my resolve not to be slaughtered.

After the release of those people it was less crowded and we could at least move about. Hours passed and still the train did not start. I scrutinized our coffin. The carriage was strongly built and there was no hope of breaking through. Next I looked at the minute windows. There were two of them on opposite sides of the wagon: small square barred holes which could be reached only by a very tall man. They were so high for me that I could not even touch them standing upright. There was of course nothing to stand on. At last I got a man to lift me so that I could look out of them. Our carriage was on the middle rails between the lunatics' wagon and empty tracks backed by an open field. Suddenly I saw a Polish guard passing by with an oil can in his hands. 'Hallo', I called, 'Tell me where we are going.' The man did not answer. 'Are we going to Treblinka?', I asked quite openly. 'Yes, that's the way to Treblinka. Your train is starting in a minute, not like that one with the lunatics. There are only two Poles, the rest of the guards are German.' Now I knew everything. Our destination – Treblinka. Departure in a short while and every attempt at escape a sheer nonsense. Still the train did not move. As our bodies were still alive, we had to turn a part of our wagon into a latrine. We were deprived of another bit of human dignity.

Eva behaved very bravely and in spite of the biting cold she never complained. Once she asked to be taken to a lavatory but when she saw the conditions she pleaded 'Mamma dear, I promise I will never again wet my pants but please, please let us go home.' Just a trifle to ask for: to go home.

There was much commotion round the train. New groups were dragged in, abuses and curses in German could be heard to the accompaniment of constant firing. A man at the window announced the arrival of a new Ukrainian detachment and some of them jumped onto our roof. Overhead we heard footsteps and conversation. We were under their protection. The train moved on at about four o'clock.

I resolved to do something. Apart from the couple Mr and Mrs G. I knew no one, but for what I intended to do they could be of no help. To do what I wanted alone was impossible for I could not even reach the window frames. I approached two strong young boys who seemed to me resolute and confided my intention to them. I told them that I had a hacksaw blade and knew how to use it and that I planned to cut the rough bars of the window as soon as it had grown dark and we were out of Warsaw. I asked them merely to lend me their shoulders for I was too small to reach the grill. The boys looked at me with a mixture of bewilderment and wonder when out of the side of my boot I pulled my precious instrument. They immediately agreed to help me.

Meanwhile we made a detour around Warsaw stopping at all possible stations. Nobody knew why. At any rate it was pointless to begin my work as long as we were in Warsaw. My associates agreed with me. We kept waiting. Our guardians on the rooftops were killing time by talking and singing. At the bars a drunken face suddenly appeared, then a hand gripping a pistol. In a flash we all shrank back pressing closely against each other trying to find ourselves beyond the reach of the pointed nozzle. I wondered why we wanted to avoid death from a bullet which would be a hundred times easier than the slow agony in a death camp. Why draw out the torment of waiting? Why did we want to miss such a decent opportunity? But that was the natural reaction of man even on the very threshold of death.

Our existence could no longer be interpreted as life, yet we still breathed, still cherished something. Hope? 'Perhaps this train would not go to Treblinka . . .' There were even people who claimed that 'the trains were going to labour camps or concentration camps. There one could at least live and have a chance of survival; the war was nearing its end!' Oh hope, blessed hope. Others had heard that these trains were being derailed and people were being saved with the help of Polish railway guards. Yes, it was true about those derailings and those Polish guards, but they were very sporadic incidents which had occurred at the beginning of the extermination of Jewry, when the entire railway workforce was Polish, moreover when no Ukrainians were placed on the rooftops. I myself knew a young man who had been saved in that way, but now there were no hopes, no illusions. I was frank with my fellow travellers, the optimists. Let us not run away from death, let us be shot dead by the Ukrainians. But the drunk Ukrainian had no intention of shooting us. Scaring us was merely his way of passing the time. And the deadly terror on our faces made him happy and so the 'molojec' (young Ukrainian) laughed. And how he howled with laughter.

Eventually we left Warsaw and were passing through fields. I looked out of the window. We were surrounded by free space, so much free space, only for us there was no place in the whole world. All God's creatures, the smallest worm had a right to live, only we had to die, for such was the will of Adolf Hitler. We had no rights but to be exterminated. Why, I asked of the immaculate white snow. Why, I asked the twinkling stars. The drunken laughs, the sound of melancholy Ukrainian songs and shots, constant shots were my only replies. That drinking overhead I considered to my advantage. I thought they would fall asleep more easily. And besides, a drunken foe was less dangerous than a sober one.

Out of the Train

WHEN MY INTENTIONS regarding the window became known to my fellow travellers I thought I would be lynched. 'A "mischugene" (madwoman) – she will bring disaster on all of us', they said. 'When the Ukrainians notice that she is sawing the bars, they will kill us all.' How could I convince them that this would be a blessed solution? So I had to explain and convince them, and the wagon eventually divided into two groups: my followers against my opponents. The two lads were on my side, ready even to fight those who opposed me. Meanwhile all became quiet on our rooftop; the Ukrainians had jumped on some other wagons to bait other passengers. It was pitch dark when I started my job. I sat astride the strong boy's shoulders and began to saw, but then it became clear that sawing off keys or handles in my flat was entirely different from cutting the bars on the fast-moving train. The cattle wagon rocked and swung in all directions, knocking my hands with the hacksaw off the bars. The job proved difficult. My fingers started bleeding, my hand became weak but I kept on sawing. Ahead, ahead, faster, faster. The boy I was perched on got tired. I climbed the shoulders of the other one, slowly progressing with the job. The blood dripping from my fingers moistened the iron, the snow-white background cast its light on my work. I went on. Sweat dripped onto my eyelids, my fingers swelled up and became terribly sore, but there was not so much left to be done. I had only to cut three bars and then bend them up. 'Mischugene', I heard from my detractors. 'Even if she cuts the bars, who will be able to slip through this small opening?', they commented. Yet I did not let myself be discouraged, and gritting my teeth, I sawed on. The job was eventually finished, the cuts practically invisible from the outside.

Now how could I achieve the next aim, how to jump off with the child? I looked at my friend from the furriers' room. 'Will you jump, too?' 'No, I want to die' – 'Dear Mrs G., I don't know myself whether this jump will save my life, but even if this way leads to death I prefer this death to that in a gas chamber at Treblinka. And besides', I went on, 'use a bit of imagination. Fancy what if while returning from a pleasant journey you leaned carelessly on the unlocked door of your first-class Pullman coach and . . .' Mrs G. smiled faintly. 'I don't have the courage to jump. I want to endure everything till the end, like my mother, like my brother.' My daughter had heard everything and understood what we were talking about. 'Mummy dear, please don't jump, dear. I promise I will always be a good girl and obey anything you say, only don't jump and don't leave me alone Mummy', implored little Eva. She kissed my hands, clutched my overcoat and, I admit, for a while paralyzed my will. I felt numb. The bars were out and yet for a moment I renounced everything. I lost my will and the power to act but I summoned up my courage to go on. I looked at the snow-covered fields and the stars and thought that if I was going to die, I would prefer death on the white snow under the starry sky to asphyxia in the gas chamber.

I knew I would be unable to throw the child out of the window. I expected Eva to resist and cry and I was sure that force would be necessary. Besides, I feared that after throwing the child I might lose courage to jump off at the last moment, and what then? No, I had to jump first, followed by the child. But who would throw her out? There was a Dr F., a tall and strong man among our group. I appealed to him. 'Dr F., you are so tall, it would be easy for you to throw the child out.' 'An impudent proposition', he said and refused. 'Do you know the consequences of such acts? To thrust a girl from a moving train is equal to killing her. You are a desperate mother, a murderess, and why should I help you? Have you ever heard about the Disciplinary Court and your responsibility before it?' 'Yes doctor, I know very well what Disciplinary Courts do but you will stand only before God's Judgement', I answered. I saw it was of no use however and turning to the young men who were among us I pleaded: 'Boys – here is my bag with provisions; bread, butter, sugar, chocolate and bottle with tea. I know you are hungry. Whoever throws out my child immediately after I have jumped will get the bag with the food.' Two lads, two religious shoemakers, agreed. I could not be certain that they would keep their promise so I turned to Mrs G. and begged her to ensure that the boys would throw my Eva out after I had leaped. I entreated her to promise. The eyes of Mrs G. brimmed with tears, she did not utter a word, only nodded her head. 'Please hand this over to the lads after Eva is out,' I implored, and gave the bag to Mrs G. I tied my coat around my waist by means of a piece of strong twine, and stood ready to jump. 'I'd like to jump first', said one of the boys who had lent me his shoulders. He put his hands against the window frame and jumped. The wind swept him off and that was all. Shots and drunken songs from the rooftops could be heard all the time.

'Mummy, mummy dear, please don't jump!' I plugged my ears. For a moment I concentrated on the technique of the jump itself and, standing on the second boy's shoulders, I grabbed the frame and thrust myself out legs first. I heard the whistle of the wind as I was whirled away. I lost consciousness.

I do not remember the moment of impact, nor for how long I lay on the ground. When I came to my senses, I found myself walking along the edge of a forest, treading on soft, white snow. The night was shrouded in silence. I tried hard to recollect how I had come to this place, alone, at night, but in vain. My bones ached, my head was throbbing but I still could not work out why. In a daze I walked on legs unaware of walking but suddenly I had the overwhelming desire to rest somewhere, to lie down. I felt so terribly tired. Yet there was neither house nor human being, only forest and snow as far as the eye could see. What time could it be? I looked at my wrist but there was no watch on it. I touched my neck to check on my gold chain and medallion – the chain was gone. Gone also was my handbag containing money which I had pinned deep inside my overcoat pocket together with some trifles which I kept hidden. It dawned on me that I had been robbed, but by whom, or when and where, I could not make out. On the edge of the forest stood a cottage. Without thinking I knocked at the window and continued to knock several times but nobody answered, nobody came out. I trudged on and came to a crossroad. I chose one of the paths in the snow and again stopped at a cottage. Once more I knocked at the window and begged 'Open, please open!' An old woman appeared at the window. 'I'd open, but I'm afraid, for so many thieves are lurking near the forest!' I trod on.

Suddenly three tall young men emerged from the forest; one was in German uniform and two were in civilian clothes. 'Stehen bleiben, Hände hoch!' (Stop, hands up), shouted the German. I stopped dead. The German started asking me various questions but I did not reply. Any answer would have been bad. So he decided to take me to the police station at the nearby town Tluszcz. We started across the forest and my blank mind could not grasp the situation. One of the civilians came up to me and said in Polish: 'Why go to the police station? Better give us the money here and we'll set you free.'* I would gladly have given them money. I pulled off my boot and took out the last of my possessions. Out fell my precious hacksaw blade into the snow. The thieves quickly snatched the money and I grabbed the saw, and at this moment everything came back to me. The train, the ghastly journey, the escape and the child.

The child – where was my child? As one insane I ran up to the robber who had spoken Polish, imploring him for help. 'Where could my child be? She should be somewhere near the railway track.' He shot me a glance. 'It's damn far to the line, and besides, don't go near the line. There you'll be caught, take my advice.' Turning to me again he asked me how much money I had on me. 'You have taken everything I had, 10,000 zloty. I don't have any zloty left.' Hearing this the thief drew from his pocket two bank notes of 50 zloty and handing them to me said: 'You'll find that useful, but don't go near the track.' In spite of this I ran like one possessed towards the railway line. My bones did not ache. I felt neither the cold nor fatigue. After a long dash I saw the rails

---

* Eva reports that her mother told her that in addition to being robbed after her jump from the train, she was raped. She also made this charge in a deposition prepared for a reparations claim, a document which has since been lost though accompanying documents refer to the rape charge. Eva believes that the shame of being raped would have prevented her mentioning it when the journal was written in 1946.

glistening. Suddenly I heard a shout: 'Stehen bleiben, *stac*!' and from a small shack two strongly built ruffians appeared. Robbers again. 'Give us your money!' 'Money, yes, I had money but they have taken it off me.' 'Who?' I described the three bandits. 'One German, two Poles, the younger had his hand in a sling.' 'That's right, they were our men. You may go.' I then understood that they belonged to the same gang of robbers. I asked them: 'Listen, please. I am looking for my child. Haven't you seen a little girl anywhere?' 'A little girl, let me think. Oh yes, some three kilometres from here a railway guard found a little girl, but don't go there, the place is full of Germans.' Again I started running like crazy in the direction indicated. An inhuman power drove me faster and faster. Oh, only if only I could be in time and not too late. Fearing I could lose my way and wishing to be quicker, I began to run in the middle of the track where there was less snow and the ground was hard. I did not care about any danger as long as I could get my Eva back. Then I was overcome. And what if the robbers had lied and wanted to trap me? And if the child was not Eva? But I shook off all these thoughts and rushed on. I felt sure that the child was my daughter. At last I saw the guard's hut and a man standing beside it holding my daughter in his arms. She was clinging to him, her small hands round his neck. 'Eva, my dearest Eva', I cried, choking with tears.

Eva did not recognize me, her golden hair was smeared with blood. 'It is nothing serious, this wound on her head. Besides I have already washed it,' explained the guard. 'I found her in the snow some four hours ago. She was crying. I lifted her up, she clung to me so tight that I did not have the heart to abandon her. I carried her to my hut, washed the wound. She would not let me go, and so I had to carry her all the time even on my rounds. I told the other guard about this foundling. The child does not know anything, only that she is called Eva. I was at a loss as to what to do with her. The Germans could come at any moment and she has held on to me these four hours. I decided to take her home after my tour of duty. God has given me two children, she will become the third. But are you really her mother?', said the man before he would give her back to me. Eva let her saviour go free very unwillingly. 'For God's sake keep away from these railway tracks. Run away from this terrible area full of German patrols. They will catch you for sure.' I thanked the good man from the bottom of my heart and walked off quickly. I did not have the slightest idea where to go. I walked on only to be further away from this dangerous place. Again I found myself wandering across the snowy fields, endlessly, helplessly. I had my precious child and freedom, yet I had no idea of what to do or how to cope.

As my feet were giving way under me I saw a neat, fenced-off cottage. Without a moment's hesitation I lifted Eva over the fence, then climbed after her and found myself in a yard. In front of me stood a big kennel. We slipped into it. It was empty. The dog had probably been too cold outside and the farmer had taken him into the warm cottage. This kennel seemed like paradise to me. At last I could lie down. My legs jutted out somewhat but that did not matter. I then started talking to my child but she lay with eyes closed and would not speak. The wound on her head still bled and I had nothing with which to dress it. For the first time in my life I was so poor that I did not even possess a handkerchief. And so in this kennel I licked my little child's wound with my tongue, like a dog would do to its wounded pup. I very badly wanted to sleep but I had to jog her incessantly to keep her awake. I was afraid she might freeze to death while asleep. I hugged her close to me, warming her body with mine, rubbing my cheek against hers and thinking about the unbelievable adventures of the previous night. Leaping off the train and hitting the ground must have made me lose consciousness. I must have lain for some time on the snow after having been robbed, for I was missing a watch, the chain and the other pieces. But why had the robbers left me my overcoat and particularly the strong, good top-boots? Perhaps they had seen that I was still alive, but why should they have stopped when they were intent on plunder and booty? Why had they not killed me, why had they not stripped off my clothes? And those second bandits, why had they not killed me, it would have been so easy in the middle of the forest? Why had one of them shown me the way and even given me 100 zloty? And what about the last bandits? Why, when I could give them no money, had they not handed me over to the Germans, but on the contrary had told me where to look for my child? And last but not least, the railway guard, a simple man of country stock, had endangered his life for a Jewish child, holding it in his arms for four hours, when at any time German patrols could pass by? That poor railway guard with two children of his own yet still willing to give shelter to a strange Jewish child? It was all incomprehensible, almost a miracle. I realized then that Good and Evil were to be found side by side in this world, or even striding together in equal measure in one person. That railway guard next to a bandit. The bandit himself, hadn't he shown some humanity? At that moment I felt nothing but gratitude. What did a watch and a chain matter – I did not need them for walking. Would I have been able to walk and find my Eva, would I not have perished had the thieves not left me the boots and coat? My little girl, by what miracle were you saved? Was it not strange that you were found at night near a railway track, picked up by a decent man and not found by German patrols or bandits? Would you have remained in your lifetime as the good man's stepdaughter had I not come in time to claim you? But for those miracles would I not have had to mourn you for as long as I lived? And those young shoemakers, those Hasidim who kept their word – I shall never know how they accomplished it for they went to a place of no return.

I knew that Eva's wound had been inflicted when she had struck the parallel railway line. While planning the escape I had had this constantly in mind, reckoning however that she would hit the snow. The gash was not big but deep, and it bled profusely. Why would she not speak? Apart from her name she would not say anything. Involuntarily, or perhaps by inveterate instinct, I turned again to God. How arbitrary was the dispensation of Providence. Why had only I been saved and the others doomed? I was no better or worse than the others, yet I was alive and they were to die in torture.

These thoughts kept whirling around in my head as I forced myself to stay awake. But I needed to think of what to do next. The stars paled before the oncoming dawn. Very soon at daybreak the legal occupant would come back to his kennel. I did not know where I could find shelter, or where I could go with my child. At daybreak I crawled out of the kennel. Numb and cold and swaying on my feet I knocked at the door of the cottage and when I was allowed inside I asked if we could be allowed to wash and get warm. I would pay. They agreed. I tried to make Eva stand on her legs but she could not. I got a shock when I saw my face in the mirror; it was grey, swollen and bruised, above the right eye I had big bumps. Such a face, without a head-covering in January, would seem suspicious to anybody. I brushed myself up thoroughly, washed my face in cold water and tore my undershirt in two. One part I used as some kind of headgear, with the second one I dressed Eva's wound. I counted on the provisional headscarf just to cover the bumps and bruises on my head. If my hosts wondered about the blue embroidered piece of silk on my head, they did not question me. Without a word they placed in front of us two cups of hot coffee and some bread. I saw that our appearance had aroused their sympathy. I drank the coffee but the child could neither eat nor drink. When she tried to bite into a piece of bread which I put into her mouth her face twisted in pain. I saw that her jaws were stiff and sore.

I learned from the peasant couple that the railway station was pretty far from their village. This could not be helped. I had to go. Thanking them for their hospitality, I set out. It was a fine day. I walked through empty snow-covered fields. For a while not a soul was in sight but after several hours I met a group of three people and asked them the way to the station. They told me that it was very far but as the roads were hidden by snow they could not tell me exactly how far. If I was not in a hurry, however, they were going to the nearby village to fetch some potatoes and from there on to the station and would show us the way. I happily agreed to join them. It turned out that my companions, a married couple with a son, were unemployed citizens of Warsaw who travelled daily to this place to get potatoes and then sell them in town. The woman immediately took an interest in Eva, the boy put his woollen gloves on her swollen hands. My hands could betray too much so I always kept them hidden. My new protectors led me to their friends in the village where they purchased their merchandise. After they had hoisted the heavy sacks onto their shoulders, we set off for the station, already good friends.

I had as yet no plan but I knew I had to return to Warsaw. For one of the 50 zloty bank notes my new friends bought a ticket each for me and Eva and together we took seats in one compartment. I was now sitting among normal people in a normal carriage, with glazed windows and doors through which one could come and go. The previous day at the same time I had been in a train too, but what a tremendous difference. My thoughts went back to my companions of the day before. Poor wretches. Who knows if they were still alive at that time. That Mrs G. who had been converted twenty years ago, and those Hasidim from the Aleksandrow rabbi, and all those others fused together by their common fate. Tears filled my eyes.

In the compartment an average wartime conversation was in progress. People were talking about the price of flour and cereal, the lack of coal and about ever-increasing seizures of smuggled goods. 'My dear, what else can we do if my husband is unemployed, and my son the civil servant gets such a low salary? Were it not for this business we would all certainly die of hunger.' Thus one person carried flour, another bacon, a third potatoes and so on. All my fellow passengers were these small merchants, carrying provisions from villages to town. I knew they were hard up, those people, with the war on, without normal work or income, running the risk of having their goods seized, even being caught in the street. But could their lot be compared to the fate of Jews denied any human rights and then doomed to the most horrific death?

· 12 ·

A New Identity

A ONE-LEGGED WAR invalid entered the compartment, clad in remnants of a Polish uniform. He made himself comfortable and began singing popular old war songs, gradually changing to newly composed anti-German hits. Strangely enough, our terrible situation and misery could be compared to this invalid who also owed his lot to the war. Driven by some strange impulse I gave him all the change I had received after paying for the tickets. Curiously, on the seat opposite mine, sat a young woman whose appearance was rather different from the rest of the passengers. This woman examined me closely, taking in my frayed coat, the strange kerchief, my top-boots and particularly my bruised hands. When I gave the money to the invalid her eyes reflected an odd sympathy. The train was nearing Warsaw when a sudden commotion stirred the whole compartment. Warsaw-Praga station was surrounded by police. There was a raid on. Why suffer, run away, if fate was against you?

Depressed, I bent over my child's head. Then my curious neighbour, while pretending to get out of the compartment, passed close to where I was sitting and asked in a whisper: 'You certainly have no documents . . .?' I shook my head. The lady stealthily handed me a sheet of paper. 'This is my document stating my name, Marianna Lukaszewska. God bless you, my dear.' And she was gone.

I fingered the certificate. How strange and miraculous! I went to the lavatory to read the document. From now on my name was to be Marianna Lukaszewska, daughter of Jan and Malgorzata née Pruchniak. I learned it by heart. Thus I got a Christian name and Aryan parents. What an unbelievable and wonderful thing to have happened, a blessing from God. I returned to my seat as Mrs Lukaszewska and under this new name I started my new life.

It was already dark when the train arrived at Praga station. 'May I go with you?', I asked the friendly couple. 'Of course, you probably don't know Warsaw.' At the station it appeared that the raid had just finished and it was safe. The potato dealers took me to their home on 12 Zabkowska Street, Flat 72. A shabby flat belonging to poor, simple people but how kind and good-natured they were. I tried to grasp the situation and think about my first move. Here I was, practically penniless, badly bruised and deadly tired, a sick child in my arms, among strangers. Yes, I was Marianna Lukaszewska who had no place to rest and no address.

I decided to ring up the factory and ask about the situation there. My hostess laid my child on her bed and I went down to phone from a little café which made money chiefly from the telephone calls. 'Hallo, Schultz & Co., furriers' department – I heard these words spoken in German by the familiar voice of my subtenant Miss Stark. When she recognized me, she burst into tears and I had to wait a long while for an intelligible answer. The Vernichtungs-kommando had definitely left Warsaw, the extermination action was over and peace had come to our factory in the ghetto. I knew very well that such a state would last for a time, so I resolved to go back there, at least temporarily, in order to have some rest and nurse the child, and then we would see. I asked Miss Stark to send the factory car for us. It was too late for that. The car could pick us up the next morning. I gave my address and the matter was settled.

I returned to my shelter and told them about my leaving the next day, asking 'Can you put us up for this night?' 'Certainly', they replied, inviting me to share their meagre supper. We talked about the war, the raids, the Germans. Luckily they did not ask any personal questions. My Eva slept in a clean bed. Suddenly we noticed some excitement in the courtyard. A neighbour rushed in.

'Jesus Christ! A raid! The Germans have surrounded this block and are arresting people.' I took my girl, thanked everyone for the hospitality and went away. I did not want to endanger those kind people. The yard was full of green uniforms. I passed unmolested between the rows of police. I found myself in an empty street at night wondering where we could shelter till the morning. Curfew hour was approaching. I simply must find somewhere to stay and had the idea that I would try to contact barrister M., my previous employer. Again I went to the small café with the telephone. 'Hallo, this is ...' 'Good evening, dear colleague,' he interrupted, 'I recognize your voice.' 'May I come to see you, sir?' 'You are welcome.' Kind soul that he was, Mr M. asked no questions, did not show any curiosity or surprise. I was well aware of my strange appearance and feared the well-lit trams. For the last 50 zloty I hired a cab and, taking all precautions, told the cabman to go to an address in Bracka instead of Nowogrodzka Street. I got off and walked the rest of the way to the house. During the drive I had misgivings about the cab driver: he was looking too closely at me, driving me in the opposite direction. Fear has big eyes, says a Polish proverb, and I was mentally broken.

When I finally arrived at his flat, barrister M. was horrified at my appearance. 'How terrible you look, my friend, what happened?' We could talk frankly because now Mr M. had his whole flat to himself. I told him everything. Only then did we examine Eva's wound. It was rather big, covered with frozen or clotted blood. I worried because the child had stopped speaking and could not walk. Little Eva accepted a cake which she licked but was unable to swallow. Barrister M. comforted me, saying nothing was seriously wrong with her. I was limping, which I had not noticed before. Barrister M. strongly opposed my return to the ghetto: especially with the child, this would have been madness. On the other hand I could not remain in Warsaw in my present state. So my child was to stay with Mrs P. who had long ago agreed to this arrangement.

I would return to the ghetto only in order to fetch some things and rest a little. We spent the night talking. In the morning I phoned Mrs P. who told me to bring Eva over immediately. Then I rang up the factory and gave my new address to the driver. I spent a few hours at Mr M.'s, played the housewife, went shopping, and all the while examined the passers-by, to make sure that my face was really Aryan enough to pass muster.

Of course I knew I could not stay at Mr M.'s. I had worked in his office for many years before the war. During the 'big ghetto', I had often been seen calling on him wearing my Jewish armband so that the caretaker and the tenants knew who I was. I had to go and try somewhere else.

My child was better. The German Karl Bruck came around with the car at noon and brought me some money from my sister-in-law. The car belonged to Mr Neumann, the German manager of our factory. The chauffeur was a soldier whom we had all feared because he used to beat Jews he met in the street in the daytime. He always used to shout: 'Daytime is for work when you are on the day shift, and when you work at night you should be sleeping during the day. You may stroll in the evenings, Jew, but before the curfew.' This German barely let us walk in the streets; and we had to talk in the car in whispers. Karl Bruck would not hear of my returning to the ghetto, he even started begging me not to destroy myself. 'How will I be able to look my wife and child in the eye after all I have seen in the ghetto?', he asked in a dull voice, burying his face in his hands. Yes, Karl Bruck was an honest man, yet I never forgot that he was a German. At last the car reached the outskirts where Mrs P. had her farm. Bruck once again asked me to ring him up at the factory if I needed anything, and left.

Mrs P. welcomed me warmly. I gave her some money, a very small amount for those times, and with tears in my eyes, entrusted my child to her. In case of my death Mrs P. promised to send Eva to my relatives abroad. On small scraps of paper I scribbled the addresses of my parents and sister in Palestine, my sister-in-law in America and my brother in South Africa. Those scraps of paper in which I begged all of them to take care of my little Eva, I considered as my will. Not to imperil Mrs P. with these discreditable addresses, I'd put them in hermetically sealed bottles which I buried in earth. I was very careful and made three copies of everything. Three bottles with small slips of paper on which I took leave from the world, sent last words of love to my relatives, begging them to take care of my little orphan, were buried in three different spots in the garden. It was terribly hard to part with Eva but I hoped I was leaving her in good care. As I was saying goodbye Mrs P. kissed me affectionately, made the sign of the cross and vowed to care for Eva as if she were her own child. I found myself in the street once again.

I went on to Nowogrodzka just once more to see my barrister friend Mr M., but found his flat locked. My former employer had left Warsaw for a few days. Apart from Mr M. I had no friends in the Gentile quarter. I knew several other people but I would not expose casual acquaintances by my call. One should not forget that Germans had published a warning that anyone who sheltered a Jew, fed him, provided him with documents or help in any other form, would be put to death. On the other hand I could not loiter for long, looking somewhat conspicuous. What was I to do?

Eventually I resolved to telephone barrister Mr S., in whose office I had also worked for some time before the war. He was considered a philo-Semite. However I had no luck, for nobody answered my call. Two or three other barristers whom I tried to contact on the phone were not at home either. Where should I find shelter? In pre-war days you could sit in the waiting-room at the station, in a park or a garden, or last but not least in a café. All these places, however, were now the most frequently searched and dangerous due to constant raids on smugglers, kidnapping for labour in Germany and continuous checking of documents. Besides, parks and public gardens were inaccessible to the Polish population, and with my appearance I could not go into a café. But I felt so tired.

I walked along Hoza Street to Three Crosses Square when my eyes fell on a church. The doors stood ajar and anybody could enter freely. Shyly I sneaked in and sat on a bench in the darkest corner. It was dimly lit inside, and a deep silence flowed consolingly onto my shattered nerves. It was afternoon but very quiet and, besides, I knew the Germans would not break into a church – I could rest there for a while. I went over and over the past few days in my mind – the blockade on Nowolipie at daybreak on 20 January, all that day I had been on my feet. Then all night I had walked through forests and roads. I had rested for a while in a kennel but then again had had to walk. Lastly the train journey, followed by the night at Mr M.'s which I had spent talking, sitting in an armchair. Today again I had been on my feet. Nothing was more tiring than such an aimless walk.

Here at least I could cry my heart out. Tears flowed down my face and I did not even have a handkerchief to wipe them away. I felt so terribly poor, so lonely and broken down. Painfully I stood up from the bench as the church was closing, and found myself in the street once more. Where to go, where to go, I kept asking myself. At the door of barrister S.'s flat I waited till the curfew, hoping that someone would come home for the night. If they, too, had left Warsaw, what would I do in the streets during the curfew? I had already resolved to spend the night on the staircase when, five minutes before the impending hour, Mrs S., arrived. My appearance immediately aroused her sympathy. She welcomed me very kindly and behaved towards me like a mother towards a child. I was given food, a nightgown, and when I lay in a clean bed I could not believe my own luck. Barrister S., however, was no longer alive. The Germans had imprisoned him in Pawiak jail and there they had murdered him, so his wife told me. Several months later she also told me that I had been rambling on all that night in a delirious fever, sawing some bars, complaining of having no shirt and still looking for my child. Mrs S. had changed the cold compresses on my head several times but I remembered nothing. I slept long and deep and awakened refreshed. I felt only pain in my thigh and I was limping badly.

Mrs S. looked at my Aryan document which proved to be a marriage certificate. A birth certificate was definitely needed and therefore she gave me her cousin's address, indicating that I should confide all my troubles in Mrs Po.

Mrs Po. indeed proved to be a most kindly, honest person. At first she scanned my appearance critically. 'You must take off this petticoat-kerchief. Here, take this hat', and she gave me a fine brown felt hat with lowered brim which shaded half of my face. 'Nobody should walk round Warsaw with hands looking like that', she asserted and gave me a pair of woollen gloves which I promised not to take off. Mrs Po. then fixed me up with a birth certificate in my new name as I had decided to remain Marianna Lukaszewska, deeming this name to be providential. Mrs Po. also promised to arrange a Polish registration paper for me, as every resident of Warsaw had to be registered somewhere. Such registration had to be backdated several years and in particular prior to the German ordinance of spring 1942, which stated that newcomers from outside the capital could not become permanent residents of Warsaw. Then I learned the technicalities of acquiring so-called Aryan documents.

Jews crossing over from the ghetto invariably came from provincial towns and even if they had been former residents of Warsaw their birth certificates showed stamps or original forms of provincial churches and towns, chiefly those later under Russian occupation. Thus it was difficult to ascertain the validity of such documents. Older Jews who, for instance, pretended that they had come to Poland after the revolution in Russia, had their forged documents issued in Russian churches, the younger ones, in Vilna, Kaunas, Lvov or Stanislawow. Assumed names and particulars were, of course, chosen at will. All this appeared rather simple in comparison with the intricate registration business which involved various municipal clerks from the Population Census offices, and area administration executives, under whose care the registration books were kept. Obviously, such documents could be obtained only for money, yet one had to admit that the amount paid was far from exorbitant. A counterfeit birth certificate with an antedated proof of registration cost inclusively about 1200–1300 zloty, an amount equal to four kilograms of butter.

Apart from those forgeries, there were the so-called 'death certificates', real documents issued by existing churches in Warsaw, easy to check in the church record books for such details as date of baptism and so on. These were birth certificates of deceased persons whose deaths, due to oversight or negligence, had not been entered into the respective church records. Such a 'genuine' birth certificate had its advantages, but nevertheless it could happen that either the person presumed dead was still alive, or that many people knew about the actual death. As it was, the price of a 'death certificate' was slightly higher because it involved the additional work of going through the church annals. Prices of those very documents were considerably higher in the ghetto because of the large number of Jewish go-betweens who profiteered on this business. All this was explained to me by Mrs Po. I had no alternative. I wanted to remain Marianna Lukaszewska, I possessed a genuine marriage certificate, the only thing which was missing was a birth certificate. All details of Mrs Lukaszewska were left unchanged. Only my new birth certificate stated that I was born in Lida, near Vilna. I hoped

that the real Mrs Lukaszewska would forgive me that little altera-
tion. Wearing the hat and gloves given me by Mrs Po. and my
overcoat cleaned and brushed as best I could, I stood before my
benefactor. After scrutinizing me she pronounced 'You look like a
poor teacher or a governess from a little town. It is even good that
you are limping, so they won't catch you for work. Looking as you
do you may walk freely about the town.' I immediately liked the
idea of being a teacher or a governess. Mrs Po. was right. A teacher
could limp in peace, it did not matter; it could even prove useful.

Thus on 23 January 1943 I was definitely transformed into Mrs
Marianna Lukaszewska, a teacher and governess from a provincial
town. Mrs Po. remained one of my closest friends until the end of
the war. On that occasion however I did not wish to bother her
any more and took my leave. I felt much safer in the streets, looking
more like other people, but the question of where to go, where to
spend the night, started bothering me again.

Warsaw, even under German occupation, was a very lively city.
Cars, trams and cabs, people running in all directions, all in a
hurry, all with some aim. Everyone had something to do, yet they
all knew that when their job was finished they could rest at home.
Why did I have to walk aimlessly in the city in which I was born
and brought up, where I graduated and had a job in a lawyer's
office? In this city where my parents owned several buildings, there
was no corner in which I could rest. Again I loitered about till the
evening. The shop windows were alight, people thronged to cafés
and cinemas. For normal people, evenings meant rest and recreation
after a day's work but for me they became a nightmare. So as not
to endanger her I felt I could not go to Mrs S.

After long deliberation I called at Mr L.'s chambers. There had
been no change in the office. The ante-room was full of people and
Mr L. was receiving clients as usual. Mrs L. was not delighted to
see me, a fact which I noticed immediately. I was a woman and
most unfortunately her junior. She did not like her husband's
cordial attitude towards me, yet for a well-bred woman it was not
done simply to refuse someone hospitality. Very unwillingly she
agreed to shelter me for the night. Just before the curfew hour,
Jerzy M., one of barrister L.'s executives whom I had met some
time before the war, appeared. That very night the Germans were
intending to carry out some arrests among former Polish officers

and Mr M. advised barrister L. not to sleep at his home. Mr L., who had noticed his wife's behaviour, asked openly: 'Jerzy, where will you take us for the night?' 'I think to some quiet flat where only old women are registered', he replied. The three of us then got into a tram and went – I did not ask where. I had already learned not to ask too many questions. We got off and made our way through those small streets which seemed to me strangely familiar. We entered a house which also seemed somehow familiar to me but due to the black-out I could not distinguish anything.

An elderly woman opened the door, put on the light and I was immediately taken aback. I was in my parents' former flat in Marianska Street where I had been born and lived till I got married. How strange that after so many experiences and homelessness I was given shelter in my own parents' home! To my kind-hearted hostess I did not betray what this house meant to me when she explained where the kitchen and bathroom were situated. The good woman complained that the flat, which she had been allotted after some Jews had been expelled from it, was in a terrible state and that all repairs had to be carried out by herself. The flat must have belonged to a wealthy Jew, for stoves and oven, even the inlaid floors had been ripped loose by bandits in search of gold and money. I felt sorry for those poor thieves who had demolished my parents' flat. I knew their labour must have been futile because my parents had not hidden anything anywhere.

All the same, the night spent in my parents' house was an experience for me. I saw in it the hand of Fate. Barrister L. jumped up in surprise when I told him in whose home we had found shelter and said: 'My friend, now I see that you will certainly outlive the war. I would like to be so sure about myself.' His words proved prophetic: Mr L. was murdered by the Germans in December 1943. At the time, however, I considered his remarks to be strongly exaggerated. The coincidence of the flat nonetheless cheered me up a bit.

Next morning we parted company. All my Aryan friends had their own griefs and troubles, great difficulties, as I later saw. I would not burden people whom I knew superficially with my sorrows, let alone have them risk the death penalty for helping me. Once again I was wandering about the streets when my gaze fell on a brass plaque at the entrance to a building saying 'Lawyer'. I remembered a pleasant, middle-aged lady, the first woman advocate in Poland, the first woman to put on an advocate's gown. I had called on her once before the war, when she had made a strong impression on me. Had I the right to call on her now, to expose that decent person to severe punishment? I brushed these thoughts away as I had absolutely no alternative.

The door was opened by Mrs W. herself, who of course did not recognize me. When I gave her my real name and profession she instantly offered me her full help, cordially asking me what I needed first. Since I thought the most sensible and advisable thing to do was to get a job, I told the kind lady that I had resolved to work as a teacher-governess, having acquired some experience during my university days when I used to give extra lessons. 'That's excellent. What a coincidence', she responded. 'Just a few days ago a client of mine, Mr B. an engineer, asked me if I knew of a reliable governess who would be ready to go to his relatives in the country. I shall phone them right away to ask whether the post is still vacant.' Soon I was listening to a friendly conversation with Mr B. 'I recommend to you an old friend of mine, a very decent person, Miss Lukaszewska, a governess from a small town.' Then I heard Mrs W. speaking highly of her dear old friend's professional qualifications. Eventually the conversation ended with 'Yes, of course she will call on you soon to settle all the details.' Mrs W. stressed that in no circumstances should I disclose my past to Mr B. He was an honest man and a good Pole, yet she advised it was wiser to keep certain things secret.

I stayed with Mrs W. till the appointed time, working on my appearance. Before I left Mrs W. put some rouge on my face, saying 'You need this my child.' As I was recommended by a well-known woman advocate, I was heartily welcomed by Mr B. at his beautiful flat at Krolewska Street. After a brief interview I was engaged as a governess at an estate in the vicinity of Sochaczew. My pupil was to be Wojtus R., a ten-year-old boy. I was to receive a room with full board and a monthly salary of 200 zloty. Mr B. invited Mrs W. and me to dinner on the following Wednesday. 'Please come. Mrs R. will bring her boy. You ladies will get acquainted with each other and we shall all drive down to Sochaczew together.'

I was overjoyed. My child was in a safe place and I had managed to get an excellent job in the country. I still had some time during which I had to pack a suitcase. Nothing would arouse so much suspicion as the lack of personal belongings. I spent the night of 24 January at Mrs W.'s flat. Both Mr and Mrs W. were very kind and treated me tenderly, like a pair of very close friends. Their behaviour was all the more remarkable as their maidservant had a German sweetheart and was generally not trustworthy. Mrs W. was visited by a woman advocate, Mrs L. The kind attitude and attentions of both ladies slowly renewed my faith in human beings and in the future.

Knowing that the telephones were tapped, I would not expose Mr and Mrs W. by connecting their flat with the ghetto, so I went to a public booth and rang up the factory. I learned that everything was in order in the ghetto and decided to return for two days to Nowolipie Street to have a good rest and pack up a few necessary belongings. It was not an easy task to enter the ghetto. I knew that various groups of Jewish labourers, the so-called 'outposts', worked on the Aryan side, leaving the ghetto every morning and returning for the night. But where was I to find such an 'outpost'? As I walked in the streets, evening was drawing in and I was still thinking of what to do.

Suddenly I heard the words and tune of *Hatykva*, the Jewish national anthem, sung on Chlodna Street by the lowest and most humiliated slaves of Adolf Hitler. It might seem incredible but in that gloomy time it became a common and daily sight. The 'outposts' were escorted by a few Jewish militia men and Germans. It was the Germans who actually made their slaves sing – 'Singen. Immer singen' (Sing, keep singing) Hebrew and Jewish songs. Why they took a special fancy to *Hatykva* nobody knew, but who could understand the sick and degenerate German psychology? The tired, miserable Jewish labourers, compelled to work, were marched along the Aryan street, forcibly singing in order to please their oppressors.

I walked through the streets like an ordinary citizen. After the *Hatykva* came to an end I heard another song, yet another which had to be extracted out of the tired throat of a Jewish slave in order to degrade him even more – to humiliate him for the glory of the German Volk. The attitude of the Gentile passers-by towards this crowd of poor wretches was varied. Some looked with pity at seeing those miserable, ragged Jews, bent under heavy loads, who

Ruth and George, in the early 1930s

Ruth and George on their wedding day, 25 December 1934

Ruth 1933

From left: Edna, Tusia, Esther, Mother, George, Ruth, Joseph, Spring 1939

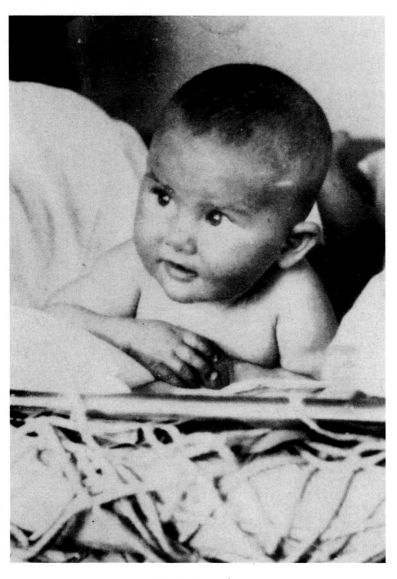

Eva at six months

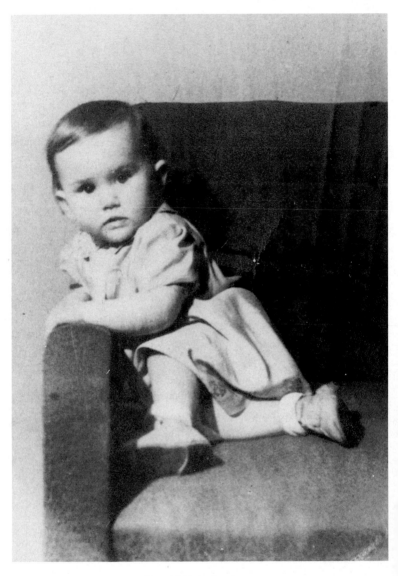

Eva, 1941, in the ghetto

Photo of Eva (wearing a cross) February 1945, sent via a South African soldier to Ruth's brother Isadore

Message to brother Isadore written on the back of the photograph (with translation)

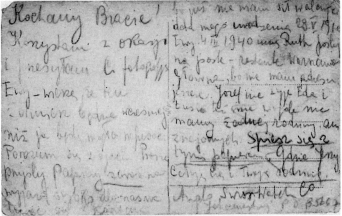

Beloved Brother
I'm taking this opportunity to sent a photograph of Eva. I trust this soldier will arrive before I could get a letter to you. Get in touch with father. Please sent the papers for our departure at once. Don't think of the cost because I haven't any strength left to fight on. The date of my birth in 29 May 1910. Eva's is 4 March 1940. Send it to the Poste Restante, central Warsaw because I haven't got an address as yet. Joseph is no longer alive. Nor Eda nor Tusia*. We have no family at all. Nor any acquaintances. Hurry with those papers. Where is George? I kiss you and your family.

*Ruth was wrong. Eda and Tusia survived. See page 232.

Ruth in 1945

Eva and Annabelle in South
Africa, 1953

were being forced to sing; others smiled at the procession walking in the middle of a road like black shadows with only their white armbands clearly discernible. For the Judenbinde, the sign of shame, had always to be clear to see. Often an urchin would mock the song, curse a Jew rudely, or throw a stone. The Germans tried to make the Jews a laughing-stock in the eyes of the Aryan spectators. The Judenbinde, the Star of David and *Hatykva* were to signify signs of the humiliation and ignominy of the Jewish nation.

The procession turned into Zelazna Street. Trying to pass off as an average onlooker, I bought a newspaper and an unnecessary book from a street vendor, but in my pocket I kept a handkerchief ready, knotted in a kind of an armband. There was not a David sign on it, but it could pass in the dusk and in the crowd. Besides, I had previously helped myself out in the same way when I had forgotten my armband. I knew that Jews from that 'outpost' would enter the ghetto from Zelazna gate near Leszno Street, so I tried to walk on the pavement as long as I could, mix with the 'outpost' and at the last moment go with them through the gate. We neared Leszno Street where the Jews stopped along the wall encircling the ghetto, waiting to be counted, searched, checked and eventually let in. I stopped near a shop, gazed at a shop window and waited, mingling with the crowd of gawpers who would invariably stand near the ghetto entrances to have some spectacle to make fun of.

I knew that some of the onlookers were dangerous characters. Informers, rabble of the worst kind, members of the underworld, the scum of mankind who loitered all day near the ghetto gates waiting for an easy prey; to grab some goods which the Germans would probably take away from the poor Jew during a search; or to buy for a few cents some valuable from the wretched 'outpost man'. Their best profits, however, were earned by blackmailing a Jew who would clandestinely leave the ghetto. Such a scoundrel would lurk for hours on end at the ghetto walls, steal up on the Jew and, after threatening to give him up to the Germans, extort money from him. There were two kinds of blackmailers, 'decent' and 'vicious' ones. A 'decent' blackmailer would content himself with a small ransom and go away looking for another prey. He would take a watch or a ring and set his victim free. He would sometimes even apologize for his deed, complaining about hard times and the impossibility of making a living. The 'vicious' one was far more dangerous. He would single out his prey, usually a wealthy-looking Jew, follow him inconspicuously to his new flat on the Aryan side, then blackmail him regularly, sometimes taking away his last penny. There were also such rascals with an 'ideological conscience', which meant that they would rob their victim of all his money and then hand him over to the Germans. Some would denounce a Jew straightaway. Apart from them there were the very dangerous informers. Posing as friends and rendering some minor service, they would gain the confidence of their Jewish prey, get his money and then betray him. I had learned about all those human beasts from the tales of their victims. I could now take a good look at them and recognize their kind, their caps shoved over their eyes, hands in their pockets. As I was standing and waiting near the ghetto entrance I probably looked so poor and modest that I did not arouse their interest.

They started letting in the Jews. The Germans searched every one, examining the contents of each rucksack. Sugar, fats, meat, all things not well hidden, were taken away. The rest the 'outpost' Jews were allowed to keep. The last moment neared – one leap from the 'Aryan pavement' on which I was standing, and I was among the Jews. In a flash I put on my provisional armband and I again became a Jewess. My new companions, immediately grasping the situation, pushed me inside the crowd, someone kindly handing me an original Judenbinde, another putting on my shoulders a sackload of potatoes. Yet another one told me that my name was Malka Rozenberg, and I was ready to pass the gate. The German did not pay any attention to me, being concerned only with the number of people belonging to the 'outpost' squad. Besides, a difference of one person did not matter, it would somehow be explained by the 'outpost' leader.

I found myself in the ghetto, once more in Leszno Street where the wall crossed the roadway, opposite the Law Court building. Reaching Nowolipie Street through rows of connected cellars and garrets, I found myself in the small street of Schulcowizna. I was terribly moved as I rang the bell of my flat and fainted on the doorstep when the door was opened. My friends took off my clothes and put me to bed and then I had a breakdown after all that I had been through. I had been strong when facing danger, but

I had been living on my nerves. Here, among my own people, in my own room, these strong nerves gave way. I became a poor, weak woman. All that night and the following day I lay in a semi-conscious state, unaware of what I was saying or doing. My friends bustled around me, a lot of people came to see me to listen to what I had been through or how miraculously I had been saved. All of them passed before me as if in a fog. Were it not for the document in the name of Marianna Lukaszewska, my sore bones and bruised hands, I would have to believe that the nightmare of the past five days had been just that – a horrendous nightmare.

For two days I lay in bed and had an excellent rest. The doctor who was summoned pronounced me quite sound except for some bruises. I got up, went to a hairdresser and packed all the things I was to take with me to the Gentile quarter. I had to examine everything very carefully, in case even the label of a Jewish dressmaker might betray me. All my real documents had of course to be left behind. It was difficult to take leave of my photographs; Marianna Lukaszewska, daughter of Jan and Malgorzata, could have no Semitic-looking parents. I could not even take Eva's picture. Her looks were not Semitic at all but what could I answer those who might ask who she was? That newly born Marianna Lukaszewska could not stand too much interrogation or scrutiny. Yet every question would need to be answered suitably and any lie or subterfuge well remembered. I left the photographs all wet with tears. Another hour, and the factory lorry would take me across the gate.

It was painful to part with my sister-in-law and my niece. My sister-in-law would not listen to any discussion about going over to the Aryan side; she resolved to remain where she was. She had spent all her life in the midst of her family and was afraid to feel strange in unfamiliar Gentile surroundings. She feared her Polish was not good enough, that her looks were perhaps not sufficiently Aryan, and argued that she might betray herself by her behaviour. I gave in, but reminded her about the promise I had given to my brother to take care of his little daughter. I had found a sanctuary for my Eva. I could do the same for my niece. As the brave girl was all for it, her mother eventually agreed.

Just before I got into the lorry, my companion Mrs Beit from the furriers' room ran up to me saying: 'My premonition has never

deceived me, I know you will survive the war. Don't forget to find
my boy and tell him that his mother will think of him till her last
breath and praise the Lord who, at least, saved him. His name is
Willy Beit and he is studying somewhere in England. Please swear
on the health of your daughter not to forget, Beit, Willy Beit.' The
poor mother went away crying. If Willy Beit is alive anywhere, let
him accept this last message from his mother.

The Schultz & Co. lorry was used every day to carry loads of fur
vests to a branch at Miodowa Street. The German Karl Bruck hid
me under the vests and thus on 27 January 1943 I left Nowolipie
Street for ever. The lorry slowed down in Rymarska Street, where I
jumped out. In a doorway nearby I brushed off the fur dust and
boldly set out along Krolewska Street to Mr B. for the dinner party.
As my hair was done and I was properly dressed, I looked no
different from an ordinary teacher applying for a job.

My future employer, Mrs R., was indeed a very kind, amiable
person and I liked the boy too. We all got on famously and there
was a very friendly atmosphere throughout the dinner. Mrs R. had
some shopping to do in Warsaw and the next morning we were to
leave in Mr B.'s car for Sochaczew. (Mrs B. was responsible for
some public works and – exceptionally – had a licence to drive a
private car.) Thus again I had one day free and decided to use this
time to find a place for my niece to get her out of the ghetto. I went
to see Mrs S., who did not recognize me, I had changed so much
for the better in the last few days. I began by asking her to shelter
my niece: 'You have such a big flat and you will not feel so lonely
if you have this lovely girl with you.' Mrs S. would not agree at
first, claiming with some justification that as she was away from
home all day long the child would remain alone in that large, empty
flat. She would not know how to explain the presence of the girl to
her friends or to the caretaker and gave many other reasons against
it. Eventually, however, she let me convince her and agreed to take
little Tusia into her care. The only thing left to do was for me to
get the girl out of the ghetto.

Departure from the ghetto was not exceedingly difficult at that
time. There were generally very few Jews left but our friendly
factory Germans, who had seen how doomed we were, simply
helped us. They helped us unselfishly without being asked, often
exposing themselves to considerable danger. To get down from a

factory lorry belonging to a German firm in the streets of Warsaw was not simple so I had to select a remote little street in which Tusia could alight from a lorry full of vests, undetected. I also had to look for temporary shelter where she would have to remain for a few hours. I went to Jerzy M. in Sienna Street. In spite of our acquaintance being rather superficial, I begged him to put little Tusia up for this one night. Mr M. and his mother immediately agreed. After taking all possible precautions, I rang my sister-in-law in the ghetto from a nearby café to inform her about the arrangements. I had to wait for Tusia at the street corner. I stood there and waited. Time passed, and still there was no trace of her. Dusk began to fall and the curfew hour drew near. I had begun to grow restless, when at last she arrived. We went to the kind Mrs M. who promised to accompany Tusia to Mrs S.'s the next day. Everything was settled. At the last moment I noticed a gold ring with some Hebrew words on Tusia's finger, which I took off immediately. Just such a trifle could bring disaster down on us both. I gave her some last directions and we parted.

I could not go away, however, without seeing my little daughter, left while she was still sick. I did not find her with Mrs P., who explained that the neighbours had shown too much interest in the pretty, nicely dressed girl with such a nasty wound on her head. The inhabitants of Warsaw knew only too well what was going on in the ghetto. Mrs P. had grown afraid of these ubiquitous neighbours and, mistrusting the driver, had herself harnessed the horse and taken my Eva to stay with her cousin, who lived deep in the country.

Yes, the people of Warsaw were well aware of the state of things in the ghetto. They heard constant firing. Each new arrival in town could be Jewish. Any sign of interest in a newcomer could be fatal. Gossip would reach an informer who could then denounce the person to the authorities. Mrs P. considered the new arrangement far safer. She did not want to give me her cousin's address. I could go there and spoil everything. I was obliged to comply although I was rather suspicious. I left Warsaw on 27 January 1943. Sad and depressed, I began my new life as a teacher-governess on Mr R.'s estate near Warsaw.

· 13 ·

The New Life

THE ATMOSPHERE IN my new home was warm and kind, the house spacious and opulent. My first evening, spent at a nicely laid table, in the company of many happy and carefree guests, was difficult. The meal was very tasty and my hosts wondered why I ate so little. 'Why don't you eat anything, Miss Maria, and why are you so sad?' Could I enjoy all this plenty and the happy company, which reminded me so acutely of bygone times at my own home, among my own relatives and friends? Could I eat when I remembered those who were still alive but had nothing to put into their mouths? I had to strive to look at ease. I had to pretend I felt all right. After a few tumblers of spirits the guests became more light-hearted and garrulous and I confess that vodka had no small effect upon me.

The topic of conversation inevitably turned to the Jews. Mr and Mrs R. began talking about a Jew who was the proprietor of the kiln in which Mr R. had been manager for many years. They kept sending him parcels to the ghetto, in great secrecy, and had now received news that the man had left the ghetto and gone into hiding. The guests carried on chatting about the Jews from their neighbourhood. Miss Lukaszewska learned how they had been sent away to an unknown destination; how the rest, who at first had managed to hide, were caught, ordered to dig their own graves, then mown down with machine-guns. The dead, half-dead and even slightly wounded were buried in the pit prepared by their own hands. And Miss Lukaszewska had now and then to add a word or two of her own to the general conversation, wary not to betray that she was choking on the tasty piece of the roast. 'How were the Jews liquidated in your home town, Miss Maria?' 'I really wouldn't know how. I left Lida when the Bolsheviks were there, and settled in Warsaw, at Praga, far from the ghetto.' I had held this information in readiness for, according to my registration papers which I guarded carefully, I had been living in Wilenska Street at Praga since spring 1942. 'Besides, in Warsaw I did not have a single Jewish acquaintance, so this problem did not interest me.' Luckily the guests would jump from one topic to another, thus enabling me to be myself for a while. At the beginning of my new career I found this constant pretence and lying very difficult. Later on I grew accustomed to it and learned to act my part.

In general I felt comfortable in this new home. I shared a big, warm room with my pupil. I had a maidservant, and the food was very good. The role of tutor was quite easy and I performed my duties with real pleasure, made even more so since my pupil was a good, intelligent boy. After a few days two other boys from the neighbourhood, relatives of Mrs R., started to attend my lessons. My mistress kept on saying that she was very satisfied with me and was happy to have a good teacher after so many disappointments. In my free time I studied the catechism, consequently teaching it at a later date to the children. I used to take any novel and put between its pages the small book of 'Catechism for Youth'. Lying on my couch pretending to read, I used to study it. I studied it in the lavatory or the bathroom, and in four days I knew it by heart and could answer any questions on the subject.

Despite this comfortable existence, I lived under constant strain and permanently on the alert. Local ladies calling on Mrs R. often used to pry into my private affairs and I was still asked various 'whats' and 'hows' and where my parents were, or why I had not yet married. I invented a fairy tale regarding my past and kept it in the forefront of my mind so as not to slip up, not even once. It was not so easy for a Jew, even for an intelligent one, suddenly to turn into a Christian with a family and a past. A Jew with Aryan papers was a human being with neither family nor past. But I succeeded in somehow evading these various problems by sometimes even bluffing for fun. I chose to be taken for a 'Miss'. A Miss was more convenient, she need not answer questions regarding her husband or children, and to simplify matters, in my story I killed off my parents and had never had brothers or sisters.

My life went on smoothly and peaceably in the R's home. In the cosy privacy of my room, when I lay down on a comfortable couch with a book in my hand I sometimes could not believe that it was me. The teaching job took me only about four hours a day, the rest being devoted to reading books which were in plentiful supply in the library. I worked conscientiously, with good results. The most trying times for me were the common meals, especially ones with frequent visitors and obligatory vodka, when I simply had to be merry. I was ashamed of my life of luxury and ease. Why had so many of my friends – nice, good and worthy women who could have been in my place – been deprived of this good fortune? Had I the right to delight in this comfort, lazing in this bed when almost all my friends had perished? Questions and problems of this kind would still creep into my thoughts. However, little Wojtus would not let me dwell upon these sad problems for long.

His antics, amusing tales or the funny faces he would make, made me laugh in spite of myself. I liked my pupil and his mother very much and we soon became great friends. We were often visited by guests from Warsaw who brought us the latest news. One day my masters threw a small party to celebrate the slaughtering of a calf. It was a real feast, because the Germans forbade the slaughtering of calves and my employers were liable to be severely punished. At this secret party numerous guests assembled both from the neighbourhood and from Warsaw. They enjoyed themselves heartily. The food was excellent and the drink abundant. I could not avoid drinking vodka in order not to offend my hosts. 'What's the news in Warsaw, Mr Henryk?' 'Oh nothing special. A well-known jewellery shop was looted, Mrs Dziuba fractured her leg while skating, and, well, I think this week they finished off the rest of the Jews in the ghetto. This time, I tell you, I saw horrible things for I was just passing by in my car.'

I sat stock-still, feeling numb. My sister-in-law and so many friends were still in the ghetto. 'Another piece of jelly, Miss Maria?' I heard the kindly voice of my hostess say. 'It's delicious, why do you eat so little?' Mr Henryk carried on with his tale without interrupting his meal, while I sat with heavy heart, listening to his account of the horrifying scenes he had witnessed in the ghetto. Outwardly I kept calm, with a ghost of a smile on my face. I knew that whatever I said at that moment would give me away. 'You know, after they liquidate the ghetto they will pull down the walls and restore normal communication in Warsaw.' Yes, I knew those German plans well, but I never thought they would finish off the remaining Jews so soon. The Jewish topic was thrashed out till the end of dinner but the remarks were more sympathetic than they might have been in the past. Jews were pitied, German methods of extermination were termed barbaric. I was sitting all the time as if on burning coals. When I went to bed, late at night, I buried my head in the pillow and wept for hours. I chastized myself for sitting at a nice table and eating a good dinner, while at the same time, my dearest ones perished, for laughing and talking gaily while they wailed and cried. I felt like the meanest traitor, an outcast. I should have shared the lot of my community and not run away like a coward and hidden under an assumed name. In tears I fell asleep at last.

The following morning I telephoned my friend Mrs L. and learned with relief that little Tusia was all right and my sister-in-law was living on the Gentile side. It turned out that Tusia had begged her patroness so effectively that she eventually found a shelter for my sister-in-law with a very decent lady in Rakowiecka Street. I know it was selfishness on my part but I felt almost happy when I received this news. At least those two were safe.

One day I accompanied Mrs R. to the dentist in a nearby town and witnessed a scene which again left unforgettable traces embedded in my memory. While riding in our carriage we passed a small, half-naked boy led in the middle of the road by two policemen. 'Go faster, please', Mrs R. ordered the coachman. 'You cannot imagine what beasts the Germans are.' Mrs R. turned to me, very excited. 'They caught him somewhere, yesterday, and now they are going to kill him. I know him, this poor wretch. He's an orphan, a beggar, he's been walking around the village for years.' I glanced once more at this child clad only in shirt and boots, the boy who was going to die a martyr's death, for the glory of the German nation – then we rode on. We had plenty to do, plenty of trifling things which filled our daily lives.

At supper the maid told us the rest of the story, the small-town news: that the Germans had led the little Jew into the cemetery, had ordered him to dig a grave, then to lie down, whereupon they buried him alive. To amuse them even more completely, both of them stamped on the earth hard with their feet, waited a while and then left the cemetery. 'It's inside, Miss Maria, that my heart bleeds. At that moment you'd have wept tears.' 'No thank you very much, I prefer honey to marmalade', I heard myself replying to the kind question of my mistress. It would have been mad to allow myself to grow pale or to let my voice tremble. Long after the story of the little Jew gave way to another topic of conversation, I still kept asking myself whether it was right to sit at that table while he spent his first night in the asphyxiating earth.

These pangs of remorse, that continuous pretence and lying from dawn to dusk made me more and more restless. The inquisitiveness of small-town society made me fear that some day I would give myself away. Regretfully I made up my mind to leave my good position. Using the excuse that the final date for arranging new identity papers, the so-called 'Kennkarte', was approaching, I left my job and went to Warsaw. I could not stand the company of strangers around me any more. I was mentally exhausted and wanted to find a small room in Warsaw where for a few hours a day at least I could be myself with no need to pretend, no need to act a part.

Once in Warsaw, however, I realized that my decision had been hasty and not very wise. It was not so easy to get a job and find accommodation for a strange newcomer from the country. Landlords were very careful and demanded references from their prospective tenants. Could I provide them with any, without endangering my friends? There were many agencies for furnished rooms, to be sure, but these were the first to be avoided. My Gentile friends told me of instances where crooks would purposely advertize furnished rooms in newspapers or flat agencies in order to lure people like me. They would carefully watch their tenants, their way of life, and after coming to the conclusion that the victims were Jewish, they would proceed to blackmail them, extorting increasing amounts of money, till they had robbed them of everything. Then, not infrequently, they would betray them to the Germans. The owner of an agency in Marszalkowska Street who was notorious for blackmailing rich Jews, enticed them into his trap under the pretext of having decent rooms to let. I was occasionally put up for the night at a friend's place. I often regretted my thoughtlessness in leaving the comfortable room which I shared with little Wojtus. Again I began my wandering around Warsaw in search of shelter.

At my friend's house, the advocate Mrs L., I met her husband's sister, Sister Maria-Janina, a nun of the Sisters of Resurrection Order from the Convent in Zoliborz Street. Apart from her duties in the convent she directed a small carpenter's workshop in a shed near the cloister. Sister Maria-Janina, upon learning of my troubles, offered me accommodation on the workshop premises, which I gladly accepted. The room was small but comfortable. Although it was very cold and lacked conveniences, I felt at home there at last. I could spend my whole time there doing whatever I liked except for a few hours during which the room served as an office. Slowly I grew acquainted with my new surroundings. Next to my room, in the kitchen, there lived a maidservant who ran the house and cooked for the boys working in the shop. She had an illegitimate son, a big brat, whom she regularly thrashed. On top of this she was very inquisitive and talkative. It was apparent that the shed was inhabited by other people as well: I heard voices through the thin partitions although I never saw anybody. In great secrecy Sister Maria-Janina confided in me that in the next room there lived two Jewesses. The older one, who had typically Semitic features, never went out, not having been registered anywhere. The younger one on the contrary was out all day, and was even employed somewhere.

Sister Maria-Janina advised me not to communicate with them. Actually I preferred sitting alone in my little room, during the long evening hours, not making any new friends. I noticed the same trait in the behaviour of my neighbours, a significant and telling characteristic of Jews in hiding: a tendency to keep away from other Jews. One could only tell the other sad stories, terrible experiences, the loss of nearest and dearest ones – there would be no end of unhappy memories. In order to live on we had somehow to forget the past and strive to become accustomed to the present.

Sister Maria-Janina, who was sixty years old, had an exceptionally beautiful character. The widow of an advocate, for the past fifteen years she had been devoting her strength and energy to the convent and public welfare. The toy workshops were designated for the poorest boys, the street urchins. The Sister admitted anybody who applied. They were coached by an expert in toy-making and carpentry, a special master would teach them all primary school subjects, and what was more, they were given free meals. Sister Maria-Janina worked hard, for it was difficult in those days to find the necessary means for the upkeep of the workshop-asylum. Apart from this she taught her boys religion and instilled in them principles of honesty and morality. It was not an easy task. Her wards were recruited from among the worst outcasts, the dregs of society who were growing up in the streets or in pubs. They would often steal, even from the workshop. Sister knew about it but she always cherished the hope that at least a few would be guided along a straight path, would learn their trade and become useful citizens. As I had no job at the time I tried to help out as much as I could. Whenever there was anything to sort out in the city I went readily. Often I was sent out to cash money in some welfare institution, or to collect provisions for the boys.

14

Uprising in the Ghetto

It was near Easter time when the insurrection started in the ghetto and the last remnants of the Jews imprisoned there took up arms against their German oppressors. While passing in a tram from Zoliborz to the city on 19 April 1943, I heard the first shots, the first signs of the uprising. Warsaw was stirred. An insurrection! The Jews were fighting. At last there was somebody who dared to take up arms against our tormentors, those seemingly invincible Germans. Jews were the first to venture; they had been the first against whom Hitler had pronounced 'Ausrotten' (Extermination).

I would pass in a tram alongside the ghetto walls several times a day, very often having nothing to do in the city, simply wanting to be nearer the fight. I tried to hear what was going on there, behind the walls. I belonged there, and not in this tram where for a few pennies I could sit comfortably among peaceful passengers. I rejoiced at every sound of fighting; *tra ta ta ta*, I heard the German machine-guns stationed near the walls; *tra ta ta ta*, answered others, fainter, from far away, the Jewish ones. My heart swelled with pride on hearing that welcome echo.

A week went by and I still passed the ghetto walls several times a day, always carrying in my pocket some letter or other to the Public Welfare or General Tutelary Board. Often I would take something for Sister Maria-Janina. I realized that at any moment my papers could be checked and I might be asked why I passed this

place so often. I might already have been observed, and a letter or
a parcel would provide a good excuse. I tried to force an uncon-
cerned look on my face but my eyes sought desperately to penetrate
the walls above which the glare of fires shot sky-high. There, behind
the walls, justice fought against oppression, man against the evil in
a green steel helmet, whereas here on this side, life went on in its
normal way, the normal life in which I was playing my part.

My fellow passengers reacted variously to the sounds of battle in
the ghetto. 'Why should the Jews defend themselves?', asked a
woman in a hat with a pink feather. 'You are wrong, the Jews are
right', I heard an elderly man speaking gravely and saw him making
the sign of the cross. 'Serves them right, those vile German cowards.
I heard that yesterday the Jews killed ten German scoundrels',
interjected a workman. The tram was leaving the ghetto walls
behind, turning into Miodowa Street. As the sounds of the battle
grew fainter the topics of conversation changed. In a while we were
passing through a normal street with the sounds of car horns,
radio, music blaring, and with neon lights flashing.

The battle in the ghetto was entering its second week. Fresh
reinforcements wearing steel helmets and gas masks and riding in
tiger tanks were sent to fight against the ghetto, using the most up-
to-date arms invented by the German war machine. A full-scale
siege was initiated against the handful of insurgents. How dare the
Jews oppose the brutal violence from cellars, rooftops or ruins?
They knew they would be killed but they preferred death in that
hopeless, uneven battle to the agony of the gas chambers. Their
deaths would be made easier if they succeeded in killing a few
Germans in the process. We owe much to our brother-insurgents
who with their blood have written these heroic pages of Jewish
history. Their unparalleled bravery earned the sympathy of all
honest Gentiles towards the misery of the Jews, and opened their
eyes to the fact that arms could be raised against the Germans.
Those fighting Jews redeemed all those weaker ones, all those
masses whom slavery had abased, whose instinct for survival had
been exploited by the Germans. Those heroes avenged – in part at
least – the martyrs' death of their brethren and by their glorious
deeds, rehabilitated other members of the Jewish community.

The sky above Warsaw was ablaze; violent explosions blasted
windowpanes in all buildings near the ghetto, keeping everyone

awake at night. Miraculously, with an increasing number of police and SS men besieging the ghetto, the Jewish fighters still held on. We will never know how many Jews sacrificed their lives in that unequal fight, but we learned that the losses on the German side were great as well.

On a quiet evening while passing by the ghetto walls in a tram I saw several people jumping from a fourth-floor balcony of a burning house. On another evening I saw a girl in a burning frock leaping from a window. That ghastly torch flashed briefly then vanished behind the wall, while the tram rolled peacefully on. The scum of society stood by the ghetto walls. Some were tempted by the possibility of looting Jewish property, others lurked for easy prey – a Jew who might try to creep over to the Aryan side through a crevice or chink in the wall. Among the uniformed policemen, manhunters, conmen and all kinds of rascals around the walls, other Poles waited too, looking out for a convenient moment to supply the fighters with arms and ammunition. A girl hungry for thrills would be waiting to convey the needs of the besieged to the Underground Organization. All of these were called human beings whom God had created in his image – the Jew-insurgent in his desperate fight against domination and the Polish comrade endangering his life in order to supply him with weapons; the blackguard, the scoundrel and the Polish policeman obligingly serving the Germans, and that soldier in a steel helmet.

On Krasinski Square, near the High Court building, unused during the occupation, there was a kind of amusement park with a merry-go-round, swings, scenic railway and terrible jangling music – all just a few yards from the ghetto walls. There was an insanity in these discordant sounds of a dying ghetto fighting for the defence of human dignity alongside such incongruous merriment. The sounds of those sacred shots were stifled by lively organ music and the sky, set on fire by the insurgents, lit up the place where pleasure-seeking crowds and onlookers revelled, splitting their sides with laughter.

After the ghetto uprising had lasted out a third week, the Warsaw population started wondering how it was that after so long the Germans could not overcome this group of fighting Jews. Loud remarks about the German inability to crush the uprising were heard more and more often on the trams. The Jewish uprising was jokingly called the second front, so much so that the conductors or tram drivers were often boldly asked: 'What's the news on the second front, how many Germans have been killed today?'

One day in our house in Zoliborz a skirmish broke out which could have had very serious repercussions for all of us. The boys were coached in grammar school subjects by a teacher popularly nicknamed 'Student'. This 'Student', as it turned out, was a Jew – a fact of which Sister Maria-Janina was well aware. Quite by accident a young man came to the workshop and recognized the teacher as a fellow student from university, a communist, with whom he had constantly quarrelled. These two had a very sharp altercation after which the visitor reviled the Sister for sheltering a Jew. It was quite obvious that the unexpected visitor was bound to turn the teacher over to the Gestapo, and the trembling inhabitants of our slum implored the teacher to leave, for a short time at least. He was courageous, however, and insisted on staying; he admitted that in any event he had nowhere else to go. Sister Maria-Janina's behaviour was remarkable. She did not give him notice nor did she tell him to quit. 'God will help us,' she said, and nobody denounced us. Yet I considered it unsafe to stay at the small house in Zoliborz and as soon as I had received another offer of a job I took the opportunity and left the hospitable shelter, but I stayed in touch with Sister Maria-Janina until the end of the war.

We were into the fourth week of the Jewish uprising when the Germans decided to apply a new strategy in their battle against the ghetto. Low-flying planes pinpointed every single building and blasted the area with incendiary bombs. Block after block stood in flames but the poor inhabitants did not even try to extinguish the fires. No shelter, no bunker could give cover – the entire ghetto burned, painting the sky over Warsaw a bloody red. The trams stopped passing the ghetto walls – the Germans forbade it. The ingenious citizens of Warsaw solved this problem. Over there on the Castle Square all kinds of carts and carriages appeared. One could get to Zoliborz by a circular route for 2 zloty. A small stretch at least had to go past the ghetto, but the uprising was dying away and there were almost no more shots to be heard.

One night we were woken by an air-raid siren. I was living on the fifth floor at the time and did not consider it necessary to go down to a shelter. I stood at the window and calmly looked at the fight in the air. It was the biggest Soviet air raid ever launched over Warsaw; flares went up and died away slowly. The sight was so tremendous that I completely forgot the danger. The fighter planes were flying low over the rooftops, defying the German searchlights. Several neighbouring blocks were hit by incendiaries and flames shot up, linking the red sky with the fires of the burning ghetto. Columns of curling smoke wound around the whole town. It was a strange coincidence that the air raid should have occurred on the very night when the ghetto was burning to death; fires here and pandemonium there. This air raid helped a few to escape from the ghetto during the apocalypse.

The Germans were always frightfully scared of air raids, immediately taking cover in panic. But the air battle ended, the night passed, then came the day, and we learned that the Soviet bombing raid had caused considerable casualties among the civilian population and had wrecked many houses. People were glad that at last the Russians had initiated action on a larger scale and that the war might come to an end sooner. As a result of such air raids, however, the fear was that not many would survive to see it.

The sky over the ghetto paled. Shots were heard no more, the insurrection died down. The victors on all fronts in Europe and beyond, as the Germans called themselves, had at last won on this front as well, and this officially heralded the complete liquidation of the ghetto. Unfortunately only a very insignificant number of insurgents had succeeded in getting away through traps and tunnels – the rest had perished. Notices in German and Polish appeared on the demolished ghetto walls, forbidding entry to the area of the former Jewish quarter under pain of death. All remnants and debris, anything that might be of any value, was to be industrially exploited. The 'Herrenvolk' published all kinds of tenders for clearing the rubble, huge posters enticed labourers to the demolition jobs. A track was laid specially to ease the cleaning of the ruins. The tram route was to be restored, the gate from Muranowska Street stood ajar.

An old Polish proverb says that nature calls the wolf back to the forest. Fully realizing the danger, I could not return to call upon Sister Maria-Janina under any pretext, but I wanted to have a last look around the former ghetto, even if just for a few minutes. And I did see it too, the empty space which had once been a part of

Warsaw, inhabited by hundreds of thousands of people. In such a short time not a single stone or a burned or demolished house remained, not a ruin, only a vast empty stretch of scorched earth, a desert. The annihilation was complete, the ghetto had been razed to the ground and was no more.

Warsaw stopped speaking about the ghetto uprising. The heroic fight was soon forgotten. There were newer occurrences coming to the fore as topics of conversation. Arrests in Warsaw were becoming a plague and unless absolutely necessary to go out, people would keep to their flats. More and more often the police would cut off a street at random and force the unwary passers-by into waiting lorries, the so-called 'sheds'. More often than not the poor pedestrian would never return home and his family would learn – after a considerable lapse of time – that their unfortunate relative had been sent to a labour office or to a concentration camp. They would receive a letter stating that the person in question had died from heart failure. Someone caught in a street raid such as this might find himself in Pawiak jail for an indeterminate period, or simply be sent to forced labour in Germany. Enormous bribes handed over in time to the 'proper' German officials, sometimes saved the innocent victim, but only very rarely. You had to walk the streets carefully, ever on the alert. I had special additional reasons to fear a street raid with its unavoidable checking of documents.

One day I had fetched a large bag of linen from my laundry and in Castle Square I boarded a tram, carrying it peacefully in the crammed carriage. As we passed Krakowskie Przedmiescie we were suddenly ordered to stop. The tram was immediately surrounded by scores of police, with two 'sheds' waiting nearby. Another tram had been forced to stop behind us and was checked first by the Germans. In a matter of minutes they would be with us. Dead silence fell upon our carriage. A young man was swallowing some paper. I was sitting motionless as I did not know what to do. My eyes fell on the parcel of laundry and I conceived a risky idea. In a flash I pushed the parcel under my overcoat on my abdomen and thus swollen leaned clumsily on my seat. My fellow travellers must surely have noticed my sudden pregnancy but no one uttered a word. Four policemen jumped onto our tram. As they were going past me, a pregnant, poor-looking woman, I could hear the pounding of my heart. Amidst cries and German curses, several people were dragged out of our carriage. The raid had ended. Within moments communications were restored and the tram went on ahead.

The normal course of events would not be changed by the fact that for scores of people life ceased to be termed life. From that time onwards I travelled by tram only if absolutely necessary. I tried to avoid such comfortable means of transport which during a street raid would turn into cages. Walking gave one more opportunities to escape or hide. In spite of taking all precautions more and more people fell victim to these raids. Those who were caught were either imprisoned in Pawiak jail – which was the worst – or placed in a special building in Skaryszewska Street, at Praga, from whence on the orders of the Labour Office they were sent on to forced labour in Germany. The Polish police gained a sad notoriety since they actively helped the Germans in street arrests and then guarded the Skaryszewska place against a possible breakout.

The Polish police had been reorganized in 1939 and they had been told to take an oath of allegiance to the new regime. Many had refused and had withdrawn from the services, but the overwhelming majority had taken the oath and had remained. They wore the same dark blue uniforms as before the war and were commonly called 'dark blues'. They became infamous during the occupation and were hated by the populace and were regarded as beyond the pale by the Polish community. Generally speaking a dark blue would readily give a hand to the Germans all over Poland. He guarded the Poles who were to be deported but could himself be bribed for their eventual release. His eagerness to serve the Germans made him more dangerous than the German himself. He would not content himself with the seizure of smuggled goods in trains or roads but would hand the unfortunate smuggler over to a German patrol. Needless to say his victims hardly ever returned home. The dark blue police were the scourge of all those who were in any conflict with the laws which were then enforced.

Of special note among many ignoble deeds was the Jew-hunt. During the German ghetto-sweeping they helped the Jewish militia. On the Gentile side the dark blues had developed into unequalled and infallible Jew-hunters, a hundred times more dangerous than the Germans themselves. Their pre-war experience – contacts with the Jewish population and hence also knowledge of certain characteristics of Jewish gesticulation or pronunciation – would enable them to sniff out with certainty the Jew shielding himself with Aryan documents. He would seldom stop at a single ransom. Having more freedom of movement than his civilian blackmailing counterpart, he would first of all extort every last penny from his victim, and then dutifully report him to the Germans as a matter of course. A Jew recognized by a policeman was generally hopelessly lost and it was no wonder that this dark blue pest was dreaded even more than the Germans. There were policemen who would accept neither bribes nor ransoms but, for the sake of their ideology, would hand over the Jews. Looking at this group objectively, however, one has to say that among their ranks there were many Volksdeutsch volunteers.

The activities of the Polish police aroused such hostility among the majority of Polish people, that death sentences were passed on several policemen by the Polish underground organizations and executions were carried out by Polish lads. We knew they would have to account for their misdeeds in the future and upon the orders of the Organization a detailed list of all policemen was kept in the Underground Offices. These contained, apart from proved misconduct, evidence of their standard of living which ascertained whether a dark blue was profiteering from blackmail or extortion. These lists of evidence were kept till the Warsaw uprising; I do not know whether they survived the insurrection.

15

My Life in Limbo

MY PRIVATE LIFE was still sad and I was very badly off. I could remain nowhere for long; I often changed my job and the area of employment. In July 1943 I was employed as a labourer in fields and gardens. I weeded the field, dug and planted, but I was always under the impression that my fellow workwomen were looking at me too closely, wondering about my presence in their midst. The work in the field was too difficult for me. I fell behind other labourers who were accustomed to this job. I stayed for only a couple of weeks.

At this time I was in touch with no other Jews apart from my sister-in-law and my niece who were now living together again. They had rented a very nice and comfortable room with full board in Rakowiecka Street. The food was excellent and their landlady took no advantage of their situation although they perhaps paid slightly more than an average subtenant would have done in normal circumstances. As soon as I had returned to Warsaw I had called the factory and asked Bruck and Schiemann to bring my sister-in-law's belongings which we had left in our flat. In strict secrecy one after another they brought us everything, including our valuables, such as they were. When I saw them for the last time they complained about their hard lot, that the factory was going to be closed and they would have to go to the front. I told them both openly what I thought of them; that the so-called decent Germans

were to blame more than the rest because they somehow should
have stopped all this and shown the 'other Germans' the proper
way. 'You don't know the terror that spreads among us', apolo-
gized Karl Bruck, 'disagreeing with the Führer is the surest way to
a concentration camp already full of German officers.'

My sister-in-law did not go out at all, spending her days reading
books. In the flat, apart from the landlady and her aged mother,
there was always a sharp-eyed charwoman whom I disliked and
feared from the moment I saw her. It was apparent that sooner or
later she would find out who her subtenants were. A pretty young
woman who would not leave the flat, obviously well-off judging by
her attire and silk underclothes, must surely be a rich Jewess hiding
under a Christian name. The facts spoke for themselves and it was
an easy guess. I was not surprised therefore when my sister-in-law
told me about a call from a blackmailer who had extorted a small
amount of money from her. From her tale it appeared that the
blackguard, an unemployed beggar, was less dangerous than other
types of blackmailer, but it was clear that he could have been
abetted only by the charwoman. After this visit my sister-in-law
tried to change flats but, finding no alternative accommodation,
had to stay on. About two months later she had another call. The
second blackmailer, also of the 'decent' type, contented himself
with a simple wristwatch which my sister-in-law was wearing. He
did not deny that he could betray the two Jewesses to his advantage,
yet pretended to have pity on them. The situation became almost
ridiculous when the man, who had come to bleed his two victims,
stayed on as guest for afternoon tea. During a friendly conversation
he even gave them practical hints about better and safer ways of
hiding their identity. He departed with a word of advice to my
sister-in-law about changing her way of life, stressing the necessity
of her getting a job.

I was well aware that this kind of blackmailer was recruited from
the ranks of young and spoiled men who needed a lot for their
expenses and were always looking for easy gain. He would not find
it beneath him to extort money from a Jew – as a rule, every Jew
was considered wealthy – and there was nothing wrong in earning
some money in this ingenious way. Nonetheless the danger lay
elsewhere. During his numerous drinking bouts he might blurt
everything out to the more ruthless types and sooner or later the

Jew would be done for. The best way out for the victim was to move to another address. We could not, however, find an alternative place to live at that time. It was much easier to take a living-in position, but my sister-in-law feared that she would betray herself while in constant contact with Aryans.

In the summer of 1943 a rumour spread in Warsaw that Polish Jews could be exchanged for Germans residing in alien countries and that for every German returning to his fatherland one Jew would go abroad. Only minor formalities were required, namely reporting to the Germans and stating your Jewish origin. My sister-in-law wanted to register immediately. I strongly opposed this. I did not trust the Germans and would never willingly give myself up into their hands, nor would I admit that my name had not been Lukaszewska. The hardest toil among the asses was preferable to going to the Germans, to confess to the race which was trying to wipe us off the face of the earth. I did everything in my power to dissuade my sister-in-law from pursuing this course of action, telling her it would be too good to be true. Much to my surprise I was supported by my niece, who although tempted by a trip as any child would have been, shared my views and asked her mother to abandon the idea.

At that time I was working as a field hand in the vicinity of Warsaw. For security reasons I betrayed neither my address nor the place at which I worked to anybody. Then around the middle of July I came to Warsaw and, using our secret code, knocked on the staircase wall, on the other side of which was my sister-in-law's room. There was no answer. I feared something had happened. Trying to leave unnoticed, I crept into the street and went to telephone the landlady next door. It turned out that there was nothing wrong and I could enter the flat freely. Once inside I found a message left for me by my sister-in-law, saying that during my absence she had decided to go abroad with Tusia. Taking a few belongings and accompanied by the charwoman, they went to the Hotel Polski in Chmielna Street, where all Jews intending to leave Poland in this way were to be assembled. The message concluded with a sentence that 'with God's help we shall still see each other'. I was in the depths of despair. I never believed that the Germans would release the Jews anywhere abroad and considered both my relatives lost. After a few days I received a postcard from Germany, addressed to the landlady, in which my sister-in-law told me that she was well and little Tusia added: 'I am happy to see a foreign country.' A few other people received similar postcards from Germany but then everything ceased and there was no sign of life from any of those who had left.

There was a rumour that all these people had been murdered. The news came from a Polish railway guard who had been transporting the Jews leaving Poland. According to his tale the Germans had stopped the train somewhere in the vicinity of Hamburg, and after depriving the passengers of their luggage, separated the men from the women. Under strong escort all alighted and the men were driven deep into a nearby forest. The railway guard did not see any more, but we knew the German methods all too well and expected the worst. Thus I now remained all alone and still without the right to visit my own child.

I got a job as governess again and once more worked in Zoliborz. The girl was a year old and did not give much trouble. Accommodation was fairly good but what was most important for me was that I could spend hours on the banks of the Vistula, all alone with the child. I would push the pram and think my own thoughts, reflecting on my present misery. Not very long before I had had a baby of my own, in just such a pram, many relatives and friends, my own flat and a good life. Now I had nothing, not even my own true personality. Only during those strolls with the pram, when I was sure that nobody was looking at me, could I be myself. I could even afford to be sad. Unwillingly I would return home and slip again into the skin of Marianna Lukaszewska. I had to be constantly on my guard in front of my masters. They treated me well but both were classic anti-Semites. At mealtimes they would not stop talking about the Jews, and I once heard my employer saying there was nothing wrong in Hitler's occupation of Poland. The war would soon end, Hitler would leave Poland which would then become bigger and stronger than ever. The fact that, thanks to the German Führer, Poland had got rid of its Jews would be of everlasting benefit to the country. This exciting topic was constantly being bandied about while I had to sit and listen. The grandparents who lived in the same house had different views. They were pious, kind-hearted Christians; they maintained that killing was not only a sin but that human creatures in need should be helped as much as possible. The old lady, who trusted me, once confided that she was secretly in touch with one of her old Jewish friends and was helping her financially.

Every Sunday I went to church, first of all in order to have two hours' break from the family, and then because I had become used to it. I did not know to which God I was praying, but I knew what I was praying for. In simple words of my own, for the health of my daughter, my husband, my parents and all my dear ones. I prayed for a speedy end to the war and saw no difference between my prayer and that of the surrounding congregation. The church organ played, the choir sang 'Gloria Gloria', and my heart cried 'Eva, Eva my child!' The words 'Pax Vobiscum' reflected my own thoughts. I would always leave the church strangely reassured and strengthened. One Sunday the Germans surrounded the church swooping down on the young people leaving. I was still in the crowd and did not know how to escape. Then the thought that I still had a slight limp crossed my mind; putting on a bad limp, I walked between the rows of police and was allowed to leave the place of danger unchallenged. During that particular church raid scores of people of both sexes were taken to waiting 'sheds'.

The local newspaper carried an advertisement placed by a family from Radzymin who were looking for a governess ready to take up a position in the country. I applied and was accepted. Nevertheless before I left Warsaw I decided to implore Mrs P. once more to let me see my daughter. I explained that I was leaving Warsaw for a long period and promised not to tell anybody about my relationship to Eva. After much discussion and pleading Mrs P. was won over. In the village where Eva lived there were some pigs for sale which Mrs P. intended to buy for her farm. I was to accompany her to help in the negotiations but before we set out I had to swear to behave like a stranger towards Eva. It did not matter that I was not allowed to hug her or kiss her; a mother like me should know how to restrain herself if she wanted to see her child. In the early morning hours we took an electric train to Regula from where we had to walk for about four kilometres. The joyful prospect of seeing my child made me hurry so fast that Mrs P. could hardly keep pace with me.

After a long walk my companion at last pointed to a large, neat brick house situated on the outskirts of a sizeable village. Just leaving the yard was a barefoot little girl driving a goat with a big stick. I recognized my Eva. We approached the farm. The child stopped and welcomed us with a Christian 'Praised be our Saviour.' We asked for Mrs C., the mistress of the house. 'Mummy is not at home but please wait inside.' She first locked the goat in the shed, then ushered us into a large, clean kitchen and after dusting the stools with her pinafore asked us to sit down. 'Mummy's in the field, but it's noon already and she'll be coming home in no time.' The child was using the peasant dialect, she looked sturdy, had grown bigger and rounder and was very cheerful. It was apparent that she felt at home in this house. Eva did not recognize me at all but showed considerable interest in Mrs P. who brought her all kinds of little gifts. How restless was that silly heart of mine, how eager to dote upon that little girl, to take her in my arms, to hug her just once. But I knew it was forbidden. Mrs C.'s old mother sat in the kitchen and was soon joined by two other children returning from school. We waited for Mrs C. to show us the pigs.

The older children told me that the little girl was called Eva. She was an orphan and they very much liked considering her to be their younger sister. I could not get over the fact that Eva had not recognized me; I wanted to be alone with her, for a moment at least. 'I think I'd better find a certain place, who will show me the way?' 'Eva, show the lady the way,' said the older girl, and Eva went out with me. 'We do that on the dung heap but I think I'll have to take you to the pigsty.' Involuntarily I smiled. How my little girl had changed during those few months – she was wholly assimilated with the peasant children.

In the pigsty with Eva I asked her various questions. I mentioned the names of Tusia and my sister-in-law with no result. The child did not remember anything from her past and I became convinced that the fall from the train had caused complete amnesia. This loss of memory was salutary for Eva, who might otherwise have betrayed herself when speaking about some incidents from her ghetto past, and our journey to Treblinka. We returned to the kitchen and Eva sat beside me, looking at the road. Suddenly she jumped up and informed us happily that Mummy was coming. A clean, neatly dressed woman entered the kitchen and was warmly embraced by Eva. 'Mummy, my dearest Mummy,' she cried between kisses. My heart turned over but common sense told me to keep still, for I saw that my girl was very happy in this house.

We were invited to share their simple meal and all the children piously clasped their little hands to say a short grace. The food was very modest but I noticed that no distinction was made between the children. My Eva ate a big plate of soup and a slice of black bread, with great appetite. A short prayer after the meal and we went out to see the pigs, the 'true' reason for our visit. We looked at the animals, complained they were not fat enough and bargained furiously, but eventually, with the business not concluded, we went back to the house. Little Eva was sitting in the kitchen helping the old grandma to shell the peas. It was getting late and we began taking our leave. 'Perhaps you'll kiss the new lady goodbye,' good Mrs P. suggested to Eva. 'Mummy does not allow me to kiss strangers,' the child replied, and politely shook hands with me. We left. Mrs P. was delighted with me. 'Miss Maria, you behaved excellently.' Mrs P. did not know that a Jewish mother had to behave 'excellently' if she wanted to see her child alive. Returning from my excursion to the village, I felt relieved and happy knowing that if I met with an accident, if I was killed by the Germans, my Eva would not suffer, she was in good honest hands.

Calm and reassured I took up my new job at Radzymin. I was a nurse to a one-year-old boy. Our house was built in a forest clearing in picturesque surroundings. My employers had been evicted from Poznan but were very prosperous in Warsaw and their house was run on a pre-war scale. After enjoying a rich meal, lying on soft grass near the sleeping boy, I would again be tormented by thoughts and questions to which there were no answers. How was it that I was so well off when so many others of my race had perished in torment? Had I the right to enjoy such a life? Strange that those thoughts would always haunt me when I felt best, when the sun was shining brightly and the grass smelled so sweet.

The boy was pretty difficult and would not sleep at night. He was rather sickly and coddled by his parents and grandparents. Just at that time he was teething and crying almost incessantly every night. Although his mother slept in the same room I had to take care of him all the time. On Saturdays and Sundays guests used to call and I was required to see that the baby's crying did not disturb their nightly peace. 'Miss Maria, do whatever you like but stop the child from crying at night!' It meant holding him in my arms all night, pacing up and down the room and humming songs because the boy had been so treated by his previous nurse. Those nights were horrible: half-conscious and sleepy, I would walk the room with the little boy in my arms. I was so dazed that often I did not know what I was doing or singing. On one such Sunday night, after draining my whole repertoire of lullabies, I caught myself singing the Jewish national anthem. Horrified, I stopped and listened anxiously to the breathing of my mistress, sleeping nearby. Thank goodness my monotonous singing disturbed nobody; after a good dinner with the usual rich amount of vodka, everybody slept peacefully. No one had noticed that Miss Marianna had been singing in Hebrew.

I was completely worn out after these sleepless nights and still in the mornings there was a normal day's work to be done, washing the child, preparing breakfast. The food was exquisite and the salary good, but several times I would hear these words from my mistress: 'I pay well and I like value for money.' The beautiful location of the house had one disadvantage. It was in the vicinity of the forest in which Polish partisans were hiding. Once I witnessed parachutists landing some 200 yards from the house. No wonder the German soldiers kept combing the whole area. One day when there were many guests in the house, they came at dawn and searched the compound. Some said they were looking for partisans, others – for Jews. My masters trembled and when a German ordered us to go outside the house, nobody moved. 'What do you fear?' asked the soldier. 'You have no arms, you are not partisans, you are certainly not Jews, so why are you frightened?' 'Miss Maria will go, I don't want to get up.' The master ordered, the servant had to comply.

I went out to the Germans, taking the child in my arms. 'There was a light on at night. You are showing the way to the parachutists,' yelled the German. 'What do you want, Lieutenant?' I asked in bad German; 'The boy is sick with diarrhoea so I put on the light to change his nappy. What could we have in common with the partisans when my master works in the German district in Warsaw? You can check around!' The Germans left with their usual blessings: 'Verfluchte Polen.' After this my masters considered me a treasure and apart from getting presents almost daily I was notified about an imminent rise in salary. However I did not wish to lose my health at this job and decided to return to Warsaw. My employers were inconsolable.

· 16 ·

Back in Warsaw

IN WARSAW I worked in several places. I could not keep any job for long; each place had its disadvantages, everywhere I felt unhappy. Long ago I had come to the conclusion that the root of the evil lay within myself. I was like a seriously sick person who, whenever resting, would feel bad. At last I took up the job of domestic servant with Mrs S. in Mokotowska Street. Mrs S. had known me well from pre-war times and there I felt comparatively well. There was no need to put up a show, to pretend, and as far as work was concerned, there was not much to do. It was obvious that all Mrs S.'s visitors had no idea about my identity and I was treated as a maid. As a matter of fact, I did my best not to be mistaken for anyone else. When cleaning I would sing the most popular songs, I would gossip about my mistress with the caretaker's wife, and with great dignity I would empty the rubbish bin. My smart French silk clothes saved from the ghetto were hanging neatly in Mrs S.'s wardrobe but all summer I would wear the same old worn-out dress. I strove to look as shabby and poor as possible. An obligatory part of my outfit was a wickerwork basket filled with some carrots, onions or potatoes. I would not go out without a parcel from or for my mistress; it was my idea of looking more servant-like. My circle of friends consisted of gas or electricity bill collectors, fitters, plumbers and the most faithful one was the coalman's apprentice from around the corner. They were very kind to me and would try to cheer me up whenever I was sad. The coalman's assistant would say 'You're sad today, Miss Maria, the old Grumble Puss must have given you what for! But don't worry, our people are coming. You don't read the papers so you can't know that the Russians are pushing ahead. Changes are coming. There'll be no servants in the future, we'll all be masters!' The kind man did not know the cause of my sadness, he did not know that I, too, awaited the Russians but for very different reasons. He would give me old illustrated papers to read, offer me fruit or a cheap flower, but could not understand why I would not go with him to the pictures. I tried to make my 'flirtation' with the coalman or butcher's assistants 'visible' to the sharp-eyed caretaker; they had always had a 'weakness' for happenings of that sort. Before leaving the flat during Mrs S.'s absence, I would often leave her a short message, never free from spelling mistakes.

Somehow my life as a domestic servant carried on pretty smoothly. It was not always pleasant, though, to walk with a wicker basket or package in my hand, to be dressed in a shabby frock when around me women wore lovely clothes. I knew I could easily become one of them but I preferred to remain the poor Cinderella until the end of the war. My appearance was so miserable that no blackmailer could have any interest in me. I thought I had changed so much that even my old acquaintances would not recognize me. Yet once, while I was strolling, basket in hand, the court usher Mr S. came up to me and looking at my faded dress said, 'Madam, I could lend you some money, you will repay it after the war.' I thanked him but declined his kind offer.

At that time an organization offering financial help for the hiding of Jews existed in Warsaw. Within the framework of the general Underground Organization of Independent Poland, a committee had been established with the aim of taking care of Jews hiding on the Gentile side and helping them with a monthly allowance. I do not know how the Organization was fundeed or who had initiated this aid but the fact that many of my acquaintances availed themselves of it speaks for itself. The Jewish relief was fixed, as a rule, at 1500 zloty a month, and it had been of invaluable assistance. For many it formed the mainstay of their existence. A Jew who did not have to pay much for his accommodation could easily manage on that money, and thus survive the war. It goes without saying that only a fraction of the Jews in hiding knew about the existence of this committee. Those who were in touch with the patriotic Polish 'intelligentsia' or people who worked in the Underground were most likely to benefit. Everything was obviously carried out in the greatest secrecy, using all available means of security. A person known to the Organization would inform the committee about the real name of an applicant and plead for the granting of an allowance.

Towards the end of the war, with an increasing number of applications, the fund was reduced to 1000 zloty, later to 500 zloty per person. The money was paid in special well-hidden places, sometimes being brought direct to the Jew in hiding. I was offered that relief but I did not accept it. I had no need of money. In the autumn of 1943 I learned by accident that my friend and fellow workwoman from the furrier's shop, the engineer's wife Aniela N., had survived with her son Jasio;* miraculously saved, she was living on the fourth floor of a house in Lipowa Street at Powisle. Her neighbours were told she was a very sick person and could not leave her room. All household purchases were entrusted to the now ten-year-old Jasio. The flat belonged to a woman on the lowest rung of the ladder, known to be the mother of an illegitimate child conceived with a German. When her lover had gone to the front and no news had come from him, she had not taken a decent job and had simply become a prostitute. For her son's sake she did not admit men into her house. Aniela cared for the flat and the child. She even used to sleep with her landlady on one couch and was compelled to listen to the stories and anecdotes of a streetwalker. I wondered how my friend could stand the company of such a woman and share the room with her, but I learned that the flat had been recommended to her by somebody who did not know the profession of the landlady. By the time she had moved in and found that she was, so to speak, in the hands of a prostitute, it was too late. On the other hand, to find a safe shelter at that time was extremely difficult. Aniela would have an occasional respite, enjoying her 'loneliness' when her landlady would leave Warsaw, which

---

* Jasio was the boy given the 'life number' by the couple who committed suicide during a selection in the summer of 1942.

she did from time to time. Whenever I was free I called on Aniela and helped her out as much as I could.

Twice during that period I saw my Eva but always on some pretext or other and as a stranger. After some time Mrs P. confessed to me that once when drunk she had blabbed to Eva's guardian that I was the child's mother and that as she had been born illegitimate I had to keep her hidden outside the town. 'Indeed Eva is too clever. People are right when they say that all bastards are clever' was his only comment before he resumed his drinking.

One day in October I phoned Mrs P. to learn that something had gone wrong with Eva in the village. She was of the opinion that the child should be taken away. It seemed that a barrow-woman from Warsaw who had been calling at the farm showed a strange interest in the child. She had been curious as to where the child had got town dresses, why Eva knew so many verses, and why, on the whole, she was different, more intelligent, than the other children. The woman became too inquisitive and the farmer's answers would not satisfy her. Soon the whole village started wondering about Eva's origin and the situation was far from good. I had no idea where to put my girl but I immediately decided to take her away from the hamlet.

When in trouble I tended to seek help and advice from the advocate Mrs W. When I called on her this time I heard about the existence of the Polish Underground Organization bringing help to rescued Jewish children. This organization was in possession of specific funds to provide the children with documents and protectors who would take care of them. As always ready to help in any way, Mrs W. immediately put me in touch with a certain man who would be responsible for accepting a child. I already knew by then how the Polish Underground worked: nobody was asked to disclose names, addresses or any particulars. If a child was to be entrusted to the Organization, no questions were allowed. The child was simply to be delivered to an appointed address at a given date and hour.

I went with Mrs P. to collect Eva. Parting with her 'mummy' was heart-breaking and the good countrywoman wept continuously, kissing and hugging my little Eva as if she were her own child. I had to promise to bring her back soon, for a few days at least. We were blessed with the sign of the cross. When we were sitting in the cart her husband came up to me saying, 'If Eva needs a place of safety please bring her back to us. Don't be afraid. I have warned the village gossip, no harm will come to the child.' Once more Eva tearfully kissed her 'parents' and took leave from the house in which they had shown her so much heartfelt affection.

Stealthily I smuggled Eva into my room, fearing the caretaker's wife. Because of some unexpected difficulties in the arrangements I had to keep Eva with me for about two weeks. I put her in my little servants' room to hide her from any callers' eyes. She had to lie in bed all day so that nobody would hear childish steps. She had to keep quiet for hours, so that nobody would hear a childish voice. With that strange child's intuition Eva knew that 'it was not allowed' and blindly obeyed what 'Miss Maria' said. But I enjoyed her company at all times. I hugged and kissed her constantly and fed her on the tastiest titbits. The little prisoner on the fifth floor behaved in an exemplary manner and nobody noticed anything.

Eventually they notified me that everything was in order, a guardian had been found and I had to bring Eva to the appointed place. Again we stole out to meet two ladies, representatives of the organization. After shaking hands without giving our names, they assured me that my child would be placed with a cultured family living on the outskirts of Warsaw. My girl would receive documents under the name of her new protectors, passing off as their relative.

I was to be informed about the name and address within a fortnight. I was to ask no questions, I was not to bother those two ladies any more. They were carrying out their dangerous task with such devotion that when I thanked them for everything they replied: 'Please, do not thank us. What we are doing is our sacred duty. If you have any other Jewish child in need of protection, give us all particulars please. We will certainly take care of everything.' I thought about those many beautiful and gifted children whom I had known, who had perished, been gassed at Treblinka, burned at Auschwitz or other places of mass murder. I thought about that girl in a burning dress whom I had seen thrown out of a window during the ghetto uprising, a human torch. Tens of thousands of children had perished, yet now the Organization of Peoples' Good Will would have been able to shelter them, would have tried to take care of them. Why so late? Why did they have to die such horrible deaths, to be gassed, burned or buried alive? It had happened because such was their dreadful Fate, or rather the will of the wicked German nation.

On Saturday 16 October I entrusted my Eva to the Organization. I knew it was best for her, yet I did it with a heavy heart. That evening I felt so terribly lonely that I could not return to my empty servants' room. I had to be near somebody dear to me. I rang Aniela, who said: 'Marysia, darling, please do come tonight. My "blind" [so Aniela nicknamed her landlady] won't be in for the night so we'll have a nice chat. Jasio will be so happy.' I left the keys of our flat with the caretaker, together with a letter full of spelling mistakes for Mrs S. informing her that I had been invited to my friend's birthday party and would not be sleeping at home. I set off for Lipowa Street with a nudge and winks from the caretaker.

Before arriving at Aniela's I had an 'adventure'. From the moment I entered Three Crosses Square I had been followed by a young man. I got onto a tram, he did the same. I took a seat – he stared at me all the time. 'Too bad', I thought, 'I cannot go straight to Aniela bringing a "hunter" behind me.' I got off after two stops in a bid to reach Aniela's flat by a circular route and somehow get rid of the man. My follower nevertheless got off too and continued to dog my footsteps. I felt sure that I had been recognized as a Jewess, but it left me strangely cold. I did not care any more for my own safety having placed Eva and feeling confident that she would survive. 'Hallo, baby, why this hurry? I'm exhausted', I heard suddenly behind me. 'Perhaps we can go and have some coffee, or perhaps to the pictures. I'll treat you, baby.' I breathed a sigh of relief; so it was only that. The chap whom I took for a manhunter had other intentions! I smiled at the man who, perhaps, was lonely too. 'I am going to see my sick mother who is waiting for me. Please leave me alone', I asked. He bowed politely and went away.

Yes, fear has big eyes, and in my constant flight from death I had remembered nothing about life and its rites. During the occupation I had many experiences of that kind when I thought that I had been betrayed or caught, and the prospective Jew-baiter turned out merely to be in pursuit of pleasure. On that particular evening when I was on my way to Aniela I was very scared indeed. Everybody had the right to do as he pleased but it was never permissible to put the life of another Jew at stake.

Aniela was waiting for me with a wonderful supper of potato cakes which I greatly enjoyed. She behaved towards me like the most tender of mothers. She knew how I was grieving due to my separation from Eva. 'I do not approve of your entrusting Eva to unknown people. You could certainly have got a job where you would have had no need to separate yourself from her. I would never do that. I would never separate myself from Jasio. Together we live and together we shall die.' I tried to explain my position to Aniela, that I knew the principle of non-separation very well from the ghetto: 'Such logic has doomed thousands of people – such reasoning means only weakness of character. First of all, according to my papers I am supposed to be unmarried, and even if Eva's presence could be explained as that of an illegitimate child, I should gain nothing by this new complication with its inevitable and constant sneers and the questions of my employers. Even if I found some accommodation for both of us, to my mind the most important factor is that such a separation is safer for the child. If recognized by a "hunter" or blackmailer I'd perish alone, but being with Eva I'd drag her down with me. Whatever for? To give way to motherly instinct or to appease one's own selfishness, to shut one's eyes to the safety of one's child. No, never. I have learned how to silence my heart, to keep quiet!' 'Perhaps you are right, Marysia dear', she conceded, 'but I wouldn't give my Jasio to anybody.'

We talked all through the night, our conversation obviously turning to ghetto topics. Aniela, with an inexhaustible fund of tales, tirelessly related stories and gossip which I had not heard, dating from the time I had already moved over to the Gentile side. 'Do you remember, Marysia, the kindergarten near the Tobens factory in Leszno Street? How we envied those mothers who would peacefully go to their work entrusting their children to the care of a teacher in the nursery?' I well remembered the end of July and September of 1942 when my child, who had whooping cough, would constantly choke in the sultry air of our furriers, while the children of the Tobens factory enjoyed the safety of their little kindergarten. Unfortunately I also remembered that day when quite suddenly a lorry arrived, which the Germans crammed with all the children, driving them off to the Umschlagplatz. Now my friend told me a sequel to this story.

'You don't know, perhaps, that the mother of one of the abducted children was my school pal, Franka. After learning that her ten-year-old daughter was among the victims she suffered a nervous breakdown, worked herself up into an incredible fury and had started ranting and raving, calling the German managers criminals and murderers. She had then been compelled to leave the Tobens factory but thanks to some big favour she got a job with us. After a couple of weeks a Polish policeman came to our factory bringing a letter stating the following: "Any man of goodwill who finds this paper should know that it was written by a girl whom the Germans are driving to her destruction. If you have a kind heart, please deliver this paper to my mummy who is working in the furrier's shop, or in Tobens factory in Leszno Street in Warsaw. Dearest Mummy, at this moment I am in the train. I do not know exactly where we are going but I guess we are going to our death. Do not worry, Mummy, I am not scared at all, and as I am the eldest here I have explained to the other children that some day all people must die anyway. As a matter of fact there is nothing wrong in our dying sooner. At present here on the earth there are only Germans, life is very hard, while there in Heaven among the angels there surely won't be any Germans. So it is for the best that we get away from the Germans sooner. The children who are with me are not even crying. I shared the breakfast we had equally among all of us. Only Janaczek regrets he did not take his overcoat with him. I remember now that I did not kiss you good-morning today, as I will not be able to kiss you any more. I cannot write more because this paper is so small. Farewell Mummy, please do not cry for me. I am fastening this paper with a hairpin. I think it will make it heavier."'

The paper was found by a Polish railway guard who, moved by its contents, had decided to deliver it to the mother at all costs. Finding it impossible to enter the ghetto he eventually got a policeman to take it to the Tobens factory and from there the letter, pierced with the hairpin, reached the hands of the mother. Shortly afterwards Franka crossed over to the Gentile side, enlisted at some office that was recruiting labourers to Germany and left for the Franco-German border. The omniscient Aniela through their common friends had already had the news that Franka was in Paris, had a job and was well off. There was no end to 'do you know this or do you know that' tales, but all of them were sad. Aniela came to know everything and in great detail. It was amazing that even while keeping strictly to the confines of her flat she would receive the latest news.

The following day was Sunday so there was no need to go back to work. 'Marysia, take Jasio to church with you. His friends have been wondering why they never see him in church.' We went to a little church at Powisle where Jasio prayed for peace for his poor father's soul, for his mother's health and for the war to end soon. We did not care for the words of the prayer composed centuries ago; we the condemned had our own Passion and our own prayer. The cross in church symbolized for us the Passion and misery of millions of human beings, even if only through symbols and metaphors, prayers could still be a comfort to us. Sunday drew to a close and I was obliged to go back 'home'.

Inquisitive by nature, Aniela wanted to know my address but she had to make do with my promise that I would phone her whenever I was free. It was known to everybody that while interrogating a trapped Jew, the Germans would beat him terribly to extract names and addresses of other Jews' hiding-places, and also as a rule their place of work. Thus further particulars would be disclosed only in case of utmost necessity. I would often repeat to Aniela: 'What you don't know cannot be squeezed out of you.' Aniela used to read two or even three newspapers daily; Jasio would always have to walk great distances to fetch them in order to avoid arousing the suspicion of local news vendors by buying so many papers. From those papers my friend learned that the Day of Atonement would fall on 29 October. The German press announced that on this day great anti-German demonstrations were being prepared by the Jews in Palestine.

As it later turned out, 29 October was neither the Day of Atonement nor did any demonstrations occur on that date, but we did not know yet that this was a simple trick of German propaganda. Anyhow, when Aniela told me about our holiday I was deeply moved. 'Come round, Marysia, we'll celebrate the holiday.' Again through the caretaker's good offices, I explained my absence: this time for a change I was going to celebrate a christening and went to Aniela. I found the table covered with a white sheet – Aniela's tablecloths had all gone long ago – and on the table –

candles! I lit the candles in deference to Yom Kippur, we ate a
festive supper, wept a little remembering our miserable lives and all
the dear ones we had lost, and we eventually fell asleep late that
night. The next day was Sunday, Yom Kippur itself. I fasted with
Aniela and in the afternoon I went with Jasio to the church. A year
ago I had been at a rabbi's, today in a church, but my prayer, as
my feelings and my life, remained the same. The change of prayer-
house was like the change in my name – superficial. We had all
been taught as children that God was everywhere. The turn my life
had taken after what I had been through, let me only doubt His
presence, but if He existed He must have been among the Jews
sunk in prayer at the rabbi's in Nowolipie Street, as well as among
this different congregation in the church. On that Day of Atonement in 1943 my soul prayed ardently and the fast was a real
expiation for my sins.

In the evening Miss Marianna went back to her job and the next
morning, while beating the carpets and dusting the furniture, she
would gaily sing all the popular hits. Weeks passed and I was still
waiting for Eva's address. The exact location was known only to
one person from the organization and that person, unluckily for
me, had been arrested and sent to jail. In vain the advocate Mrs W.
knocked at various doors – nobody knew the address and there
was small hope of getting the person out of jail. An apparently
light-hearted Marianna sang cheerfully, cleaning windowpanes on
the fifth floor, but inwardly she was grieving. I was afraid that if
anything happened to the imprisoned lady I would never learn
where my child was. I had no idea what new name little Eva had
been given.

One day my friend Halina L., also an advocate, gave me a yellow
blouse which was too small for her and a piece of blue fabric. She
urged me: 'Marysia, make a dress for Eva from the blouse and cut
out some nice blue flowers, but each flower simply must be hand-
embroidered. It will be grand.' 'But darling, such embroidery would
take weeks and I do have to do six rooms and cooking!', I replied.
'Never mind, I assure you that before you are through with
embroidering, Eva's address will be known.' Good, faithful friend.
She tried to cheer me up although she was likewise anxious and
restless. In my free time I would embroider one flower after another,
the work was progressing but the lady was still a prisoner and there

was no news about my Eva. I would telephone: 'Halina dear, I have nearly finished the dress.' 'Why this hurry, have pity on your eyes', she would advise. 'Better let Marianna have a good wash, wear a deeper décolletage, and come round. There will be gentlemen at the party', my friend would jokingly reply, inviting me over to her. Dear Halina! The Germans had murdered her two brothers. She could not practise her profession and was compelled to deal in some small trade, yet she would always be cheerful, striving to encourage and make others happy. Marianna would put on a fresh blouse and, armed with her inseparable basket, go to Mrs L.

The gentlemen whom we'd mentioned on the phone were her husband, who had definite reasons for hiding and was passing himself off as her friend and adviser, and an advocate whose name was on the Germans' blacklist of people to be shot. Apart from them, two ladies were present, both advocates of Jewish origin, now professionally baking cakes and pastries. So the company was well chosen and everyone had interesting stories to tell. The two ladies were having continuous troubles with blackmailers and had changed their names several times. Their flats were 'hot' – having become known to undesirable people which made it necessary for them to move. Again I was satisfied that my choice had proved the best. I had descended to the lowest classes and assimilated myself with poor maidservants and nannies. I had succeeded in making my appearance so commonplace and insignificant that no blackmailer would have wasted his time on me. There in my friend's flat I was given plenty of practical hints regarding aspects of staying in hiding. I was warned about the members of the former official ONR party – the Polish Fascist Organization – who had not learned their lesson either from the war or from the Germans. I was told how the radical ONR youths, with little sword emblems in their lapels, upon discovering a Jewish hideout would persecute and ultimately murder the wretched inhabitant. Ignominious, but true. The conversation eventually turned to the latest political gossip and the news, which we found to be a more cheerful and optimistic topic. The curfew hour was imminent. All of us criminals with death sentences, we left our hospitable friend.

1944: A New Year

On 20 JANUARY 1944 I celebrated with a big feast. It was the anniversary of my escape. Having heard further rumours of the Russian offensive, I was in a very cheerful mood and started believing that we would survive the war. I went to visit Aniela with a bottle of wine, stopping short as I came across the Star of David painted on the entrance door of the apartment. This meant that a flat had been occupied by a Jew. I hurried upstairs and immediately told Aniela about the star. I learned that some minor incident had recently occurred, but it made me very frightened. In the grocery shop where Jasio did his shopping people had begun asking him about his mother. Somebody had mentioned that in his opinion there were Jews in the block in Lipowa Street. The news spread. There was no danger from the decent grocer but the news might have reached other ears. Later on it turned out that there were indeed two Jewesses living in the house and the shopkeeper warned them that they had already been sniffed out and advised them to be on their guard.

Poor Aniela dreaded possible searches and was having sleepless nights. Little Jasio had had his experiences too. The boy already knew not to undress in the presence of other boys and would always decline communal bathing in the nude. One day he came to tell his mother that his friends were having fun playing a betting game to see 'who pisses furthest'. It was too late to back out so it

seemed that Jasio would be compelled to participate in the compe-
tition. The clever little ghetto child, the miraculously saved and
cunning protector of his mother who already knew how to cheat
the Germans, had an ingenious idea and shouted just at the critical
moment: 'Shame on you, pigs! If I tell my Mummy she won't let
me play with you.' 'Oh you little lord ladeda', his comrades taunted
Jasio as he turned away in tears. I was very worried by this story as
I could imagine that some day, instead of 'Oh you little lord', a boy
would shout 'Jew' and then both mother and son would be
doomed. Insistently, I started to convince Aniela that something
had to be done about this.

In Warsaw at that time it was whispered in the strictest confidence that some surgeons could 'mend' the after-effects of circumcision with excellent results. The operation was said to be relatively
painless. This operation would be performed mainly on men with
non-Jewish features whose only distinguishing Judaic characteristic
was a circumcized penis. If the Germans suspected someone of
being a Jew or had the slightest doubts on the matter, they would
never hesitate to carry out their examination in a doorway, in a
shop or even in the street. The best Aryan papers or doctors'
testimonials would be to no avail – the man would be lost. After
asking around in the greatest secrecy for such a surgeon, I eventually obtained the address of a doctor at St Lazarus' hospital.

I took Jasio there and after explaining that the boy was badly
off, asked the doctor to operate on him at a reduced fee. The
surgeon, a very decent man, agreed and later carried out the
operation under local anaesthetic. All through his ordeal and later
during the dressing of the wound the boy behaved bravely. He
understood without being told that all was being done for his
benefit and did not utter a sound. I do not know exactly how and
what was done and how it looked later, but I heard men praising
the results. Nobody felt embarrassed to discuss these subjects at
that time. Aniela was not too delighted with the result, saying 'it
was not like new', to which I would simply reply that nothing
remade was ever like new. Anyhow, all signs of the circumcision
were obliterated and the boy could move about freely.

The surgeon was the saviour of many men, particularly those
who would enlist for jobs in Germany in order to get lost in a
foreign environment. All applicants had to undergo a medical

examination, which obviously no Jew could pass successfully. Thanks to these operations many tragedies were averted – at least until such time as the Germans, with magnifying glasses, started publicly examining any male suspected of being Jewish.

Around the end of January 1944 the lady from the Organization for Aid to Jewish Children was at last released – due to payment of an enormous bribe. Mrs W. gave me Eva's address, where I went immediately. My child had been placed in a villa at Molotow. The ground floor was occupied by the owner, a physician's widow, wholly unaware of this business, while the first floor was occupied by Mrs Maria with her nineteen-year-old daughter Halina. This was my Eva's haven. My heart pounding, I introduced myself to Mrs Maria. Looking at her strong yet pleasant and kind face, I knew at once that little Eva had been lucky yet again. Mrs Maria was an intelligent, energetic kind of woman. Her husband was a writer, a lawyer by profession, then a prisoner of war in a German camp, the so-called 'Oflag'.

Eva looked fine. When I asked her whether she would not like to return to me she replied: 'No, I like it here at aunt Maria's.' Mrs Maria had provided my daughter with a birth certificate in her own name. Eva had been supposedly born the daughter of Mrs Maria's brother-in-law, in Lvov, then under Russian occupation again. Thus checking the document's authenticity was rendered more difficult. The landlady at Mrs Maria's was told that the brother-in-law had been killed during the war, after which the little girl, having no other relatives, had been sent to her aunt. Mrs Maria wrote to her husband in the 'Oflag' that his niece was healthy and doing fine. Although he had never had either brother or niece, he took the hint immediately so that in his letters he would ask after his niece, urging his wife to take proper care of the poor orphan. Mrs Maria kept these letters as confirmation of the child's presence and the references to Eva would occasionally be shown to the landlady.

Once a week I called on Mrs Maria, where bit by bit I learned the habits and secrets of the household. In a pram lay little Jedrus whom I was told was a distant relative. Then I met two girls aged twelve and fourteen, relatives of Mrs Maria as well. One glance at the girls immediately confirmed my suspicion that they were my own compatriots. A young nurse whom I met in the house was easily identifiable as the child's mother on account of her attitude towards the boy in the crib. The maidservant also belonged to the same 'category'. After a few weeks I had a clear picture of the situation in the house. Together with Eva it contained in total five Jewish children, the nurse, plus somebody else who was hiding in the attic. For the time being I did not know who that was.

A fifteen-year-old girl helped in the household. As I was later told she had been living under the staircase of a block of flats for a long time, eating whatever she could beg, until she met a woman from the Organization and so found herself at Mrs Maria's. There was another thirteen-year-old girl from Lublin whose father had put her to board at his Aryan friend leaving him some jewellery for her upkeep. This acquaintance had kept the girl for about six months after which, allegedly having no more money for her maintenance, he had turned her over to the care of the Organization. The beautiful fourteen-year-old brunette called Marysia had been placed there by Mrs Maria's friend, a French teacher. The girl's mother was hiding in Warsaw under an assumed name. Little Jedrus was indeed the son of the nurse. Mrs Maria cared for the whole flock and it required a great deal of cunning and diplomatic skill to explain the presence of so many different people in the house and to invent a plausible history for each occupant. On top of all this Mrs Maria had placed several Jewish children at various orphanages and boarding-schools, passing them off everywhere as relatives. It should be understood that in those times no orphanage or boarding-school would accept anybody without a vouchsafing certificate.

Mrs Maria treated all her wards with motherly, loving care. The children were always neatly dressed and well fed. What is more they were coached in French by a lady popularly nicknamed 'Madamcia', who worked in the Organization. A friend of Mrs Maria's, a fellow student from her matriculation class, also taught the children grammar school subjects. Mrs Maria's flat was open to anybody in need of help or refuge. Once when I was under threat – it later turned out to be unsubstantiated – I went without hesitation to spend the night there and was welcomed with open arms. That night I struck up a closer relationship with 'Madamcia', who had also come to sleep there for some reason. She proved to be a paragon of virtue. Fourteen-year-old Marysia had stayed for a long time in that lady's flat and could obviously not go out into the street. In summer it had become unbearable for the girl to sit indoors all the time and during 'Madamcia's' absences Marysia would sometimes sunbathe on the balcony. After the eviction of Jews the block filled with all kinds of miscellaneous citizens and soon the neighbours started gossiping about the black-haired girl who would not leave the flat yet could be seen sunbathing on the balcony. The caretaker, luckily an honest man, summoned 'Madamcia' to point out that the tenants had been sniffing out a Jewess in her flat. He advised her to avert the danger before it was too late, and to send the girl away.

Marysia was thus entrusted to Mrs Maria's care and 'Madamcia' would teach French to all the girls. Not content with doing just this, she would provide them with documents, find suitable flats and generally help as much as she could. Being very knowledgeable about Jewish problems, 'Madamcia' considered my way of hiding to be the safest. Nonetheless in case I was caught by the Germans she agreed that I could refer to her as a relative; my mother was to be her aunt and in case of necessity she would take an oath on this relationship. She was supposed to have often visited our house at Lida and been on very friendly terms with my father Jan and her aunt. It was very cleverly devised for our documents 'betrayed' no such relationship. A genuine Aryan relative was priceless to a Jew at that time. The best documents could prove worthless if a crafty Gestapo man asked: 'It's all right with your papers; they are in order and I believe you to be an Aryan. But give me some names of your friends or relatives who have known you for a long time.' Such a Jewish Gentile, a human creature with no relatives and acquaintances would then be lost.

I now had two relatives. Sister Maria-Janina had consented to be the first, and her deposition would arouse no disbelief. Now I felt much safer. I had my family, I was working as a domestic servant – the caretaker would testify to this without doubt – and my papers were genuine. At the beginning of my career as Lukaszewska I had bought a book describing north-eastern Poland and the town of Lida, in order to learn about the countryside and the town in which I was supposed to have been born. I wanted to be prepared for all events and tried to avoid any slip-up. In a short time I knew more about this town than its average inhabitant. Then I went to the

Post Office in Nowogrodzka Street and asked for an all-Poland directory. I knew that a directory was like a town's mirror. I studied the book for a long time and learned names of the streets in my home town, what cafés and cinemas there were, doctors, barristers and pharmacies, and a lot of other details, and the most important detail of all, which school I had attended. All this information cheered me up considerably and helped to instil some self-confidence.

Aniela's half-sister once told me that when the Germans had caught her friend they had subjected her to a very thorough examination from the catechism and asked particulars regarding the confession. I was thus to be well prepared for any examination and resolved to go to confession in order to learn its ritual so as to answer any questions if the need arose. Just before Easter 1943 I put that plan into action and went to church. It was evening. The church was dimly lit. Only a few people were present. They came to account for their deeds and hear from the confessor's mouth the words of absolution or condemnation. I knew how attitudes towards the sacrament of confession could differ. Many regarded the act as a formality, while many simply sinned anew after receiving absolution. I went to the church with quite different intentions, wanting simply to learn what was unknown to me, to understand an alien ritual.

I awaited my turn. Before me a young woman knelt weeping silently. Candles were burning on the altar, the church was already nearly empty and dark; near the trellis-work a gentle whisper could be heard. The serenity of concentration and repentance came over me in spite of myself. I was forgetting my reasons for being there. When my turn came and the priest behind the lattice asked what was burdening my conscience, quite against my will I started to tell this stranger a true incident in my life, a deed which I considered a sin against a fellow creature. The priest listened intently without once interrupting my tale, and after I had finished asked me: 'Did you behave thus because of your vanity?' 'No, not vanity drove me to it. I had good reasons,' I replied. He absolved me. Then I understood what a big psychological effect the confession and absolution must have on sensitive people. Lost in thought but strangely consoled, I left the church. What a powerful weapon is religion.

Warsaw became a dangerous place. A few of my former acquaintances had been caught, among them Aniela's stepmother. While standing peacefully at a tram stop in Marszalkowska Street, she was recognized by her former neighbour with whom she had squabbled about some attic key many years previously. The mean woman did not hesitate to take her revenge and denounced Aniela's stepmother to a passing policeman. She was taken from the street and later murdered at Pawiak. At approximately the same time my colleague the woman advocate A. was caught in the street. She was pointed out to a guard by her former opponent in a lawsuit who claimed to have lost the case, hence a great deal of money, because of her arraignment. She disappeared without trace. Another acquaintance of mine, also a lawyer, was betrayed to the Gestapo when she asked a woman to whom she had entrusted her belongings for the return of her expensive fur coat. The vile woman had simply wanted to rid herself of the Jewess in order to gain possession of all the 'treasure'. This acquaintance also perished, murdered at Pawiak. My former employer, the advocate M., told me about the tragic death of a good friend of his, a very wealthy woman who was denounced by a dressmaker's assistant, because the Jewess had been very finicky when choosing styles and had not tipped the assistant sufficiently. These and so many similar stories abounded so that one became inured to hearing them.

The Jewish Gestapo men who remained alive were very dangerous. Their eyes were penetrating and Jews pointed out by them were lost without hope. A little car often seen passing slowly along Marszalkowska Street, always keeping close to the pavement, became notorious. Once I was walking along this street when suddenly I heard the shout 'Szma Israel', followed by the sight of a man dragged struggling into the car. It transpired that the cry had come from the slowly driven vehicle, causing an elderly gentleman passing by to stop and look back instinctively. It was final proof for the manhunters. They must have been observing their prey for some time and, having reckoned that only a Jew would react to these words, had successfully used their subterfuge. A friend told me that the most unexpected shouts could be heard from this car.

Another time, while walking in the street, I heard behind me a low humming of the *Hatykva*. For a moment I wanted to look back but I overcame this desire. The singing individual overtook me. He was a young fellow in a little round hat with a feather. This hat meant the same as a Gestapo uniform as we learned at the end of the war. Unfortunately under this hat was the cheeky, carefree face of one of my university colleagues – a Jew. The degradation of some people had plumbed such depths.

Aniela received a farewell letter from her stepmother. A calm, dignified letter full of clever, practical advice for her stepdaughter. It had been brought to an appointed place by the jail warden, a decent woman who described the last hours of the unhappy Jewess awaiting execution. She had been terribly beaten during her interrogation yet refused to disclose her daughter's name or address although she was promised freedom. Another message was brought by a girl whom the Germans had caught as a Jewess. The evidence against her had simply proved insufficient so the beasts had limited themselves to beating her many times until she had lost consciousness. They had beaten her so monstrously that she had ceased to feel the blows. In spite of this torture she had not confessed to being a Jewess – she knew that such an avowal would have meant death. When she lifted her skirt I shrank back in horror and revulsion. I never imagined that a human body could ever look so ghastly and yet the girl lived on. The Germans certainly knew how to treat their victims. What is more their cynicism knew no bounds for before her release she had to sign a paper stating that she had no claims against them. No claims – although she was mutilated and disfigured for life.

More and more of my friends were having all kinds of 'mishaps' and were compelled to change their names and addresses. Considering Aniela's flat none too safe, I started looking for another shelter for her. My friends gave me the address of a certain lady in Ceglana Street where I went very unwillingly. This former Jewish street was now inhabited by scum of all sorts. Besides, it was rather unpleasant for me to walk in the area where not long ago my parents had lived, where I had spent my childhood. In the recommended flat in Ceglana Street I was received by an elderly aristocratic lady. 'Yes, I might accommodate a cultured Jewess with a boy, but I presume, madam, you understand, it must cost . . .', and the aristocratic lady named such a fantastic price that it left me speechless. The sum was four times what Aniela was paying at that time and I thought she had been overpaying anyhow. The lady talked profusely about the dangers of letting a room to such a subtenant and without any suggestion on my part stated: 'It is absolutely impossible to let the room for less because it would not pay.' I thought about a poor washerwoman I knew who had for six months harboured my colleague, an advocate, at the cost charged by this lady for one month. I thought about a poor tram conductor who sheltered another friend of mine, taking only the actual cost of her upkeep. Mrs Maria had received just 1500 zloty per month from the Organization, for every child. This covered all sundry expenses for room, laundry, upkeep and that greedy 'lady' – supposedly from the best society circles – demanded 6000 zloty monthly, otherwise it would not be worth her while. I remembered a German saying from my schooldays: 'Im Volke, diesem Meere der Menschheit, da leben Adams Kinder von jeder Sorte' (In a nation, this sea of mankind, live Adam's children from all walks of life).

· 18 ·

Retributions . . . Sentences

THE COURTS OF the Underground Organization sentenced several Poles to death not only for political collaboration but also for economic help given to the Germans. The sentences were carried out very boldly, often in the busiest streets. We read in our illegal press about Poles and Volksdeutsche executed for blackmailing hunted Jews or for denouncing them to the Germans. Such notices would always describe in detail their list of crimes, pointing out the motives for the death sentence and condemning the ignominy of their villainous deeds.

Several German criminals were done away with in such a masterly manner that the authorities felt completely helpless against the perpetrators. The manager of the Arbeitsamt had been killed by a would-be client almost under the noses of his clerical staff while sitting in his study during office hours. A lorry carrying a huge amount of cash, with an armed guard, driven in the middle of a convoy, had been kidnapped in the centre of town. Political prisoners on the way to interrogation were rescued in broad daylight in the streets of Warsaw despite their strongly armed escort. The head of the Gestapo, the bloodthirsty Kutschers, had been kidnapped in his own car and killed. Many assassinations, especially of obnoxious Germans, heads of some departments or institutions, were carried out, but the perpetrators were never caught. Acts of this kind would result in retaliation by the Germans.

The numerous arrests which followed every such exploit would unavoidably end in mass executions. The Germans would not flinch from acts of the worst brutality.

In such an atmosphere the Germans went to extraordinary lengths to protect senior officers. One morning they ordered the evacuation of the whole district of Powisle. Without being given any reason, just the portentous shout 'Fort', absolutely all inhabitants of the vast area had to move out within a few hours, leaving behind all their belongings. Coming to help Aniela in her removal, I witnessed the terrible scenes which took place when the wretched people were compelled to execute this order. Aged people, sick and paralyzed, were carried out. Incriminating papers were hurriedly burned; people tried to save the smallest quantity of their possessions. On the other hand they chopped up the furniture and damaged anything they could not take away, so as to prevent the Germans taking advantage of their misfortune. For love or money it was impossible to hire a cab or even the shabbiest cart in Warsaw that day as the people of Powisle held every one of them. During the afternoon it became known that some very powerful German, whose life must have been highly valued, had to be driven along that part of Warsaw; it was therefore considered safer to remove every living Pole. In the evening of the same day the inhabitants were allowed to return.

Despite all these drastic security measures the lives of senior Nazis remained unsafe. Derailings of trains carrying important German officials or troop transports became a daily occurrence. Many soldiers going to the front died under the wrecked wagons and although Polish lives were also lost during these acts of sabotage, work carried on. After the assaults on trains the Germans took to burning the neighbouring villages and carrying away all their inhabitants. The same method was applied to those places where partisans were known to shelter. The Germans knew that the partisans were supplied with food and clothes – willingly, or even at revolver point – by the peasants, and as revenge a scorched earth policy would follow.

The forests of western Poland provided relatively good shelter for the partisans. The Germans were terrified of the densely wooded areas and no German, not even those well armed, would penetrate their depths. Our underground press informed us that the forests, especially those on the eastern frontier, hid many Jews. Some of them had joined the partisans and formed a part of the underground forces. Some were hiding on their own land but were keeping in touch with the partisans, benefiting from their help when it was needed. There were, however, instances when the Jews avoided the partisans, whom they feared as they feared the Germans. It should be pointed out that the forest partisans consisted of varied groups with different ideologies. We knew about all their exploits against the Germans from the underground press. We often read about real battles between Germans and partisans, both parties using all kinds of arms. The casualties and losses inflicted upon the Germans were largely a result of the admirable heroism and excellent organization of these guerrillas.

We knew that many monks and priests worked for the Independence Organization and that many Jewish children were hidden in orphanages and Catholic institutions. One day the Germans swooped down on a boarding-school directed by the Silesian Brothers at Powisle and arrested a number of priests and pupils. Some were released on the spot but the rest were dealt with in a particularly bestial way. In Leszno Street, where once the even-numbered side belonged to the ghetto and was now completely wrecked, they hanged the arrested Silesian Brothers and their young foster-children on the balcony of one of the highest burnt-out buildings, opposite the Courts of Justice. Their tragic bodies were left hanging for several days. In the business area, in a bustling, thriving street, with its trams, cars, cabs and people hurrying in all directions, living their otherwise normal daily lives – there on the balcony, in full view of everybody, still hung the blackened corpses of the heroic priests and boys. People tried desperately not to look, yet they were compelled to see them, to think about them, and those who still did not know, had to learn to feel hatred and revenge. After several days, having considered the frightening example sufficiently effective, the Germans took the bodies down.

Now and again the Germans devised new distractions for us. Since more and more incidents occurred where Germans were killed by Poles, they issued a proclamation that for each German killed, ten Poles would be shot: such announcements were made both in writing and on the notorious 'bawling cans', as the loudspeakers were contemptuously called. Without any particular provocation, new mass arrests were started, merely for the purpose of having a number of hostages handy. First of all notices in German and Polish appeared on lamp posts to the effect that due to the killing of X Germans, X Poles had been taken hostage. Their names and surnames, addresses and professions were clearly stated, and it was said that they would be shot unless the culprits were caught by a set time. Obviously the perpetrators were never found, thus within a few days we would read on the same posts the names of hostages already shot. These notifications grew more numerous, the lists of names longer. They were read anxiously by relatives and friends of the condemned.

The executions in Warsaw were carried out publicly. We all knew the big lorry and its special crew; in front there stood a German in a steel helmet, in his hands a big horn. Every few minutes he would blow it in the same fixed manner. On side-benches in the lorry were seated twelve Germans armed to the teeth. Behind this vehicle was another, smaller one, containing the victims condemned to death. The sound of the horn filled us all with terror. We knew that people were being driven to their deaths. The lorries would stop in the streets with the densest traffic, the hostages would be dragged out to be mown down by machine-gunfire. After the execution the Germans would drive the vehicles back, the horn would sound again and on the pavement would remain the bloody corpses of the victims of German bestiality. The street traffic was not to be interrupted.

The corpses would have to lie there until the municipal lorry of the Sanitary Department arrived. This was the same lorry that was used to clear garbage from the streets and onto it the still twitching bodies were sometimes thrown. Once when walking in the street I unexpectedly heard the Polish anthem sung loudly by several male voices. The song grew louder, stirring the emotions of the passers-by. I stopped with the others. 'They've brought the hostages', somebody explained, and in a while we heard a fusillade. The song abruptly died. My heart stopped beating. The men standing nearby uncovered their heads. Yet again we heard the cursed horn, the starting of the engine and the Germans, their deed performed, drove away. A few moments later, however, flowers appeared near the bleeding bodies, white roses and lilies dyed with red. In a short while the corpses were buried under the flowers showering down from all sides, despite the strict interdictions and danger.

In this way the Warsovians would take leave of their unfortunate brethren. Another time I happened to be at my sister-in-law's former landlady in Rakowiecka Street, when the executions started at Pulawska Street, in our immediate vicinity. Standing in a seemingly invisible place at the window we could see everything, a sight which froze the blood and which one would never forget. We were apparently spotted from the pavement for suddenly a shot rang out, the bullet piercing a hole in the pane just above our heads.

The Germans realized that the last-minute singing of the Polish anthem, other patriotic songs or shouting anti-German slogans made the hostage's death easier, so they devised new torture. On the morning of the execution they would shave the doomed wretches and fill their mouths with a mixture of plaster and cement in order to prevent them from uttering a sound. In the busiest streets of Warsaw the Poles would now be executed naked from their waists and die mute under the executioners' bullets. The 'Herrenvolk' would exterminate its enemies using means of murder which Satan himself had never invented. We had to look on helplessly, praying for an end to it all.

Anti-German posters and slogans started appearing on walls, fences or advertising boards placed there by unknown hands during the night. From the 'bawling cans' one could sometimes hear a Polish patriotic song or a news bulletin broadcast by the secret Polish Underground Station which would steal its way into the German system. Little boys would jump onto moving trams and sing all kinds of prohibited hits, the most popular being: 'An axe, a pick, a glass of home-brewed vodka, By night an air raid, by day a street-catching, An axe, a pick, yes, yes, yes, When Hitler will go to hell.' The words were simple and each of the singers became an author, changing the words to whatever seemed more appropriate at the time.

The song of the urchin became a national demonstration in the lively streets crowded with German troops, police and all sorts of informers and blackguards. 'Pigs have flooded the country', the German passers-by were mocked impudently (the song of a nine-year-old boy). 'Haili, hailo', boisterously sang the Germans. 'When will Hitler go to hell?', the urchins of Warsaw would answer. Very popular too were the street bands consisting of surviving war wounded or unemployed musicians. For *Song of Warsaw* or *My Heart in a Rucksack* played in Hoza or Krucza streets, the passers-by would give their money generously.

But Warsaw, being a big city, was inhabited by many kinds of people. While some, full of sadness and despair, would clench their fists upon reading the lists of murdered hostages, others, inhabitants of the same city, would jostle one another in a queue before a cinema booking-office. The Underground Independence Organizations boycotted the cinemas from the very moment of German occupation. This was partly because some of their revenue went to the German Rearmament Fund and partly because going to the pictures meant that one was compelled to see the German newsreels, which consisted of victorious marches of the German army, battles won, liquidation of the enemy and endless pictures of the Führer. No decent Pole would look at all this or listen to the German anthem sung or played. There were, however, people who would not bother with unimportant things like these and would wait, often for hours, in order to obtain a ticket. And this in spite of versed inscriptions saying 'Only pigs Go to the pictures, To the theatres Go the rich swine,' printed on small posters to be found pasted all over places of entertainment. Yet the cinemas and theatres were sold out.

A lot of people would also go to the races. The Germans allowed them only in Cracow, but lovers of racecourses and bookmakers could content themselves in the squares of Warsaw, where a full report of the races and major events was broadcast. Those races were an obvious German 'ersatz' but for a lot of people it would do. Only certain types of people could enjoy themselves in that way. In circles considered to be the noble part of the Polish community one would hear: 'We cannot enjoy ourselves or dance when our soldiers are dying on all fronts, and our brothers are being tortured and murdered in concentration camps.'

On a hot summer's day, the Germans swooped down on the Vistula beach, cordoned it off, and not even allowing the sunbathers to dress, loaded them all onto lorries and drove to Skaryszewska Square and thence to the labour camps in Germany. This incident aroused very little sympathy: 'Why should they sunbathe in these hard times' and similarly sour comments were heard. This raid did not, however, deter some people from frequenting the beach and the Germans repeated the catch. Enraged that at a time when their soldiers were fighting desperately yet some carefree Warsovians were still enjoying themselves, they raided several big cafés and bars.

On the other hand, they purposely encouraged the Poles to get used to drinking, especially the youth. Vodka was issued to workmen in all factories and German institutions. It became the means of remuneration for all kinds of activities, including overtime work or even catching a Jew. A Jew-hunting gang operated on the Warsaw–Otwock railway line. They were given a few litres of vodka by the Otwock police for every Jew caught. I know of an incident when a 'pure-bred' Aryan, unfortunately black-haired, was apprehended at Falenica by such a 'hunter'. When the man tried to explain that he was no Jew the villain cynically replied: 'Probably you are not a Jew, but first of all I'll get my vodka for bringing you in. And when after checking it turns out that I was wrong, you'll be freed anyway.' Apart from the factory-produced vodka, the so-called 'bimber' vodka, illegally brewed in homes, cellars or attics, was very widely consumed. Addiction to drink spread equally in towns and villages and drunken twelve-year-old boys were not an uncommon sight.

There were different types of children and youth in Warsaw too. Some attended underground schools and studied diligently, transporting illegal newspapers or at nights scribbling 'Hitler Kaput', 'The year 1918 is approaching' or similar anti-Hitlerite slogans on the walls. Other Warsaw children would cram into the entrances of apartment blocks playing cards and drinking vodka. After the fall of the ghetto they would lurk outside the walls, near manholes, and spotting a Jew crawling out would shout 'Jude, Jude'. The Jew on the threshold of freedom would often lose his life because of such a young scoundrel.

Lawyer M.'s daughter, who was hiding in Warsaw and who had rather pronounced Jewish features, was recognized by a former schoolmate while walking in the midst of a busy street: 'Since when do Jewesses walk about without an armband?' By a stroke of good fortune there were no informers nearby and Miss M. escaped. The same Miss M. attended matriculation classes with a couple of other girls who, although well aware of Miss M.'s origins, had never harmed her but were always helpful. When Miss M. had problems and was forced to change her lodgings, the mother of one of her friends sheltered her. The kind lady was a pensioner's wife and far from rich, yet she charged very little and made Miss M. feel at home.

One day when I called on Mrs Maria, I found her upset and worried. 'I have no more strength left, the whole thing is too much for me,' she said and revealed to me the mystery of the small attic room. She was hiding a ten-year-old boy, whose distinctly Jewish features meant that he should not be seen by anybody. He was a dirty, lousy street beggar who had been sent to Mrs Maria with a request to be given refuge for some days only, until another protector could be found for him. Mrs Maria argued against this arrangement, saying that there were already too many people of that kind in her house, but it was pointless – the boy could not be abandoned on the streets. Six months had elapsed but nobody had picked him up and none of the Organization ladies had agreed to accommodate him. All were afraid. The boy was still at her home, always hidden upstairs, but sometimes the child could not bear his cage and would be allowed to come down to the kitchen. 'Only today the landlady has seen the boy and recognized him to be a Jew. She has ordered me to remove the boy immediately, she is terribly frightened. I have promised, but where should I send him?' That was the cause of Mrs Maria's worry. Mrs Maria, the guardian angel of seven people, sentenced to death. I admired her superhuman courage but unfortunately I could not help. She was very religious and had a deep faith that God would not forsake but fortify her in carrying out the task she had undertaken. Her favourite saint was St Antony, to whom she would pray for the lives of her seven Jewish wards.

What cleverness and diplomacy she must have displayed in order to explain and justify the presence of so many different people in her house. What difficulties she must have had in those times with the upkeep of such a numerous family. 'My children sit at home all the time. They have no pleasures or entertainment, they must at least eat properly,' Mrs Maria would say, and with an effort would make ends meet. I do not know how she could cope with everything and keep the children well cared for on the small sum of money she received from the Organization, especially when there was no allowance for little Jedrus. 'It will be all right somehow, St Antony will help and the war will soon be over', she would say cheerfully.

A young doctor, obviously aware of the situation, would often call to examine all the children. 'Eva must go to a specialist for an X-ray of her lungs', Mrs Maria told me one day. Together with Halinka, Mrs Maria's daughter, I went to a well-known specialist in children's diseases who did a 'Pirquet' test and X-rayed Eva's chest. I do not know whether the physician guessed who the child was, rooming with two different aunts, or maybe he just thought we were very poor but whichever it was he totally refused to accept any money from us. My child's 'Pirquet' was unfortunately positive. The photograph of her chest showed that her lungs were damaged and in the physician's opinion Eva needed to be sent to the country. I did not know what to do but Mrs Maria did and she managed everything. 'We'll send Eva to my mother in Zakopane. Although the Germans now forbid the Poles to live in the Zakopane area, my mother has a piece of land where she has been living for decades. Eva could go there as my mother's granddaughter.'

At Easter 1944 Mrs Maria obtained a travel pass, without which Poles were not allowed to go by train, and accompanied Eva to Zakopane. With aching heart I again parted from my little daughter. I did not wish to know the name or address of that grandmother as I simply feared that if I knew such details I could have them 'beaten out' of me. I knew of incidents when people of really strong character were unable to endure the excruciating pain, thus giving away their dearest ones. Aniela again found fault with my behaviour when I related the news about Eva. 'A fine mother you are. I would never part with Jasio', she snapped. It was difficult to explain to her that it was not my life at stake, but the child's health and very life.

I remained alone once more, yet I was strangely happy knowing that Eva was in the safest place so far. I still called on Mrs Maria. Several times we helped each other and when once the need arose to assist some of my friends, complete strangers to her, she did not hesitate to do so with the utmost devotion. I stayed on at Mrs S.'s in my capacity as domestic servant. I got used to my job and felt relatively happy. As there was not much to do in the afternoons I would spend the time reading. Anyone looking by chance into the servant's room would catch Miss Marianna studying an encyclopaedia: I read nineteen thick volumes thoroughly from beginning to end. It was a tedious but engrossing pastime which did not leave me time for morbid thoughts, for pondering upon my helpless situation, the tragic mess in which we were all stuck. Then I would also reread many books which I had read some time before the war and was pleased to see that I could understand them fully at last.

The terrible war years and my many experiences had made me more truly mature. I came to understand other people's situations and experiences as I would never have done before the war. I could not have understood what hunger meant, and to what desperate lengths it might drive someone. We think that we all know the feeling of hunger. 'Mummy, I'm so hungry I could eat an ox . . .!' In the streets of Polish towns before the war beggars could be seen asking for alms, and stammering: 'I am hungry.' In some poor districts one could see undernourished children and famine would often spread in villages where the earth was barren and the peasant was the father of a big family. Yes, there had been some really hungry people before the war, yet during the war I understood the real meaning of hunger. Hunger gnawing the entrails, hunger leading some to listlessness and apathy, others to crime; hunger which drives even a man of very high ethical standards, who in a former life exercised self-restraint, to steal food. The same happened to some other principles which had until then seemed abstract to me. In normal circumstances it was not easy to penetrate the psychic torments of a doomed human who feared the police or dreaded courts and jail. But who could begin to understand the vexation and torment of a wretch who not only feared troops, militia, jail or court, but was afraid of anybody and anything and yet must live on among the people he dreaded and make the best of a bad bargain?

My employer in Zoliborz told me once, 'Miss Marianna, you speak so loudly in your sleep that one can hear you in the next room.' Before the war I had never talked in my sleep. 'Too bad', I thought, 'I must take care of it!' Sleep became my enemy because I might involuntarily betray myself, so on top of my other troubles I was deprived of the peace of a night's rest. From the moment I heard that remark I started sleeping very cautiously and until the end of the war I would turn sleep into a dozing, nervous cat-nap.

Many a writer has endeavoured to describe the turmoil of a human soul, the feelings of a man before he is to die. Not one of them had the wealth of inspiration that could be found on the Warsaw 'Umschlagplatz' in 1942 or 1943. Nobody had seen so many hundreds of thousands of people dying simultaneously. The reaction of these doomed, famished, tortured creatures would have been a real surprise for all sages and philosophers. 'There is nothing new under the sun', said the author of Ecclesiastes, but I could answer him: 'You are foolish, you have seen nothing.' Hitler's butchery was something new, something never to be understood by anybody, and the human tongue is unable to express it properly. I tried to think as little as possible, I wished time would fly faster, ever faster.

· 19 ·

Nearing the End

During the entire period of their occupation the Germans sought to win the approval of wider Polish opinion, taking special pains to induce the Poles to provide them with recruits, always with negative results. After the outbreak of the Russo-German war they would openly write in the newspapers that except for Poland all other nations under their rule had supplied them with troops and had actively fought on all fronts. The Quisling press could not understand that Poland, directly imperilled by Bolshevist Russia, would not consider it her sacred duty to fight against that impending threat to culture and Christianity. To gain the Polish masses the Germans puffed out the 'Katyn case' and tried to convince the public that the Russians, as the murderers of 12,000 Polish officers, deserved to have the Poles against them. But public opinion remained unmoved by the German propaganda. The entire community suffered deeply because of this slaughter of 12,000 Polish officers, but it made little difference whether the murderers were Russians or Germans.

In the spring of 1944 Allied victory seemed imminent which put us all into a mood of feverish expectation. I would read the German papers with the greatest interest, yet I would always buy a newspaper far from where I lived in order not to arouse the vendor's curiosity. To be careful could never do any harm. In my room, when nobody was at home, I would unfold the big political

map belonging to the late barrister S., and meticulously follow the
course of the front line. 'The Army Supreme Command announces
. . .' became familiar to me. I went diligently through all news
bulletins and was delightfully inspired by the often-repeated
euphemisms to the effect that the German troops, unmolested by
the enemy, had retreated from this town or that, of course after
demolishing all military objectives and food stores. The Germans
would often add that in abandoning the town the front line had
been straightened. They did not conceal the fact that the town had
been left 'after a fierce and inexorable battle' and my heart rejoiced
in reading these words. I would also read the obituary notices with
great pleasure.

German newspapers did not of course print all obituary notices
on account of their growing numbers. I noticed that the only ones
printed were those of higher officers of merit, awarded various
honours. 'My beloved younger son Johann has fallen for the Führer,
Nation and Fatherland, following the example of the soldierly
death of his father and brother', wrote a 'proud mother'. 'My
sunny twenty-year-old only son sacrificed his life for the Führer
and Great Germany', wrote another German woman, and I read
these notices with some satisfaction. What had come over me, what
had the Germans brought about that I could rejoice in the death of
these youngsters, that I could be delighted at another mother's
terrible suffering at the loss of her youngest or only son? For me he
was only a hateful German and I was glad that by his death he had
made the German ranks smaller. Every day more German officers
fell. It even got to the stage that when reading the name of an
officer honoured by Hitler and given the Cross of Honour, I was
waiting for his obituary notice. I invented a game which consisted
of noting down the names of these distinguished officers and later
finding them on the list of the fallen. They were all airmen. In my
soul I had become a murderess. On leaving the house I would
carefully erase all traces of my ghastly game. The map was hidden
in my mistress's room and the newspapers destroyed. I had to bear
in mind that in Marianna's servant quarters only kitchen fiction or
a prayer book could conceivably be found.

There were funny, or rather tragi-comic moments in my new
profession. Once my mistress announced that a friend was coming
to stay with us for some days after a quarrel with her husband. She

arrived, a nice, cultured lady who seemed to be almost too polite. The fact that she sat all day long in her coat and veiled hat was very quaint. When I served dinner or supper the conversation at the table was suddenly interrupted. My ladies were obviously afraid to talk in front of me. The guest room was adjacent to mine and when I met the visitor on her way to the bathroom next morning, I noticed her confusion and quick retreat. I thought it very strange. When only half an hour later, while serving breakfast, I saw the lady in her hat and veil, my suspicion changed into certainty. Although she tried to hide her face from me I examined her closely and came to the conclusion that our guest was a hunted Jewess.

I did not wish to pretend in front of my mistress and I told her immediately that I knew who her visitor was. Indeed I was not mistaken. She was the wife of an engineer, a Jewess denounced by her former servant, who had had to vanish from her flat for some weeks. Since the poor lady looked Jewish, the hat with its lowered brim and veil proved to be a good camouflage. Her husband Mr R. used to call round. I had known him before the war when as a client he had often come to the office, and my superior advocate S. was his counsel in a case before the High Court. Naturally he did not recognize me. He visited us not in the guise of Mrs R.'s husband and everything turned out all right. I waited upon Mrs R., cleaned her room, helped in every way and I felt very glad when she praised my cooking or admired her well-polished shoes. It was painful that she was forced to put on an act, to wear this veiled hat, to fear me. Many were the times I wished to disclose my identity, to reassure her that there was nothing to be afraid of, to calm her, but my mistress forbade me to do so. 'It's better to leave things as they are, Marysia. Mrs R. is a very frightened woman and the less she knows the less she can blurt out under stress.'

Thus for her I still remained a servant girl, one to be feared. Mrs R. tried to win my favours with sweets or some fruit and always marvelled that Miss Marianna did not have a sweet tooth. After a couple of weeks she left our home, tipping me exorbitantly. Obviously I could not keep this money taken from a Jewess in hiding, meant as bribery against betrayal. With it I bought two pairs of nice slippers and gave them to Mrs Maria for the two sheltered girls. I knew that the poor children needed only house slippers, they never stepped out into the street. I promised myself to talk this funny story over with Mrs R. after the war and have a good laugh together, but I never met her again.

My mistress was also taking care of her late husband's former clerk and his family. She hid advocate G. at the home of her trustworthy washerwoman, who in exchange for a small sum kept him together with his nine-year-old son, who had very Semitic features. Lodging with another subtenant, a woman employed by the Germans, she had to take pains to keep the boy unseen. The boy, very vivacious by nature, suffered tortures during the time the other lodger was back from work. With no other hideout available he would be put into the bed underneath heaps of pillows and eiderdowns and with only a narrow chink of space for breathing. Without a sound, he had to lie motionless for hours. Since this was proving to be unbearable my mistress began looking for alternative accommodation for him with some decent family, while putting him up for a few days in our home. The boy had known me very well before and it was important that he should not recognize me. Mrs S. would sit with him at home, but going out she would lock him up in the drawing-room, handing the key to me. The child was terribly bored and asked incessantly through the locked door: 'Miss Marianna, when will Mrs S. come back, when will she be back?' He would repeat this question several times an hour, but would not ask anything else, being forbidden to talk to the maidservant. In any case the boy himself feared strangers as he knew he was in deadly peril. The poor child suffered and I could not help him. Many times I wanted to open the door, to take the boy to my room, to console him, hug him and show him a bit of tenderness, but common sense prevented me from the imprudent step of divulging my secret to a nine-year-old child. I would buy him sweets, cakes and other titbits which I would hand to him through the half-opened door, keeping my face hidden. 'Here you are darling. I've got some sweetmeats, these are for you.' I tried to ease the boy's lot at least in this way.

Mrs S. eventually found a place for him in a little suburb near Warsaw, but his future protectress stipulated that she had to see the boy before she would accept him so Mrs S. had to arrange a visit. I admit I feared this journey a bit. Within a few hours, Mrs S. returned agitated and annoyed with the boy. 'Miss Marysia, you must vanish for a few days!' On regaining her composure, Mrs S.

explained what had happened: the boy had not seen the streets for many months and, drunk with freedom, had let out an incessant stream of questions. He had talked aloud in the tram, drawing attention to himself. Mrs S. had noticed that they were being observed by a suspicious-looking individual. When they had alighted from the tram this person had got off too, and had followed them. Mrs S. had started wandering about in the streets trying to dodge the manhunter, but failed to shake him off. He then came up to her and told her that he was arresting her for looking after a Jewish child. Mrs S. begged for mercy for the poor boy and implored him not to destroy the child, but the scoundrel replied: 'You are both liable to the death penalty'. He wanted to take them to the Gestapo in Szucha Street. After long negotiations he let himself be 'persuaded' for the price of a gold watch of sentimental value to Mrs S. However, he knew Mrs S.'s address and the scene had been witnessed by the caretaker's wife. Luckily the incident had no harmful repercussions.

Our flat became a meeting place for several young men. As she trusted me implicitly, Mrs S. disclosed that they belonged to the Underground Organization. Every Thursday I would open the door to the fixed pass-code of knocks. Although the visitors tried to behave very quietly, Miss Marianna could hear everything in her room. One day when only a few young men were present, somebody rang the bell and knocked in a way that sounded suspicious. One of our most frequent visitors rushed into my room, very excited. Handing me a bundle of papers, which I immediately concealed under my dress, he said: 'Miss Marianna, you are not in any danger. If anything happens you tell them we've just come to pay a visit.' Very calmly I went to the door. Fortunately it proved to be a false alarm. An absent-minded member had forgotten the code. I knew that my shelter was becoming unsafe but I had endured so many dangers that I feared nothing more.

Another day when the young men were gathered in a room in our flat, a German for whom the same room had been requisitioned, arrived unexpectedly. Opening the door to an unusual knock and seeing the German, I knew that danger was threatening us all. Outwardly self-possessed and with an innocent smile, I said to the unwelcome caller: 'How nice of you to call. Madame was so anxious to see you. Do come in', and let him into the study, closing the door behind him. I rushed into the meeting room and shouted 'Scatter immediately!' The boys did not need to be told twice and quickly and wordlessly dispersed. As if nothing had happened, I opened the windows, took dusters and brushes and pretended to clean the room. I was however, terribly nervous because I thought the German might have noticed the overcoats hanging in the hall. After some five minutes the German, on leaving, saw the maid quietly preparing his room. I then realized how very careless we had been and how easily we could have got ourselves into deep trouble.

This carelessness was revealed in several rather bad jokes we shared, for example the following telephone conversation: 'Good morning Janek, have you got the jam?' 'Yes, thank you very much indeed.' 'And how do you like the jam?' 'Oh, it's very tasty, only it gets jammed.' This was of course a reference to rifles which were supplied. Or another one: A young man comes to a flat on the third floor and asks: 'Excuse me, would you like to buy some butter?' 'No, no butter is needed', they answer him. The young man belongs to an underground organization and the question is the password for entering the flat. He waits at the door. After a while another young man arrives and ringing at the same door asks: 'Do you want to buy some butter?' And again the same answer. But after a third lad asks the same question, the annoyed tenant shouts: 'No, no, I don't want to buy any butter, don't bother me so much. The place you want is on the next floor and after all, I am a Volks-deutsch!' The jokes were merely jokes yet there was a certain amount of truth in them. In reality undercover activities were extremely stressful and required a great deal of steadiness and concentration. And because it had gone on for so many years, it was exhausting even to the strongest individuals and led to many casualties.

The spring of 1944 was exceptionally fine and although any spring would have inspired us with new hope, that one decidedly lived up to our expectations. The Russians were nearing our border in great strides and on the second western front the Allies were gaining further successes. Although the Germans themselves knew that they had lost the war, not for a moment did the frightful terror in Warsaw abate. Executions in the street and mass shootings in Pawiak jail carried on as before. If we were to believe what we read in the illegal press and the English war bulletins, the end of the war was only a matter of weeks away. Yet, in the mean time, each day of German occupation resulted in further hundreds of victims. Prayers for the dead, for the peace of their souls were being held daily in numerous Warsaw churches attended by relatives and friends. I attended some of those services and pondered upon the fact that nobody prayed for the peace of the souls of murdered Jews, nobody remembered them. There was not even a single rabbi or a synagogue left because the last one had been demolished by the Germans after the final liquidation of the ghetto. The date generally considered the anniversary of the death of over 400,000 Jews – 21 July – was approaching. None of us had records of these events, nobody knew exactly on what particular day the Jews had died.

I was anxious that there should be a memorial service to pray for the peace of the souls of murdered Jews. In the records of St Jan's Cathedral, if they survived the Warsaw uprising, there should remain a note from the priest (to whom I had given an offering) saying that on 21 July at seven o'clock in the morning before the main altar there was to be a divine service 'for the peace of souls of all my brethren who perished on 21 July 1942 in Warsaw'. Knowing how extremely hurt and upset Aniela would be on that anniversary I went to see her. She still dreaded leaving her flat. 'Jasio will accompany you and will pray for the souls of all our dearest ones.' The only persons who knew the true reason for the service were Aniela's faithful friend, her former governess, little Jasio and myself. I was to meet the boy at half past six before King Zygmunt's statue near Castle Square. I spent that night in meditation remembering those who had first been deprived of freedom and dignity and were later butchered in a most inhumane manner.

On the morning of 21 July, when I was walking along the Three Crosses Square, I noticed some feverish activity in the traffic. German motorcars, vans, motorcycles were rushing at high speed returning from the direction of the Vistula. Tanks, ambulances, field-kitchens and cannons of all kinds were dashing at a furious pace along Nowy Swiat and Krakowskie Przedmiescie. At six in the morning the traffic was already heavy. 'Look, ladies and gentlemen, the Germans are taking to their heels', cried out a fat woman in our tram. I wondered why people were showing so little joy while witnessing their deadly foe in full flight. More and more carts appeared in the streets, loaded high with trunks and suitcases. Cars were piled with bundles of all sorts, bedding and even furniture, topped by groups of women and children. In Krakowskie Przedmiescie the traffic jam of cars, tanks and armoured vehicles was so thick that our tram conductor had to ring uninterruptedly and even then could move on only very slowly. I got off the tram as I simply wanted to observe everything. I wanted to touch the reality, to have tangible proof of the great event. The day before there had been no panic in Warsaw, but on 21 July there was panic, the deathly fright of Germans trying to get away. With little Jasio in tow I went to the Cathedral. There were many people in the big church that day, but none of us knew for whose souls this service was being held and for whom we were praying. I know that in normal conditions a Catholic church is unsuitable for prayers for dead Jews' souls and that a Christian priest is by no means appropriate. Nevertheless as there was neither a synagogue nor a rabbi, and God is everywhere, external features are of little weight. Most important is what a praying person feels and experiences.

Jasio, sunk in his prayers, remembered his brother, his beloved daddy and granny. I had in mind my late relatives, friends, and all that multitude of unknown Jews who had perished in torture. When we found ourselves in the street once again watching the fleeing Huns, we could believe that at last justice was being wrought.

I spent all that day in the streets, totally unable to stay indoors. My joy was marred by the sad news of the arrest of my friend Mrs L.'s husband and his confinement in Pawiak prison. The situation was worsened by the panic which overwhelmed the Germans. There was nobody to talk to about Mr L.'s release, there was no one to be bribed. Together with Halina's husband some hundreds of people had been arrested. A few were set free a week later, among them was Mr L. The rest were shot. This was the last German achievement.

My friend Aniela was very excited in those last days of July. She imagined that she would soon be leaving the hateful flat in Lipowa Street. She had already phoned the tenants of her pre-war apartment, and was thinking about the dresses and coats she would wear. She hoped to be restored to life very shortly. 'Now you see,

Marysia, that your caution about Eva has been exaggerated. Warsaw will be declared an open city and will not be bombed. Eva could have safely remained with you, and now, as it is, who knows when you will see each other?' Still I felt that Aniela was wrong and we would yet have to suffer before we got rid of the Germans.

Shops were besieged by customers. People started hoarding food. The Post Office stopped functioning, even telegrams were not accepted. Trains were running irregularly. People were expecting heavy fighting on the banks of the Vistula. The Germans issued a proclamation stating that the enemy was approaching the capital and that Warsaw must be defended against the Russians with the active co-operation of the population. All the Warsovians had to assemble in a body for digging ditches. This call drew no reaction as nobody answered it. No one would co-operate.

The noises from the front line could be heard at night. Dull, resounding thuds, increasingly distinguishable reports of heavy guns made our hearts rejoice. People from the neighbouring districts were swarming into Warsaw, considering the capital to be safe. Others were leaving Warsaw for villages, assuming the country to be quieter. I felt happy that Eva was at Zakopane. I was certain that in the mountains there would be no front-line fighting, no bombings. Nonetheless, I asked Mrs Maria for the name and address of her mother in Zakopane. Mrs Maria was then without any resources for, as a result of the feverish conspiracy work being done by the Organization towards the end of July 1944, she had not been paid for the upkeep of the children. To help her out, at least in some small way, I took a few kilograms of fat, bacon and sugar to Mrs Maria. Her pupils had started thinking about their future, what to do with themselves, where to go.

Food became short. Grocers either sold it at exorbitant prices, or kept it hidden for the black market. Those merchants who had grown rich during the war wanted to exploit the situation in order to gain still more. During the panic, and for the first time, people were not saying, as they had in September 1939, that the Jews were setting up a black market by concealing provisions. At the end of July the soldiers of the Home Army were being ordered to be on the alert. This was, however, cancelled. The sounds from the front died away, the artillery fire grew weak and everything became ineffably sad.

· 20 ·

Warsaw Uprising

In the late afternoon of 1 August, we heard quite suddenly in the streets the first shots fired and shouts of 'Down with the Huns!' What we had been anticipating for so long happened – the word became deed. The Germans instantly vanished from Three Crosses Square and Mokotowska Street although this quarter belonged to the so-called German district. Within a few minutes of the outbreak of insurrection, the Germans were nowhere to be seen. As if by the touch of a magic wand, red and white flags appeared on the balconies of buildings, as well as national armbands on the arms of men and women. Girls and women wore the sign of the Red Cross. The feeling was sublime.

On the subject of the Warsaw uprising much has no doubt already been written and much, I presume, will be written still. It will be the task of experts, of historians, to give a very accurate, documented and skilfully written account. But not even the most sensitive reader, unless he or she was present at that time in Warsaw, would ever understand or feel what we experienced and felt. Let the writers and historians relate as much as they can, let the poets sing about the insurrection. Every tale and every poem would be a further step to testify to the truth. But no pen would ever be able to render what we saw or experienced. I shall only try to give an account of some of the events which I observed, and which will be locked in my memory for ever.

At about five o'clock on the afternoon of 1 August, I walked in Three Crosses Square and gazed as if in a dream at a red and white flag fluttering from one of the balconies. Only a short while ago there had been Germans here, and now I saw young boys with rifles over their shoulders marching boldly ahead, eighteen-year-olds in civilian clothes, one with an ordinary rifle, another with two grenades on his belt, a third with a pistol and yet another with a simple axe in his hand. That was our army in the first hours of the Warsaw uprising and on seeing this the well-trained, fully equipped knights of the Third Reich took flight! It was the miracle of that day, and nothing that happened afterwards would ever wipe out the unparalleled bravery of those lads who first came out to fight the Germans and who drove them off the Warsaw streets. 'Don't loiter unnecessarily in the streets. Keep indoors, please!', ordered the boys and very unwillingly I had to go home.

How charming I found my little servants' room! It had turned into my castle in which I dreamed golden vistas of freedom. So God had granted me life to see this moment of German defeat. There were no Germans around. Our boys had driven them out! The war was coming to an end. Mrs S. and I wept tears of great emotion for the dead who would never see such a day.

The streets of Warsaw that night began to take on an entirely different form. A barricade had been erected across the roadway at the corner of Mokotowska and Wilcza Streets, and from the windows of our flat we could clearly see similar barricades along the whole of Mokotowska Street right up to Redeemer Square. Another barricade separating Mokotowska Street from Three Crosses Square was raised at the corner of Mokotowska and Hoza streets. On a balcony opposite our windows a boy of perhaps ten was sitting, playing the *Song of Warsaw* on a mouth organ and from the banisters waved a large red and white flag. At the entrance to that building stood a man with an old-fashioned shotgun. All around was still and quiet. I quickly went down into the street. In the entrance of our house some people were standing, reading a newspaper.

After five years this was the first patriotic Polish press to be read openly and publicly. Obviously I too wanted to read it, but the tenants looked at me in an unfriendly fashion. Was it a domestic servant's business to know what was written in a newspaper? 'You Miss, better go home, look after the housework. Your Missus will read the paper and then she'll tell you what's in it.' I left the building resolving not to live there any more. Now, during the uprising there was no more need to pretend to be a servant, to masquerade and put on a show. I went to Halina L. I was already known to some people as Mrs L.'s friend, which meant a person from society. I read the first edition of the newspaper edited by the Polish Socialists' Party. I was moved. Can anybody who has never lived under oppression understand our emotions on reading a Polish newspaper?

'Citizens, the hour has come. We have driven the Huns out of Warsaw.' My eyes filled with tears as I read. The contents of the first articles were inspiring. All citizens, with no regard for their class, religion or political creed were called to fight the enemy. Building after building was searched for Germans who might still be hiding there. Those caught, including Volksdeutsche, were taken prisoner. More dailies appeared and kept us informed about the streets now in Polish possession and those still in German hands. Our strategic position was not bad. At the beginning the uprising was quickly suppressed only at Praga. The Germans did not move, choosing rather to adopt wait and see tactics. As we had had our wireless sets confiscated by the Germans as far back as 1939, we listened to the news bulletins in several flats abandoned by them. The members of the Polish Government in London certainly did not know that while listening to them for the first time after nearly five years we wept, hardly believing that this was a real radio message and not the hated 'bawling-can'.

At the very beginning all tenants of a building were entrusted with the task of organizing life in their area. Guards were put at the entrances, taking it in turns to check all those who entered, for fear that a German or Volksdeutsch who had run away from another house might try to hide where he was unknown. In case of fire on the roofs or in attics, pails with water and sand were prepared and two voluntary wardens were continuously on duty. Trenches were dug, connecting buildings with one another so that one might walk considerable distances without emerging on the street. Directions, names of streets, and numbers of houses were clearly marked by inscriptions on the cellar walls. In some places tunnels were even built under ground to facilitate crossing from one pavement to another in case of shelling in the street.

Care was arranged for people who would accidentally find themselves in a certain area and were unable to return home. Some people who had come only to fetch their laundry from the washerwoman or to call a doctor on 1 August had intended to stay for a few minutes and had remained for two months, unable to reach their homes at Praga or in districts held by the Germans. Although at the beginning the food situation was difficult, it was unthinkable to let a stranded person go hungry or homeless. I was amazed by the spirit of kindness, understanding and brotherly love that pervaded everyone around us.

Much was expected from those wireless broadcasts: the much-desired approach of the Russian line, the long-awaited Allied help for Warsaw. Yet in the mean time the Russian front was moving away and there was no help from the Allies. After a few days when German activity intensified and they started shelling particular streets, people were being killed in doorways. Then news came over the wireless that Paris had been liberated from the German yoke. I am not jealous by nature. I always wished only the best to the Parisians cherishing beauty as I did, and still do. I was really glad that the Germans had not demolished that wonderful city, yet why was it that we were to be burned down under German fire, why were our houses to be destroyed, why us? We could only ask the dumb wireless cabinet. This question could be seen in everybody's eyes, but in the first days of the uprising nobody dared voice it aloud, nobody dared to show doubt about the outcome of the revolt. It would not do to be down-hearted.

Field hospitals were established at several strategic points in our district. I saw such a hospital in Mokotowska Street and Ujazdowskie Allee and even two in Hoza Street. The hospitals were built up from practically nothing. Everything from bedding, dressings and first-aid remedies was generously supplied by the people of Warsaw in the first days of insurrection. Collections were organized in every building and not even the poorest would fail to donate at least a pillow, a towel, a bottle of alcohol or iodine. These donations often involved great personal sacrifice for the benefit of the hungry and homeless, for hospitals or medical supplies.

I will never forget the first letter that I received at that time, care of the advocate Mrs L. It came from Aniela from Lipowa Street, brought by a ten-year-old boy. It bore an inscription on the envelope: 'Boy Scouts' Post'. I was moved to learn that as early as the second or third day of the uprising the Boy Scouts had organized a postal service to carry letters from outlying parts of Warsaw, even from the districts held by the Germans. The 'Post Office' was established in a private flat in Hoza Street and letters were accepted by a small lad. 'We have no stamps as yet and for the postage we take donations of books for the youth organization; so if you have one, we'd be delighted', said the little Post Office official to me. Would anybody believe such a thing? Little boys who carried letters under enemy fire, with disregard for their own safety, accepting books for future Boy Scouts' libraries in lieu of payment. Halinka* and I went through her library and picked out all suitable books which she had received from her parents, grandparents or aunts on various occasions. We wrapped them for 'post duties'. At the same time letterboxes appeared at building entrances in Hoza and Krucza streets. They were of quite imposing dimensions, provided with huge letter-slits, since letters carried heavy, often very thick 'stamps', fixed to them by a cord.

In her first letter Aniela wrote: 'I am happy, beginning to live at last.' She went on to inform me that she and Jasio had moved to her neighbour's on the ground floor, and that a communal kitchen had been organized with everyone sharing food provisions. For the time being there was peace at Powisle and sisters from the Convent baked bread which was distributed among the citizens. The main thing was, however, that the Germans were nowhere to be seen. I immediately 'posted' a small food parcel to Aniela. The Boy Scouts' Post was at that time the only means of keeping in touch because telephone connections were cut off.

A detachment of our troops lay encamped in the vicinity of our building. Every evening at dusk they would make a sally in small groups, stealthily drawing near the German positions. They were always accompanied by a few volunteer nurses. The hospitals began to fill with the first casualties, young boys and girls hit by enemy bullets while on duty. All doctors instantly applied for work. As well as professional nurses and students of underground

---

* Halinka is the affectionate diminutive of Halina.

vocational courses, many untrained women volunteered for duty. All wanted to do something to help. Blood donors were in abundance. At a physician's in Krucza Street I had to queue for an hour but then I was happy that my blood belonged to group 'O' – universally suitable. I kept that 'blood certificate' for many years.

In the streets the odious 'bawling-cans' were replaced by new loudspeakers. We at last had our own radio which kept us informed about the situation on our inner city front. The boys accomplished acts of unparalleled courage in both aggressive and defensive battles. We had successes which at the time seemed really great. The capture of the Post Office building in Koszykowa Street, I think, resulted in many casualties but it was a very important strategic point. The taking of the 'Cedergren' building in Zielna Street intoxicated us with pride and joy. I do not remember now exactly when and which buildings were captured, but the smallest success would fill us with elation, while the loss of a house or (worse), of a human life was viewed with deep concern. The St Lazarus Hospital in our immediate vicinity changed hands several times. A pitched battle was still raging for the House of Commons building. Many of our boys gave their lives there.

The food situation deteriorated and supplies were gradually exhausted. It became difficult for me to get a loaf of bread even from the baker's assistant, although he knew me as 'Miss Marysia', his equal. 'The master now accounts for every loaf of bread. I can give you only half of my own', said my friend, stealthily handing me a piece of hot bread. The baking of bread for the civilian population was discontinued – all went for the troops. We understood very well that a soldier in action should not go hungry. Only some of the bakeries would accept flour and the following day one could obtain baked bread from one's own supply.

Thanks to my profession as maidservant, I had many acquaintances in my previous district – in certain circles of course. By chance I discovered a few kilograms of flour in an old sack at our grocer's. 'This flour is stale, I only use it as glue for paper bags. Had it been all right I wouldn't have kept it for so long', he told me. Nevertheless I thought I'd try it out so I bought eight kilograms of it for a ridiculous price. The baker's apprentice weighed the flour, constantly smelling it to examine its quality. 'Mr Felus, please don't sniff at it, it's not perfume', I scolded. 'There's exactly eight kilograms', said Felus and the next day I received that amount of fresh tasty bread. 'Among 500 kilograms of good flour eight kilograms of stale doesn't matter', said my friend, 'and besides, the master always mixes something to make it go further and produce more loaves.'

During the insurrection I actually lived at my friend Halinka L., but I would come faithfully to the flat in Mokotowska Street. The block of flats had a second entrance from Ujazdowskie Allee and standing there I had a good view of that boulevard as far as the German positions. Once, standing in the doorway, I saw a German tank trying to cut through to Three Crosses Square. Near me two boys were watching. They quickly threw two bottles filled with petrol at the passing tank. Their aim was precise and the tank burst into flames. Two SS men with their hands up jumped from the burning vehicle. It was an exciting moment when the two Germans, trembling with fear, stammered 'Pardon, pardon'. I looked at the boys – neither had any weapon. The SS men stood dazed for a moment, uncertain about their fate. They looked at the boys, the boys looked at them and eventually the Germans, their hands still raised high, their frightened eyes still staring at the lads, started slowly retreating in the direction of Szucha Street where at last they began running wildly. I gnashed my teeth in powerless anger. One of the boys was on the verge of tears. The tank was still burning on the roadway.

As the uprising continued, however, more of our soldiers were better armed, often they could be seen carrying machine-guns. A grenade factory was established in our area. Many weapons were captured from the Germans. The Wehrmacht soldiers who had given themselves up, or others captured in battle, were taken prisoner, but SS men, police and all kinds of informers and spies were shot. I do not know how much truth it contained, but a rumour was spread in our district that a Jew who had been kept prisoner by the Germans had reported to the authorities, requesting permission to hang the Germans. 'It's a waste to use bullets for condemned Germans', he was credited with saying, presumably repeating the phrase so many times used by the Germans about Jews. The German prisoners were directed to work. Once I went to a house in Krucza Street to have a look at the Germans in captivity.

I saw them doing some light work. They were well treated and guarded by two boys who also protected them from possible attacks by the population. We were not even allowed to spit in their faces. At the same time the Germans would shoot any Polish soldiers without mercy, even civilians taken prisoner, denying them the right of combatants.

Our newspapers informed us about the procedure Germans applied to the inhabitants of a captured house. In most cases they were driven out of their flats without being allowed to take anything with them, the building set on fire, while all young men were carried off to an unknown destination. We read that on the so-called *zieleniak* the Ukrainians had raped women under the eyes of their husbands and children, then murdered the defenceless people. The German tanks would appear more frequently in Marszalkowska Street, Redeemer Square, Jerozolinska and Ujazdowskie Allees, and soon more direct hits were scored with petrol bottles, setting them on fire. Then the Germans fell upon a satanic expedient: they would drag women and children from a captured building, seat them in tanks and drive on with them in front as safety cover. At around the end of September 1944 these reinforced tanks invaded the Warsaw streets. Did any regular soldier ever have such a tragic dilemma? At the end of the uprising I talked to an advocate's wife who had been placed with her daughter on a tank in just this way – the woman had escaped death by a miracle, yet after nearly six weeks was still unable to regain her mental equilibrium.

In the mean time our lives were being further organized. Militia were established from which all 'dark blue' policemen were banned. The courts started functioning properly. Offices of the insurrection were situated in Krucza Street and the Security Committee had its headquarters in our neighbourhood. Food stores and all kinds of military equipment depots were established. Much needed soldiers' canteens, seamstresses' shops and other institutions were all quickly and efficiently organized. Courts started dealing with offences, even those relating to pre-insurrection times. Germans, Volksdeutsche and Poles were tried for all kinds of transgression. If a German or Volksdeutsch was not guilty of any special crime against Poland or Poles, he would be considered a prisoner of war. To all other crimes the judgement applied was based upon laws which had been in force at the outbreak of war. Sentences were published in newspapers. We read about many citizens condemned to death for collaboration with the Germans and actions detrimental to the welfare of fellow citizens. The 'dark blues' were sentenced for their zeal in serving the occupying forces and some death sentences were passed for Jew-baiting, taking advantage of their weakened position in hiding, and betraying them to the Germans. It is obvious that only very few cases were brought to the attention of the Court, but all were dealt with under the full severity of the law.

Apart from these Courts we had our own little laws. Women who were known to have had intercourse with Germans were caught. Their hair was shorn and an inscription 'For Germans Only' was placed on their clothes. These women were not allowed to leave their rooms without this inscription.

It was still relatively quiet in our district, but refugees fleeing from other areas related stories of terrible atrocities. Our friends from the neighbouring Mokotow found shelter in our flat. They told us that the Ukrainians set all captured houses on fire and brutally murdered the remaining inhabitants. Other tenants of our block of flats sheltered people from Sienna, Sliska and Grzybowska streets because almost all buildings and houses there lay in ruins and were under constant heavy artillery fire. The Old Town fell. Its heroic defendants found their death under the debris of ancient buildings. Only a small number of survivors, dejected, blackened and prematurely aged, forced their way through the trenches and canals to our area. The number of tenants on our block increased greatly.

At night we started to rebuild and reinforce the surrounding barricades. The huge concrete roadway slabs were heaved up by means of big iron levers and used as material for barricades. It was a hard, heavy job. Two women could hardly lift such concrete slabs so men set to work lifting them. Between slabs we would leave small slits or holes for embrasures while large empty spaces would be filled out with sand bags. One of these reinforced and excellently built barricades was erected near our doorway, the result of all-night work by tenants from neighbouring buildings. My bruised hands were bleeding, but a feeling of pride in our achievement overwhelmed me when I gazed upon the barricade in the morning.

The streets of Warsaw began to look rather odd. Overturned

trams across roadways, telephone poles broken, pavements without concrete paving. Shops, many looted, gaped their emptiness, glass splinters from shattered windows strewn everywhere. Yet from the balconies the red and white banners still fluttered, and the loud-speakers broadcast communiqués and national songs which the Germans undoubtedly heard in their adjoining positions. The radio would play, the bullets whistle, but despite our ever growing hunger we still felt very happy. Our district was subjected to heavy artillery fire. We learned to distinguish various kinds of guns by sound and we experienced a new German weapon at first hand. In our district it was named 'the roaring cow' (or simply 'the cow'), in other parts of Warsaw 'the cupboard'. Both names were apt: 'cow' because before it was discharged one could hear what sounded like a stifled mooing, then something like winding up, followed in a few moments by a terrible roar as the missile would fall; and 'cupboard' because the sounds accompanying this winding up before the shot was fired were like the noise made by a cupboard shifted on a wooden floor. The name was irrelevant. The weapon inflicted terrible damage to the buildings and killed a lot of people. A few days after shelling had begun on Krucza Street, not a single building along the whole street remained undamaged.

These projectiles could tear off a complete roof or the whole top floor of a building, thrusting it into the distance. The biggest buildings were completely wrecked after a few hits. People within reach of the missile got horribly burned. I saw a woman, for instance, whose face had been left greenish-brown. Mercifully she died soon afterwards. Many casualties were victims of snipers. Germans or Volksdeutscher hidden somewhere in attics, chimneys or other inaccessible places would now and again shoot at passers-by. Constant searches were carried out for these snipers. Sometimes a German would be found with his weapon.

One day a little friend, a Girl Guide who often brought us letters, came to us most upset. 'Today they are amputating my friend's hand in the hospital, she is a Girl Guide too. The bone was shattered by a bullet, gangrene developed and now the hand must come off. My friend is not afraid, she only asked to have flowers by her bedside when she awoke from the anaesthetic.' We looked at each other, Halinka and I. How worthless and small we felt in comparison with that little girl. But where to get the flowers? Some months ago there had still been beautiful flowers on our balcony but now everything was covered with plaster and rubble. Who would think of flowers in these days. We went onto the balcony, however, shoved away bits of brick and wall and found a few half-faded blooms. We revived them with water and bound the spray with a pretty ribbon. Our Girl Guide was happy and carried the flowers to the hospital with pride.

'The cow' roared on daily, causing ever greater damage. The hospitals were full and a great many people died. In Hoza Street, near the hospital, there was a small garden which soon filled up with graves. The first victims were buried very solemnly, the graves kept neat. A carpenter from Wspolna Street was kept busy making coffins but the demand for his services grew too great. Wood was needed for crutches and artificial legs for the crippled and so the dead were soon buried without coffins. The cemeteries grew ever bigger, the graves dug close to one another became less neat, flowers were no more to be seen. Only here and there the hand of a mother or wife would place a pot with a wilted flower, or sometimes only a few green leaves. Graves of young boys filled all available squares and gardens, while every courtyard became a little cemetery. 'Here lies in peace twelve-year-old Janek X. He died on liaison duty.' I have seen so very many of these inscriptions to the little heroes and heroines who were often not older than ten years of age. These children of Warsaw, pupils of various underground schools, these most courageous young knights in the battle against the German invader, were falling like flies. I asked myself 'Why, what for?' Soon living conditions became unbearable. Famine took hold, epidemics spread, gas, electricity and water supplies had been cut off long ago.

What I had feared most eventually happened. The Germans began to demolish and burn Warsaw from the sky. One Sunday, at the beginning of September, low-flying planes dropped several blockbusters on St Alexander's Church at Three Crosses Square. The church was completely wrecked and the Germans thus gained an unobstructed view of the whole district. Commanding the high building belonging to the Polish National Bank on one side and St Lazarus Hospital at Three Crosses Square on the other, they could have a clear view of our troop movements. From the day the church was wrecked we knew no peace. Artillery fire was directed at our street without respite and the planes dropped incendiaries and blockbusters.

The hospital in Hoza Street was crammed when all wounded had to be moved to the cellars. This was a terrible sight during those days of unabated bombing. The damp, low-built cellar, its darkness lit only by a few candles, with the wounded lying on the floor ... the dirt, the complete lack of bandages ... all added to the sense of horror. And in this dim, confined space surgeons were performing the most complicated operations, practically without a break, to the constant accompaniment of the roaring of the 'cow' and the deafening noises of the falling bombs. Dysentery spread through the hospital and doctors stood by helpless; the exhausted sisters were unable to clear away the excrement due to lack of water. Getting a pail of water from a well on which the fire was directed meant certain death, and the hospital needed so much. The doctors, sisters, all the workers were hungry, stumbling with weariness, but they worked on. They worked without interruption.

By night we would stand guard on the roof of our seven-storey building with a supply of sand. At this time the Germans would drop midget incendiaries which could be easily put out with a few handfuls of sand, if spotted in time. The night guard duty on the roof was considered to be the most dangerous, but as I was young and strong I took up the job of fireman most willingly. My companion was Mr Janek, a bailiff's clerk. His wife and little boy slept peacefully as well they might; we would certainly save the house from the little incendiary bombs. Night after night for three hours we sat on the roof, gazing at the sky, watching. One night we could clearly hear the front line shouting and the droning of artillery. 'Mr Janek, do you hear, the Russians are approaching!', I cried. 'What of that, I know I'll not outlive the war', he answered. I laughed. 'The uprising is at its end but the Russians could come any day.' My friend Halinka L., with her aged mother and two other aged women who had come to us from a bombed-out part of the town, was almost constantly in the cellar, emerging only in the evenings when it was quieter. In the neighbourhood of our building, bombs were now falling incessantly and our flat was brightly lit by the fires of burning houses. A huge red and white sign was painted on Three Crosses Square to enable the Allied airmen to drop weapons and ammunition.

We still expected help. We did not want to believe that they could let us become the prey of the Germans. Once with baited breath we listened to the broadcasts from London whence came words of encouragement asking us to stand firm, praising our bravery and – nothing else. At the risk of endangering our lives we would go to listen to the news. Hungry, thirsty, often wounded, we would stand in the courtyards, frequently under a hail of bullets, to hear at last a voice bringing real help. We listened, we waited, but in return we received only words. Not only empty, but often painful words. Warsaw was in flames, the soldier-child was dying in the hospital cellar, and the Polish authorities in London were transmitting pathetic songs to give us strength! Sometimes we thought they were mocking us. After listening to these broadcasts we would return with heads bent. We would go back to our posts and duties, work in which nobody believed any more. We all knew by then that we were sacrificing our lives for a lost cause while London sent only promises of support. We must give credit, however, to the diplomats who had granted us the rights of combatants. From now on, in theory at least, the Germans would no longer shoot the captured fighters but consider them prisoners of war. Even this small diplomatic success came late, very late.

Carrying on my night-time duties, I sat listening to the artillery battles. All around me fires were raging and from the roof of the seven-storey building one could clearly see which district was burning. The light was so bright that the winding Vistula was distinctly discernible, beyond which little lights flickered and died away. In the purple sky there appeared little twinkling pinpoints, the planes from which one could see what looked like a handful of golden sovereigns falling every few minutes. Those were the flares. 'Miss Marysia, let's go to the staircase, at least. They'll burn us like bugs', said my companion one night. Involuntarily I shivered at this comparison. I had heard it once before. Then, in April 1943, when the Germans had begun burning the ghetto from the air, a woman grocer from Mokotowska Street said to one of her patrons: 'I live near the ghetto and I see what's going on there. They're burning the Jews like bugs.' And now history was repeating itself, the same was happening as in April and May 1943. The Germans were using the same infallible weapon and they were burning the town from the air. I knew that this was the end.

My night duty was nearly over. Soon another shift arrived, whereupon I went to have some rest. Some rest, when one had to lie fully clothed expecting an emergency which might include having to run away. No sooner had I fallen asleep than I was awakened. 'Marysia, they have come from the hospital. They need blood, quick.' In a moment I was up and ready. A little liaison girl led me to the hospital in Mokotowska Street. But we arrived too late – the man would never again need a blood transfusion. I was about to go back home when a new transport of wounded was brought in. 'Miss Lukaszewska, please wait,' I heard the doctor say. I waited while he examined the wounded. 'Yes, this boy has suffered a big loss of blood, a transfusion will be necessary ... Are you ready? Group "O", excellent, sit down please.' A light prick and my blood flowed slowly out, directly into the veins of the wounded youth. I looked at the boy to whom I was giving my blood. He was perhaps seventeen years old, on his face barely the beginning of a dark stubble. 'We collected them after a night raid,' explained a medical girl orderly, while dressing her own wound. I was happy that my blood had proved useful in the fight against the Huns. I did not know the name of this 'relative' of mine, but it was all the same to me. 'Thank you, that's enough,' said the doctor and ordered me to rest a while. I went home and avoided talking about the amount of blood given in order to spare my friend's nerves and unnecessary worry.

My friend Wanda P., also a Jewess, was a nurse at a hospital in Ujazdowskie Allee and asked me to call on her sometime. Mass was celebrated every Sunday in the hospital. I had never attended such a service and on one quieter Sunday I went there. I entered a house in Mokotowska Street and from there by means of several complicated, concealed passages I came to a big courtyard of an old villa in Ujazdowskie Allee. From the balconies hung beautiful carpets and all around were attractive flowerpots. The field altar was modest; in front of it wounded soldiers sat or lay on stools, benches and stretchers. A little further behind stood the lightly wounded and the healthy soldiers. The priest was in uniform, a soldier served at Mass and two officers in splendid uniforms knelt nearest to the altar. It was the first time I saw soldiers of the uprising in such splendid attire. The Mass was being celebrated quietly. Suddenly we heard the terrifying whistle of a missile. I looked at the praying people but nobody stirred. The missile fell somewhere nearby. After the first one came the second, then the third. Whizz after whizz, explosion after explosion, yet nobody moved, only the heads of those kneeling bent lower, the words of the prayer spoken louder. The devilish cannonade came to an end at last, the Mass was concluded in peace. Lost in thought, I emerged from the hospital courtyard, richer in one more experience.

In our building, a tiny chapel was concocted out of a staircase alcove window. Simple, modest statues, a few artificial flowers, that was all it contained. Every morning and evening the tenants of the house would gather here for prayers. In these horror-filled days, religion and prayer were a great refuge and solace for the harassed people. 'Thy will be done', whispered the crowd, heads humbly bowed. I could not understand that part of the prayer which says 'and forgive us our trespasses as we forgive them that trespass against us'. How could it be that we were to forgive the Germans their sins? No, never, no religion could demand this from us. The city was in flames with everything falling in ruins. Thousands of innocent people lay dying under the debris, women and children were burned alive. Those feeding the flames of our hell, those hangmen and executioners were the Germans. Were we to forgive them their sins? 'From fire, hunger and war, deliver us Lord; from sudden unexpected death, save us Lord.' How meaningful were these words then. The prayer always ended with remembrance of the dead and a patriotic song.

In almost every house, there were similar small chapels, everywhere prayers were sent to heaven, but in response a hail of bombs would fall from above. One evening a bomb fell nearby tearing the head off a statue of the Virgin. Still prayers carried on at this mutilated chapel and the words 'and forgive us our trespasses as we forgive them that trespass against us' acquired a new, tragic meaning.

The German position, with St Lazarus Hospital now permanently in their hands, drew very close. We were separated only by Three Crosses Square. The German fire became almost unbearable and we were compelled to sit in cellars. A blockbuster demolished one of the neighbouring buildings and from under the debris could be heard cries and moans for help, however faint. 'Hurry to help save the buried' was the order. Collecting a few men I left the cellar.

Usually only men were asked to do the digging, and although they looked at a woman with some hesitation, I somehow got a shovel. Evening fell and we stole carefully to the wrecked house. I stared with awe at this mountain of bricks and rubble which was to be dug up. We started working but the job proceeded very slowly and I was certain that we would not be finished before daybreak. The Germans must have spotted us because from St Lazarus Hospital, or from the Polish National Bank, they began attacking us with machine-gun fire. We carried on anyway. From the nearby barricade, however, the boys started shouting at us: 'Get away, you civilians, don't loiter. They'll mow you all down and we'll only have trouble.' We had to give up. Very sad, I went back while the faint moans of those buried alive could still be heard.

The evening broadcast from London cheered us up with the news that the French had driven off the Germans almost completely, that the Belgians and other nations were regaining their freedom and that the situation on all fronts was very satisfactory. But not so for us. Those parts of the city we still held were diminishing daily. We were losing one district after another and it was clear that the insurrection was dying. After the fall of the Old City, Powisle fell. Small numbers of insurgents fled to us and to Mokotow through the sewers. In Ujazdowskie Allee near Wilcza, boys and girls would wait near a manhole to help their comrades climb out. Dirty, soaked, run down to a state of exhaustion, they would crawl out – the knights of Staromiejska, Swietojanska, Dobra, Lipowa. There was no fright in their eyes, no fear, only resignation. They knew our cause was lost. For the time being they were all placed in one of the neighbouring houses in Wilcza Street. They were to get some rest before having to fight on.

The water shortage was becoming acute. Several people would get killed daily just standing in the queue. We tried to eat all our food from the same plates in order to save washing-up water. The water with which we had filled our bathtub several weeks before was unsuitable for drinking, full of plaster and brick splinters, but it could still be used for our daily wash. The third floor of a shelled area was not a safe place for the morning wash. I informed my friends that 'I'd like to go to the other world clean' and would stubbornly scrub myself down every day. On two occasions the accompanying shell-blast took off some bits of my garments and

my friend laughingly cried: 'If the bombing lasts any longer, all our
knickers will be gone!' Poor Halinka, who during the entire
uprising had no news of her husband, stranded in the endangered
part of the city, had to console and take care of her eighty-year-old
mother. In spite of this she was as good-natured as ever and cheered
us all up. Instead of complaining about the many inconveniences
we suffered, she would take everything in her stride. 'It's just as
well that our hands are black from constantly sitting in the cellar,
at least that way nobody can see that I have no manicure', she
would say, ruefully looking at her dirty hands.

Because of the lack of water and the time needed for washing up,
we started eating our soup directly from the pot. This Halinka
enjoyed so much that once, when we were all sitting sadly in the
cellar, she announced in a loud voice: 'I am offering you all an
exceptional bargain! Whoever wishes may have my beautiful china
dinner service free. I have come to the conclusion that soup eaten
directly from the pot tastes much better!' Good humour and jokes
diverted our attention from the miserable reality of our existence
and we all tried to avoid any allusion to the sad events.

One day Aniela's step sister, Marysia, came to us. She entered
our rooms proud as a peacock, dressed in uniform. It turned out
that this nineteen-year-old matriculation student had taken part in
underground activities during the entire German occupation.
Although garrulous by nature, she had never betrayed this fact even
to her own sister. Now an experienced soldier, she had been
entrusted with some very responsible duty, having been stationed
at the Polish Savings Bank; this building, although demolished,
harboured in its cellars the command headquarters of the insurrection. The position in the heavily shelled bank building was very
difficult, but keeping it in our forces' hands was considered of
paramount importance.

The uprising was dying out. The Germans began dropping
leaflets urging the population to surrender and leave the city. The
pamphlet threatened the complete destruction of Warsaw resulting
in great suffering to the civilian population. In order to enable the
people to depart, the Germans would call a ceasefire for some
hours during which the civilians had to go to the nearest German
barricade, waving a white handkerchief to signal surrender. The
population would be granted life and their freedom after a compul-

sory short stay at a staging camp at Pruszkow. Leaflets to this effect were dropped every few days. The first ones found no takers. 'We will not surrender', the tenants of our building unanimously declared while we awaited the further turn of events. Low-flying planes began strafing us from the air even more ruthlessly. Building after building fell in ruins. In our immediate vicinity several blocks of flats were ripped apart, killing hundreds of people who were later found in the rubble, a fact which jolted the neighbours into considering the need to leave the capital. We had several hungry, sick children in our midst whose parents were forced to look helplessly at their misery. Also among us were a few aged people, a few sick. Defeat was inevitable, what did they have to wait for?

· 21 ·

Our Building Falls

STEALTHILY, SLYLY, people made their retreat and crossed over to the Germans. We learned afterwards that they were safe. I myself would never willingly surrender to the Germans, begging for their mercy by waving a white flag. Besides I knew that sooner or later a bomb would hit our house, too. On 15 September, while I was washing myself in a few drops of water, I heard a terrifying noise and a strong blast threw me from the bathroom to the kitchen. I was only bruised as the bomb hit the neighbouring block. 'It will be our turn next', I thought, and quickly put on my clothes. I could not leave the flat yet because our soup was cooking on the little kitchen stove and was too precious to waste. Eventually the soup was ready and I carried it down to the cellar to enjoy it together with my friends. 'Halinka, be quick. We might not eat it in time and I don't wish to go hungry into the next world; it wouldn't be good manners', I joked, but I saw that the situation was serious. They were obstinately bent on getting us this time, the planes droned on as if directly above our heads and the rattle of the engines deafened our conversation. We just knew it was to be our turn next. We did not have long to wait. There was a hellish roar, everything in the cellar shook, plaster and pieces of wall began to fall on us. Women started to cry. I can still hear the voice of an old woman ringing in my ears to this very day: 'Januszek, Januszek, where are you, why did you tear your little hand away?' With sinking heart I knew I was buried under the rubble of a seven-storey building. The air became stifling.

In the cellar there were a few men from a police post which had been stationed in our house. They comforted us and tried to work out some means of rescue. I was strangely calm, feeling rather like an onlooker and not someone taking an active part in this disaster. I was sure that we would get out of this cellar. 'Please be quiet. Our fellow police on the outside will certainly come to our rescue', we heard one of the policemen saying. We waited in the pitch darkness – we could not see one another. Someone murmured prayers, there was a cry, while the deafening noise of the planes' engines still roared overhead. Every minute seemed an eternity.

At last we heard some voices outside. The police had arrived with help. We crawled out through a crevice in the shattered wall and breathed fresh air again. The street was dark from the smoke and dust. The bombs had hit several adjoining blocks, wrecking them completely. We ran. We had to get as far as possible from what was now the most dangerous district. Through the ruins and rubble, tumbling over burning beams, choking in the stifling air, we ran on. We did not know where to go. Halinka suddenly remembered that it had been comparatively quiet in Noskowski Street where her sister-in-law lived. In any case we had no choice. Finding the way there was very difficult and slow, walking through still-smouldering ruins, mountains of debris and glass, over bomb craters and cracks. Clinging to each other we could not help laughing. We were all black, but so completely black that we resembled Negroes. Even Halinka's mother's white hair was black. It was a long way to Noskowski Street. We had to walk through several cellars joining different houses, two underground tunnels under heavily shelled streets; after what seemed like an eternity, we arrived at the place.

Noskowski Street near the Engineering School was half in Polish and half in German hands. The even-numbered side was Polish, but the entrances were locked and barricaded from the inside. We could get in, however, from Lwowska Street through openings cut in the outer walls of adjoining buildings. So we were on the border line, but it had its advantages as those buildings were not bombed since the Germans would have had to hit their own positions, thus killing their own soldiers.

It was comparatively quiet in Halinka's sister-in-law's house. She was the engineer N.'s wife. Although I was a stranger to her, she welcomed me warmly, offering to accommodate me together with Halinka and her mother. Here we rested and regained our mental equilibrium. Mrs N. employed young Miss Helena as a governess for her little daughter. One brief glance told me that this girl was Jewish. In the course of conversation with her my guess proved to be correct and I, too, disclosed my secret to her. We were soon great friends. I was told at the outset that Miss Helena's aunt, a lady in her mid-forties, was staying with Miss Helena. Since Miss Helena had no other relatives in Warsaw, Mrs N. agreed to put up her aunt during the uprising. That aunt seemed to be strangely solicitous and tender-hearted. I soon understood her behaviour when she turned out to be Miss Helena's mother. When accepting the teacher governess, Mrs N. had had no idea of Miss Helena's origins, but had learned about it soon afterwards. She had kept her on and for two years employer and employee were well contented with each other.

In the house in Noskowski Street I had the opportunity of direct contact with the soldiers of the insurrection, a better insight into their incredible bravery, self-denial, devotion and endurance. I must admit that observing those soldiers had a great effect on me as I learned a great deal from them. I was staying in a flat with paneless windows facing the German side, but I slept peacefully, secure in the knowledge that there, in the basement and on the ground floor, our boys and girls kept constant watch with their fingers on the trigger. They were starving, but fought on, sacrificing their lives although they knew in those last days of September, after the fall of Molotow, that the situation was almost hopeless.

At long last the Russians took Praga. Again we started reading the newspapers pasted over the walls of every courtyard with enthusiasm. I would again attend all radio broadcasts. Our rescue now seemed only hours away. We waited for this, mostly in the courtyards.

During this period of time-killing, I made the acquaintance of a young Jew. He told me that he had been imprisoned with a large group of Jews at Pawiak, and had been freed by the insurgents who had given them lodging and clothes. He had parted with that group of Jews after a few days and had come to stay with a good friend in Noskowski Street where he was given food and shelter. 'Now I have everything, but what is going to happen when, God forbid, the uprising fails and the Germans come back? Look at my features, my terrible Semitic features. Have I regained my freedom only to lose it so soon for ever? I must confess that I pray daily for the success of the uprising not for my sake, but because of the insurgents who set me free. Even if my freedom is short-lived, I shall remain eternally grateful to the boys for the few weeks of freedom that I have had. I give almost all my food to our soldiers. I got used to eating very little in jail anyway. Practically every night I keep watch with them, happy to be allowed to share their jokes and keep company with them.' I saw the lonely young man pacing the yard. He would always be the first to read the paper on the wall. He would know everything first and had a good grasp of our situation.

Day after day we waited, looking steadfastly at the sky. One fine, sunny morning, the Allied planes came and circled around our block, flying low. People crowded the courtyards waving to them and shouting in Polish, English, French and Russian: 'Help, come and help, we are perishing.' Grown men wept out loud. Everybody was overwhelmed by a nervous excitement. Intelligent people who knew they could not be heard by those in the planes cried and shouted in all possible languages: 'Come on, help us, have mercy on us!' They seemed imbued with a collective frenzy. In the eighth week of the uprising we must all have been on the verge of nervous breakdowns for a scene like that to take place. The planes then flew away and the exhausted people slowly dispersed. Later we learned that the airmen had dropped several tons of cases with food, medical supplies, weapons and ammunition, but the majority had fallen on the German side. We waited on. The centre of Warsaw was only partly in Polish hands while all around were the Germans. Food reserves were already drained and hunger weakened us more and more. I was so feeble I could hardly walk, and my head was constantly throbbing.

We were told that big stocks of barley lay in the Haberbusch breweries and one could take as much as one could carry. People made collective expeditions to fetch this barley so I decided to join a group to get some. At the N. family's home I felt like an intruder, an extra mouth to feed in time of food shortage. We assembled at a police station in Poznanska Street from where we set out, provided with passes and a guide. The way to Zelazna Street was very difficult and dangerous. The Germans were stationed in the Telegraph Office building at the corner of Poznanska and Nowo-grodzka streets and were shelling that whole area. We wandered for several hours through tunnels, cellars and all kinds of ditches. While going under the roadway of Jerozolinskie Allee we heard German tanks rolling over our heads. In Zlota Street near the Atlantic cinema, German corpses barred our way. A few minutes before the place had been hit by artillery shells. But in defiance of this ordeal the soldiers stood on guard and our passes were checked several times.

At the Haberbusch brewery I got some barley from relatives of the engineer N. and two loaves of bread. On top of this, I was lucky enough to buy some rancid 'edible' oil and with a full sack bearing heavily down on my shoulders, I set out to return to the meeting point. In Panska Street I heard the roar of the 'cow' but I had nowhere to hide. There was literally not a single building left nearby. I lay down on the ground. The missile fell somewhere further along, the blast throwing up huge clouds of dust which covered me completely. I ran on. By some miracle the building housing the Workers' Sick Fund had remained intact. The house in which I spent my childhood was totally burned out. Streets like Wielka, Sienna, Sliska and Zlota were damaged to such an extent that I had no means of making out where I was. I eventually reached the meeting place whence we were to be walked back in groups again to the other side of Jerozolinskie Allee. With my precious load I arrived in Noskowski Street late that evening, after a long and ghastly passage. The barley had to be ground in a coffee mill, which was a long and tedious job but worthwhile, since from barley flour one could make cakes to fry in a pan. The cakes, however, were stored away for a rainy day and for the time being we had to put up with nothing but watery soup, three times a day. I was permanently hungry.

Twice I made a dangerous trip to my friend's flat in Hoza Street to fetch some clothes and other belongings. I learned there that when the building had been wrecked, in the very cellar where we were buried only two steps away from us, fourteen people had been killed, without us having the slightest notion of it. A part of the cellar had collapsed, burying them under a pile of masonry in an instant; the poor wretches had had no time to utter even the slightest sound. My companion's sad premonition during the night watch on the roof had proved right. He had perished under the debris, together with his wife and little son Januszek. His old mother wandered among the ruins, almost completely mad, still looking for her family. It was the old granny who had held little Januszek's hand. It had been that old voice I had heard calling 'Januszek . . . Januszek . . .' I also heard that a few people who had so narrowly escaped death with us had taken shelter in one of the neighbouring houses, but an hour later a bomb had fallen on that house too, burying them all under the ruins. I shuddered. By some miracle I had again survived.

The house in Noskowski Street was like an oasis of peace but leaving this shelter meant certain death. Carrying water was particularly dangerous, as one had to stand in a queue for sometimes five or six hours under unceasing German fire. The adjoining little square grew into a cemetery with every bit of earth a grave. At the well on Lwowska Street I often met German prisoners, neatly dressed, with rings and watches on their hands. Nobody bothered them, nobody stood over them with a whip or weapon. When a German would help a woman to pump water from the well, he would hear 'Danke' in reply. What strange creatures, and how different was this behaviour to that doled out by the Germans. I simply feared to think what the Germans' behaviour would be if the situation were reversed. The Poles knew that very well but would not and could not behave differently. They followed their sense of honour and humanity.

As the end of the eighth week of the uprising drew to a close, demoralization grew more marked. People would charge 50 zloty for a cigarette and rich scoundrels would sell a few kilograms of flour or peas at the price of 5 roubles or dollars in gold. Only sugar remained cheap and plentiful during the uprising and we simply sucked at it all day. This at least gave us energy but played havoc with our teeth.

The word 'capitulation' became more and more familiar to our ears. The Germans dropped new leaflets. They wrote that in view of the present state of affairs, when only the city centre was held by the insurgents, the question of finishing the uprising was completely dependent on their will and wish. They maintained that they were able to range their heavy artillery in such a way that within a short time only a heap of rubble would remain. The war operations came to a standstill and we presumed that during this lull negotiations regarding the capitulation were in progress. I would not believe this but the rumours persisted. I still waited for something to happen. My heart was heavy. The papers could no longer conceal the fact that the situation had turned very serious, while appealing to the public to keep calm and remain in the city. The trend of the articles was: 'Abandoning the city could mean death. Don't you remember the fate of the Jews carted away by the Germans? The same fate awaits us.' Finally on 2 October came the terrible news: Warsaw had capitulated. The failure of the uprising became a fact, all soldiers were to go into captivity while the civilian population would be compelled to leave the city. The tragedy was made the more painful since we all knew that the end of the war was imminent. In October 1944 the Germans had practically lost the war to the Allied forces, but against Warsaw they could still be victorious. The suburb of Praga was already in Russian hands and this suburb was so near and yet so far. Just like the distance between life and death.

The date set for the surrender of arms was 2 October. These arms, concealed for years in various hideouts at the risk of human life, arms captured from the Germans in bloody battles at the price of many casualties, arms dropped from the long awaited Allied planes, when every piece would cost many lives – all these arms were to be laid out under the feet of our brutal victors. Although we had to leave the city I tried to postpone it until the last moment, still waiting for some miracle to happen and hoping that we would not be forced to go to the Germans. The soldiers were already walking out. One of the last groups included a relative of Mrs N. The boy had a fiancée whom he wanted to marry before they parted. I witnessed their tragic wedding ceremony. In a hastily composed chapel in the cellar, an insurgent priest married the young people, who had to separate within the hour – perhaps for ever. After the ceremony the young wife and guests saw the bridegroom off to report for roll-call at a German barricade. The bride did not even cry.

The barricades, built at such enormous sacrifice by hopeful

patriots, now had to be pulled down under German supervision by the last groups of soldiers. Looking at all this I cynically concluded that such was the price of righteousness if not backed by force. Justice, truth, sacrifice and the highest heroism lay in ruins. Fresh graves were trampled on by the heavy boots of German soldiers. One of my fellow advocates, a Jewess by birth, committed suicide by jumping from the fifth floor of a building in Noskowski Street. Her nerves could stand no more. We buried the unfortunate Misia in a small garden with the help of the caretaker. She was buried without a coffin, without even a sheet – only a bottle bearing her name was put into the shallow grave. I could not even weep. The Germans started going from house to house chasing out the remaining inhabitants. There was no alternative. We had to leave.

We were to be sent to a staging camp at Pruszkow, and from there – God only knew where. We were warned that we would not be given any food at Pruszkow, therefore everyone had to take food for about a week. We made some cakes from the barley flour with the rancid oil, took a few bottles of black coffee, some sugar, and the most essential medical dressings. We had to remember that we might have to march several kilometres to Pruszkow itself, therefore we could not take many clothes in order not to make our rucksacks too heavy. On 6 October, together with Halinka, her mother and the family N., I left the house. Within a few minutes we were already under German 'protection'. I tried not to look at them so as not to see those accursed green uniforms. I wished to shut my ears not to hear that hated, too familiar shout 'Fort, fort, schneller, schneller'. At the border the Germans distributed bread. I did not take any as it reminded me of the procedure at the Umschlagplatz when at the beginning of the liquidation the evicted Jews had been given bread and jam. The Germans, as they stood on both sides of the long rows of tired people who were bent under the weight of heavy rucksacks, were taking care that no one slipped away to hide. We could now see the full extent of Warsaw's ghastly devastation. We passed through areas now completely evacuated while all around was a wilderness gaping with ruin and desolation. Women and children, the old and the crippled, had to march ahead, always quickly, while our German guards laughed to burst.

We were suddenly imbued with the defiance of people who had

nothing left to lose. A wish not to show the Huns how broken we were. 'Halinka, let's take it easy. The weather is fine, the sun is shining, we have come out of the uprising unhurt, damn it! Perhaps it won't be so bad. If we leave Warsaw laughing, I assure you we'll be back soon. I can't expect anything bad anyway. I've been dead since 20 January 1943. This march is terrible, but it is an idyll in comparison to a journey to the Umschlagplatz and these guards are lambs set against those beasts from the Vernichtungskommando. Cheer up, Halinka, it'll be all right, and the Germans will be damned anyhow.' In a mood of calm I saw we had arrived at the Western Station, or rather at the place where there had once been a railway station. After several hours waiting we were crammed into cattle wagons but we managed to stay together in one group. We rode past the summer resorts. Everywhere it was quiet, with people strolling about peacefully. The uprising had been only in Warsaw. Outside the city people had not suffered at all. The lying, misleading propaganda had proclaimed that the surroundings of Warsaw had been evacuated. Our train eventually drew into a separate part of Prusznow. Guards and SS men encircled us and hurried us to the camp. Nobody knew what was going to happen, what they would do to us. We stood in front of the overcrowded camp barracks. 'You are lucky,' a Polish stretcher bearer called out to us, 'you'll be segregated today and maybe even taken further.' I tried to find out more, perhaps there was a chance to escape. All I was told was that the healthy and strong-looking prisoners were to be sent for 'voluntary' labour to Germany, while the old and sick were to go somewhere else, destination unknown.

While observing the groups of people marching by, I noticed that the young and healthy were guarded by strong detachments of SS men, whereas the weak and old were left practically to themselves. After several hours I decided that those who were unguarded would perhaps be set free. I expressed my view to my friends and we decided somehow to mix in with one of these groups as soon as it passed by. Time was running out. Soon our turn would come and we would be segregated. Once surrounded by SS men we would have no opportunity to escape. Almost at the last moment a group of women with children, the old and unfit, passed by. In the nick of time we jumped into this crowd and quickly mingled with them. The SS men shouted at us, yelled and threatened, but could not leave their own group, fearing its dispersal. In the mean time our group trod quickly ahead, entering a barrack filled with people definitely unsuitable for work in the Reich. Our success was tremendous. We felt triumphant.

We found ourselves in Barrack No. 4, which had been a factory shed and was now overcrowded with people who had been there for weeks awaiting transport. They waited on the floor with their families or in groups, surrounded by dust and filth. With great difficulty we found a piece of floor for ourselves in a dark corner. Representatives of some welfare organization distributed soup and coffee but one had to wait in a queue for several hours. Afraid of being spotted by a German while standing amidst the old and sick I preferred rather to give up my ration. Again it turned out that we were lucky as next day was destined for the transport of those confined in our shed. Night fell, and I had to spend it standing up because there was not a bit of floor space left on which to lie down. One could not even take a step without tumbling over people lying on the floor. Suddenly we heard a siren alert. That was all we needed – an air raid. Crammed tight in the locked shed we waited. The roar of exploding bombs shook everyone awake and scared people senseless. The sick wailed, children cried, and the only thing we could do was wait. At last the air raid ended, the nightmare was finished, and day dawned.

We started to get ready for the journey first thing in the morning and I noticed a group of people standing nearby. One look at them convinced me that they were Jews. Only such a big gathering of people and the prevailing upheaval could explain the fact that they had remained undetected until now. All the informers, blackguards and other scoundrels had too many troubles of their own at present to remember the Jews. My friend tugged me away from them. 'Marysia, leave off, you won't help them and you may make things worse for yourself,' she said, and I had to agree with her. During preparations for the transport the medical orderlies came in to tell us that before the march another selection would be performed by the Germans: all the young, healthy and fit would be taken away. The only thing left for me was to get sick. I dipped a piece of cottonwool in iodine, covered it with gauze, then applied this dressing to my right cheek by means of coursed strips of adhesive plaster. I bound my hand with bandage, made a sling and put my hand into it. Thus decorated I hoped to pass German scrutiny. I reckoned that as they were in a hurry they would satisfy themselves with a superficial inspection. All my friends tried to disfigure themselves and look old and ill. Mothers and fathers of little children felt the safest because the Germans would release them. There were known incidents of kidnapping a child to secure such a selection. The gate of the shed was opened at last, and SS men appeared in the yard. We were lined up in fives, following which they took stock of us like cattle.

I must have looked pitiful because an SS man even gave me a tin of condensed milk. This milk, donated by the welfare organization, had been destined for children and the sick, thus when we passed the selection I gave it to a really sick person. The Germans picked several people from our rows whom they considered fit for work in Germany, and the rest were marched to awaiting open wagons. It was difficult to reach the high steps of the wagons but nobody pushed us, nobody beat us. After several hours of waiting in constant fear that another elimination might take place the train eventually pulled out. In the last moment two girls jumped in. They had bribed a German with two gold 5 rouble pieces and he had let them go.

We passed small stations. I drew out a map which I had taken with me in order to work out the direction in which we were travelling. It was quiet all around. On the way we passed people evicted from Warsaw who threw loaves of bread, onions, apples, even sausages into the wagons. It was a friendly gesture, and greatly moving. I realized that no danger threatened us as the whole train was escorted by only a few guards who behaved pretty decently. We could not enjoy our journey, crammed as we were and standing all the time. Some of our fellow travellers would relieve themselves by climbing the wagon ladder and sticking their behinds outside. We tried not to pay attention. The journey had already lasted ten hours when I noticed that we were going back, passing the same places as before. The guards eventually stopped the train and allowed us to alight. We were permitted a few minutes to do everything we needed – publicly and under the watchful eye of the guards. I went up to one of the guards to ask where, in fact, we were going. He replied that they did not know themselves. Very soon an order arrived directing us to the vicinity of Cracow. We travelled all night and feeling very cold we huddled together for warmth. The night passed by somehow and at about noon our train stopped at Jedrzejow station. We were set free! Near the railway station tables with bread and milk had been set up, and the temporary office proceeded to register the evicted. Those who had somewhere to go were provided with a paper directing them to their chosen locality. That paper was like a train ticket. The rest could remain at Jedrzejow and its surrounding villages.

Along the railway track peasant carts from various neighbouring villages waited, and the peasants simply invited the refugees to their huts. I could not believe my eyes. I would never have imagined that help given to the unhappy citizens of the capital would be so swift, so efficient and so unselfish, moreover that this help would be provided by the peasantry. We were told that the bailiff was placing the refugees among the peasants who had to provide the poor victims with full and free accommodation. Of course if a refugee had means, he might pay a modest remuneration to the peasant. Halinka and her mother remained in the village where for a ridiculously small sum they obtained a room with full board.

22

To Zakopane and Eva

I TRIED BY EVERY means to reach Zakopane, to see Eva. I knew that Zakopane was 'Polenrein' (cleansed of Poles), that no Pole was allowed to enter that area, but I decided to try nevertheless. For the time being I went to Jedrzejow. The small town was full of refugees who swarmed to the few restaurants open on Sundays, buying up everything in sight. I entered the first flat at random on the ground floor, wanting to buy some food. I was invited inside and fed bountifully. My hosts allowed me to have a wash and rest. They gave me many practical hints, but refused to take any money from me. Out of my rucksack I now pulled out the precious cakes made from barley. The good lady of the house wondered that people could have been eating such muck and straightway threw the cakes to the hens and ducks, but even they would not eat what I had acquired with such great hardship and pain during the uprising in Warsaw. Next morning I left via Cracow for Zakopane. It was doubtful whether I would reach Zakopane, since I was told that all newcomers were checked on arrival and that only permanent residents were allowed in. At daybreak, however, I reached Zakopane without incident and left the station without being challenged or detained by anyone.

The little town was still asleep when a sledge took me to the house of my daughter's foster-granny. I knew Zakopane well from pre-war days and had always loved it. But now, after all I had been through, after the hell of the Warsaw uprising, these quiet, dignified moments, the fluffy, deep snow, these sleighs with their little tinkling bells seemed to me just a dream. In the pale light of dawn Zakopane seemed more beautiful than ever. My frayed overcoat and the poor rucksack reminded me that I had not come for leisure to a luxurious hotel, as I had done in the old days. With pounding heart I knocked at the door of Eva's sanctuary.

The door was opened by an old lady to whom I introduced myself as Eva's mother. Grandmother was happy to see that I was alive, because she had heard that I had perished during the uprising. She lived together with Eva in a shabby little room. The child was sleeping peacefully on a home-made bed. I was very warmly welcomed and grandmother assured me that everything was all right as far as Eva was concerned. All the neighbours were convinced that Eva was her real granddaughter. We resolved not to tell anybody the truth – it was easier, as Eva knew me from Mrs Maria's place in Warsaw as 'Aunt Marysia'. To all acquaintances I was to be introduced as a friend from Warsaw. After a few hours a friend and neighbour, Mrs Zosia M., called on granny. She had leased a villa nearby. Mrs Zosia instantly offered me accommodation but would not hear of receiving any payment. 'You'll pay me after you've earned something; for the present I will not accept any money.' I was then given a beautiful room in the nicest spot in Zakopane, treated like a sick child by my hostess and later cared for as a sister. It felt like Paradise. I saw Eva daily, but always behaved with the utmost restraint. Although granny assured me that all her women friends were decent people I preferred to keep my secret and be constantly on my guard.

Granny told me that since the previous July she had not been receiving any allowance for Eva's upkeep. All her friends were helping her as much as they could. Many local ladies would often call on her while I was there, keen on news, gossip and especially newspapers. Granny would please them by pulling out from under the cupboard or sideboard the latest edition of an underground paper. All these women would caress and fondle little Eva. Only I behaved like a complete stranger towards my beloved child. 'You certainly don't like children, Miss Maria', Mrs Zosia once remarked. 'We are all so fond of Eva and try to help the poor granny.' Although I helped granny as much as I could I still feared people's prying eyes, and regarding fondness for Eva, well . . .

First of all I began looking for a job to acquire a work permit. Without much effort on my part, I was taken on as a waitress at one of the most fashionable local restaurants which, since it was frequented by Germans, issued my work certificate promptly. The job was rather easy, the food excellent and I received a salary. I felt almost happy. My child was healthy and blooming nearby. I could see her daily. The job was not difficult, I was well off, around me I had good, kindly people and it was obvious that the war was nearing its end. I enjoyed the natural surroundings and in my free time I would walk to the same places which, before the war, I had visited in my husband's company. The same mountains, the same grandeur and beauty, the same nature, but how much had the world changed in the mean time.

A fragment of an old poem came to my mind: 'The forest was there, we were not. The forest will be there, we shall not.' Everything material and emotional in this world will be gone, both previous happiness and our present troubles, but the mountains and nature will remain the same. In all respects I was well off in Zakopane. My employer was a really good, obliging woman while my landlady, Mrs Zosia, one of the kindest and most pleasant creatures I have ever known. I took to her very much indeed. Her one very grave fault was that she hated Jews and would talk about them at every opportunity. She would constantly mock Jewish expressions, ridiculing Jewish customs and practices. In my opinion she had an unhealthy obsession with the subject. Since I was unable to have a heart-to-heart talk with her, I could never understand where this ill-will towards the Jews came from, and what its real cause was. Being a kind-hearted woman she would always speak with sympathy about the deaths of her Jewish acquaintances. She was of the opinion that killing people was too brutal and cruel a means of getting rid of them, yet she was glad that even by these inhuman methods, the Jewish question in Poland was settled once and for all.

To this day I cannot understand how a person who in all other respects was so aware, kind and gentle could be so wrong. Notwithstanding this she would never actually harm Jews. Several people from Warsaw settled in our villa and among them was the widow of a doctor with her daughter. Mrs Zosia suspected that they were Jewish, which I did too, though I did not admit it. Landlady and tenant often quarrelled about the use of kitchen and money and Mrs Zosia bitterly complained about 'the Jewesses'. When somebody suggested giving them notice, however, Mrs Zosia to my surprise replied: 'God be with them. Be it as it may, I would not wish to make their lives more difficult.' And as a matter of fact she tried hard to make their lives easier. At that time I learned that all Jews from Zakopane had been sent to Nowy Targ and there, outside the town, had been slaughtered, mown down by machine-gun fire. Their houses had been destroyed, leaving no trace of their existence.

At the end of October Mrs Maria came from Warsaw and was put up at her friends in Nowy Targ. She was accompanied by her daughter Halinka, wounded during the uprising. Then came one of the 'relatives', Hala, the housekeeper and that boy who had been kept hidden in the attic for such a long time. I was deeply moved at being able to embrace Mrs Maria again, and to listen to her latest experiences. During the uprising Mrs Maria had established a small infirmary in her flat where she worked day and night. The nurse, little Jedrus's mother, and the remaining girls were very helpful. Wounded Halinka had been carried by her comrades through sewers and tunnels to her mother's flat at Molotow. I learned about the tragic death of our beloved 'Madamcia', who had died while on duty, hit by a German bullet. As the bombing increased in intensity the infirmary had been moved to the cellar, where work carried on as before. The owner of the villa, the woman whom everybody had feared, turned out to be a great patriot and a very efficient co-worker.

After the collapse of the uprising, Mrs Maria had left Warsaw with her substantial 'family' but along the way had lost two girls, while the nurse and her son had remained in a little town, where she took up a job in a hospital. The biggest problem was caused by Janek, with his pronounced Jewish features. Mrs Maria bandaged his head and half of his face and somehow got through all the German control points and the camp at Pruszkow, where she had stayed for two weeks. From there she had come to Nowy Targ, but Janek caused problems again. He could not stand the bandages, tore them off and would stealthily creep out.

After a few weeks Mrs Maria's hostess openly declared that she was afraid to keep him. Compelled to leave Nowy Targ, Mrs Maria found refuge at one of her friends at Poronin. At first little Janek followed orders and kept to the house, but after a few weeks the same thing happened again. It was not surprising that the poor boy, after such a long confinement in Warsaw, could not endure this new imprisonment. The neighbours started gossiping. The landlord, who had nothing against the boy and who was Mrs Maria's faithful friend, became anxious and they had to move once more. Now with the whole family she rented a secluded house on the outskirts of Poronin, where little Janek was again locked up in an attic. In the mean time the two lost girls were found. They wrote to Mrs Maria at her mother's address that they were in some small town under the guardianship of the local vicar. The mother of black-haired Marysia (one of the girls who had got lost on the way) came to Poronin with a friend of hers. Both ladies were put up by Mrs Maria. This resourceful woman started up a small infirmary once more and soon received some financial aid from welfare agencies. The landlord, a Highlander, supplied dairy goods free, some provisions were received from the Guardians' Council General and life in the little house on the outskirts of Poronin somehow stabilized itself.

We were talking about the uprising when Mrs Maria, always frank with me, disclosed what disgrace the extreme radical nationalistic youth (who wore the little sword emblems in their lapels) had brought upon themselves. On some occasions these people, blinded by hatred, would even kill Jews met by chance during the uprising. 'How painful and sad this is to every decent Pole', complained Mrs Maria. And I later learned that my colleague, the advocate G. who had gone through so much, was murdered with his wife, son and a whole group of Jews, by just such home-grown followers of Hitler. I tried to console Mrs Maria, but how could I tell her that her heroic deeds, and those of her ilk, would never be forgotten, that they would never be lost in the sea of wrongs and injuries suffered by the Jews at the hands of the German and Polish evil-doers who in their ideological blindness, or driven by the basest instincts, willingly or unconsciously helped the hangmen? Besides, human nature would rather remember Evil than Good.

The little infirmary became too small and Mrs Maria rented two big houses, establishing a full-scale convalescent home. I admired that remarkable woman's talent for organization. When I came to see her achievement I found myself in spacious, sunny and airy hospital halls, usually fully equipped with nurses to take care of the patients, mainly our boys from the uprising who felt most comfortable there. They knew they were at home, there was no need to feel embarrassed. A cheerful song about the soldier who went to the attack and laughed at the rain of bullets because he had in his rucksack a spare heart in store was sung by everybody! They could feel comfortable and safe in Mrs Maria's home because that ingenious lady had acquired the right to mark her establishment with the sign of the Red Cross and the Germans feared to enter.

At the end of 1944 the food situation at Zakopane became very difficult. The action of the partisans hidden in nearby mountains and forests, aimed at derailing the trains to paralyze the German communication system, aggravated the food supply from Cracow and its vicinity. In granny's house, there was nothing to eat and I had to provide some food. I took two days' leave and set out with a group of professional women smugglers. In a small town, Miechow, near Cracow, I bought flour, peas, buckwheat and fats. I returned to Zakopane with a thirty-kilogram load. The Germans would often swoop down on food smugglers, but in spite of this danger I tried my luck many times until granny's pantry was fully stocked. Naturally all my friends were sure that my trips had been made solely for profit. Nobody ever guessed any connection between Eva and me. Since her arrival at Zakopane Eva had been bathed every Saturday by Mrs Zosia. One Saturday, as she was very busy, Mrs Zosia came up to me and asked shyly, 'Marysia, would you mind very much if I asked you to bathe Eva?'

There were not many Germans left in Zakopane by then since German rest-houses, orphanages and other establishments had been evacuated following the rapid Russian advance at the end of the summer. People said that during the occupation there had been so many Germans that the Polish language was hardly heard at all, and Poles were almost nowhere to be seen. Those allowed to live there were compelled to work for the Germans. The Nazis unleashed fantastical anti-Polish propaganda and succeeded in convincing backward Highlanders that they were not Poles but 'mountaineers'. The propaganda, backed by considerable terror

tactics, was able to create a misconception of 'Goralenvolk' (a
mountaineers' nation). It did not dispense, of course, with local
traitors among whom a Highlander, Krzeptowski, was of greatest
help to them. He enjoyed the confidence and esteem of other
Highlanders and many were lured by his poisonous propaganda. A
member of Goralenvolk would get more food on his ration cards,
more milk for his children, and would enjoy other privileges. This
Krzeptowski was sentenced to death by the Underground Organization and was later hanged by his fellow Highlanders from a tree
in his own garden.

In Zakopane we always got hold of illegal newspapers and we
learned from the English war bulletins that the war was coming to
an end. However, the German terror still persisted. Now and again
someone was arrested by the Gestapo and from time to time people
were carried away to Germany for forced labour. People still
received a summons to the Arbeitsamt. One night the Underground
Organization raided this labour office and burned all the registers.
The raid was successful but in the shooting that ensued, two
members lost their lives and their bodies had to be left behind.
Next day Mrs Zosia told me in secret: 'Just imagine – one of the
raiders was a Jew!'

23

The Last Round-up

A<small>T SIX O'CLOCK</small> on the morning of 9 January 1945, we were awakened by vicious kicking and banging at the door. I turned to the window and in the pale dawn light saw green uniforms. My first reaction was to try to escape but seeing how many policemen there were I understood that this would have been hopeless. Mrs Zosia opened the door and the house immediately filled with the all too familiar yelling and shouting. The Germans ordered her to bring out all the people who had come from Warsaw. I breathed a sigh of relief – so they had not come to fetch only me – it was a mass arrest. They inspected room after room and soon they were checking my papers. My Arbeitskarte proved of no use, neither did the certificate of exemption from digging trenches. I was arrested and put under the guard of SS men and Ukrainians, and we were all marched off to the Arbeitsamt where they checked our Kennkarte only and detained all former residents of Warsaw. We were bustled into a building which before the war had been the fashionable hotel Morskie Oko and were locked into the big ballroom. My female friends were in despair, yet I took the whole affair in my stride. My God, what evil could befall me now, at the end of the war and in Zakopane, the most fashionable of locations? I sat down on a comfortable chair and picked up some long-forgotten book. My attention was attracted by a young man nervously pacing the floor. He had an intelligent, firm face, but showed more fear than the rest of us. His woman companion seemed strangely familiar to me and I was certain that they were Jews. I looked around the hall but saw no more obviously Semitic faces. I waited, curious to see what would happen to us. The day went by and the night was also spent in the chair as we carried on waiting. The representatives of the Guardians' Council General (GCO) arrived next morning, bringing us a canteen with soup and coffee. I managed to see some armbands with the inscription GCO make their way from the arms of their legal owners to the arms of those arrested. In this way some of the detained, carrying the canteens, went out to freedom. At regular intervals the mugs with coffee which nobody drank were being brought in and more and more people, friends of the GCO, would leave our ballroom. I had no friends among the GCO dignitaries, no backing, so I had to think about a means of escape for myself.

From a seemingly friendlier officer from Alsace I learned that these arrests had been carried out under orders from Cracow, which had decided to make a thorough purge among the 'revolutionary elements'. Since all inhabitants of Warsaw as insurgents belonged to an undesirable element, they had to be isolated from the rest of the population before being sent somewhere deep into Germany. I remembered the appeals of Governor Frank in which he announced that the refugees from Warsaw would be given all possible facilities. Nobody else but Frank urged the populace to be generous to the stricken survivors, to give refuge, accumulate relief funds for them, and on top of that he initiated a public collection of money. I had never believed in the sincerity of German intentions and their sympathy always seemed false to me, but I never imagined that they would go to such lengths against people whose native town they had burned down. So till the last moment of their stay in Poland they offered us ample opportunity to study their perfidious character. Fearing the authorities from Cracow, no guard would free anybody, even for the largest sum of money.

We were informed that a Polish physician had arrived and would examine all who were sick. Having nothing to lose I decided to try this way out. I told the doctor that because I had a weak heart I was not fit for any work – besides I had to care for a little child. To back my arguments I put a sum of money on the table. The physician pocketed the money, and handed me a small chit of paper with the number '3' written on it. Anxiously I asked him: 'Doctor, what does this mean?' 'It is all right, you will not go to Germany.' I was astonished to see the same scrap of paper with this mysterious number '3' in the hands of all those who had undergone the medical examination. I saw that the 'generous' man had made a fool of us, for the number indicated fitness for labour in Germany. (I have kept this little paper with the doctor's signature till today, as a souvenir.) Having learned about my impending deportation, Mrs Zosia brought me the rucksack containing my belongings and some food.

By now I was furious. On 10 January I was to be sent somewhere near the front to die. This seemed foolish when perhaps within a few weeks the war was going to end. No, I said, and refused to give in, resolving to escape by hook or by crook. Taking care to study the layout of the building and to watch when the guard was changed, I waited for an opportune moment to flee. Morskie Oko had been a big hotel with many porters, waiters and maids. We were imprisoned in the ballroom on the ground floor. The doctor had been on duty on the first floor. The upper floors were occupied by the Germans and were inaccessible to us; the second floor was guarded by four policemen. I asked for permission to see the doctor. I had noticed that in the confusion they had not written down the names of persons already examined. I had in fact to be accompanied by a guard to the physician's office, but I succeeded in getting rid of the tired officer on the half-landing. I passed two maids armed with brooms, pails and dusters who were allowed to go to the upper floor. One of them had already gone up the steps but the second put her things to one side. I saw her ingratiating herself, chatting flirtatiously with one of the soldiers. Without a second's hesitation I took off my coat and rucksack and thrust them under a door. Picking up the pail, dusters and brooms I boldly passed the policeman guarding the entrance to the upper floors. Struck by a moment of fear I would have hesitated but my legs had already taken me to the third floor. Then I left the maid's paraphernalia and climbed higher.

On the fourth floor there were small, neglected rooms. I entered the first one I came to which resembled a cell, empty and quiet. I spent several hours there but was going blue with cold as the windows were paneless and I had no overcoat. Night was falling and I felt terribly worn out. Deciding to look for another shelter I eventually found a room with two beds in it – one was empty while the other was piled high with mattresses. I overcame the temptation to lie down on that empty bed, cover myself with a mattress and go to sleep. Instead, I put one mattress against the open window, then unscrewed the bulb as a precaution against anybody switching on the light. After locking the door I pocketed the key. At last I then crawled in between the heap of mattresses on the other bed. Almost suffocating and feeling very uncomfortable I moved a little closer to the wall in the small space between it and the mattress. Now at least I could breathe. Feeling more comfortable I fell asleep in this strange position.

I have no idea how long I slept but I remember being awakened by the sound of steps in the corridor. I recognized the sound of heavy soldiers' boots. Somebody opened the door with a key. I felt that two people had entered, a soldier and perhaps one of the maids. The mattress stifled their conversation but I heard the maid's vulgar laugh. Fortunately the visit did not take long for soon I heard the sound of the door locking. I fell asleep again. I awoke feeling terribly hungry. Very cautiously I crawled out of my hiding-place. It was already daylight. I looked at my watch – seven o'clock. This meant that I had been under arrest for forty-eight hours, all the time without food. Somehow I felt very calm. I expected that the Germans would soon take their victims away, after which I would be able to regain my freedom. At about nine o'clock I heard noises coming from the street, German shouts and curses. I guessed that the prisoners were being led out. Then I waited for another hour before emerging into the corridor. Everything was calm. Both lower and first floors were quiet and had been cleaned by the maids. All was still in the hotel with no guard to be seen. In the place where I had left my coat and rucksack I found nothing, but it did not matter.

The main thing was that I was free! Calmly and peacefully I walked out into the street, heading straight for home. Bone-weary, incredibly hungry and grubby, I nevertheless felt elated. Passers-by stared at me with undisguised curiosity, because a woman wearing neither overcoat nor head-covering on 11 January presented a very strange sight indeed, but I was so enjoying my freedom that I was almost oblivious to the cold.

I was in excellent spirits as I entered Mrs Zosia's house. At the sight of me the good lady had a fit of the giggles, for I apparently looked very funny with bits of straw from the mattresses stuck all over my hair. I was so tired and hungry that I could not even think about the loss of my belongings. Food and rest were uppermost priorities at that time. The consequences of my flight did not scare me in the least, since the Germans had not made any lists of the people they had arrested. Therefore they could not possibly know who had been deported and who had remained. Mrs Zosia went into town to glean some news, returning within half an hour with my rucksack and overcoat. It turned out that the GCO had instructed their men to search the ground and first floors of the Morskie Oko and to store everything they had found with the Organization.

In the middle of January the Russian offensive forced the Germans to leave Zakopane. The Gestapo were the first to leave, hurrying to vacate the houses and villas, rushing off madly in the direction of Cracow. It was a grand sight. The SS men remained in their headquarters until the last moment, the long black flag waving dully outside. The remaining SS men and German civilians who had failed to leave on time, finding all ways of escape cut off by the Russians, committed collective suicide. A small detachment of German motorcyclists dashed through the town. Their task was to demolish all objects of military importance but in fact they only managed to blow up a few little bridges over mountain rivers before they fled.

On 29 January, when I went down into the kitchen I was met by two Russian soldiers. Zakopane was occupied by groups of partisans who had come down from the mountains. All day long Russian troops marched through town. I watched their comings and goings in disbelief, as the moment to which I had been looking forward for so many years had finally arrived. The realization that the Germans had left never to return had still not fully sunk in. I would never again hear their horrible bullying orders, their shouted insults. 'Los! Fort! Schnell! Laufen! Dreck! Schwein! Verflucht!' were almost the only words we heard issuing from the mouths of the 'Kulturträger' (purveyors of culture) for nearly six years.

In spite of the hard times we now experienced, the lack of sufficient food and other essentials, I felt happily relieved to know that I would be able to contact my husband and parents, to resume a normal life at last. Unfortunately, the Post Office was not yet functioning while the damage to all bridges on the road to Cracow meant that it was impossible to leave Zakopane. I waited for another few days before setting out on foot, on 8 February, intending to make it back to Warsaw. The only capital I took on my journey was biscuits and sugar as our money had lost all its value, and no one would accept it. Later on, every holder of a Kennkarte received 500 zloty, regardless of the amount of money he or she possessed. The rest could be deposited in a bank for their eventual revaluation.

The first 60 of the 110 km to Cracow, I covered on foot. Later I was given a ride on a Russian tank, then a military lorry. After four days' journey I reached Zawiercie where I remained for two days, working at a Refugees' Relief Point at the railway station. Many people were to be seen on the road treading wearily on their way. Prisoners from German jails, camps, those returning from forced labour, prisoners of war. The largest group, however, comprised the inmates of Auschwitz, or what was left of them – shadow-people, scarecrow-like skeletons, teenagers, old men, little girls tinged bluish-green – all this pathetic humanity trudged on resolutely, filling the highways in order to put some distance between themselves and the places of their martyrdom. Everyone wanted to hurry back to their dear ones, their homes or huts, their own normal life. Although I had thought I had seen all the horrors there were to be seen here at this Relief Point, I was still to discover new proof of German bestiality.

I saw starving people who were unable to hold a cup of coffee in their wretched trembling hands and they had to be fed like babies. I saw men with ears cut off, men without noses, a woman with two big holes in her cheeks burned through by her tormentors. The sight of all this made me forget my reason for hurrying back to Warsaw. I wished to help these wretches, if only in some small way. To think that these scraps of brutalized humanity were the 'healthy' prisoners who had had the strength to leave Auschwitz under their own steam. The sick or dying had remained in the hospitals, too weak to be moved.

At Zawiercie railway station I saw the British prisoners of war. They looked different, dressed in their neat uniforms, well equipped, healthy and well fed. During the course of my conversation with them I learned that at Auschwitz the English were treated better than the French, but that the worst lot fell to the Russians. Obviously the Germans treated the British and Americans with more respect. I met a soldier wearing the emblem of the Union of South Africa. He was from Johannesburg, about to fly back home via Odessa. I told him that I had a brother living there who had had no news from me for almost a year. He promised to visit him for me and deliver a letter which I quickly wrote. He really was true to his word, for well before foreign mail service was resumed, my brother had received my letter together with the photograph of Eva that I was able to include.

Upon reaching Cracow, I made for the Jewish Committee. There I again encountered the sickly inmates of Auschwitz, camping in every available space in rooms, corridors, stairways and doorways. Still dressed in their paper-thin striped pyjamas, wooden clogs on their bare feet, were people from France, Italy, Hungary, Romania and all other countries clamped by Hitler's iron fist. (The majority, however, were Jews from Poland.) Men from different countries, speaking different languages, coming from various social classes, looked equally broken and in dire misery in this crowded place. For the most part they had nowhere to go, no relatives, no friends, no money. They did not know what to do, where to turn. Freedom is surely a great thing, but once it has been achieved, one realizes the need for so many other things and then liberty loses its desirability.

During the second half of February I went back to Warsaw again. The crippled city welcomed me with its stumps of burnt-out buildings and I walked through streets gazing left and right, stunned at the ghastly destruction; when we had left the city there had still been some undamaged buildings left standing. I distinctly remember Mokotowska with buildings untouched. On the day of our departure, 6 October, the building in which I had lived had been intact. It turned out, however, that after our exodus, when the city was deserted, special squads of Germans had gone from building to building, setting them on fire. Thoughtless, useless destruction, *ars pro artis*. Till that day the word 'vandalism' had been the term used for aimless ravaging. I knew then that this expression was out of date, far too mild for the mindless sadistic destruction wrought by the ardent followers of Hitler. It was a terrible ordeal for me to walk the streets that formed an inextricable part of the memory of my former life. 'Warsaw, my dear Warsaw, you are in my dreams', sang a crippled invalid, leaning on a crutch made from part of a green fence. He sang amidst ruins and still smouldering ashes, expressing the mood of all returning Warsovians at their first sight of their native city in ruins.

My pre-war flat was burnt out. Although one of the buildings belonging to my father was still left standing, I could not remain in the debris-strewn city even though I had the chance of obtaining a small flat in the property. I wished to visit my friend Halinka who was living in Praga, a difficult place to reach, as a cart took one only as far as the banks of the Vistula. There was no bridge open to the public, but since the river was frozen solid we were lucky enough to cross over on foot. I found Halinka cheerful as ever. She made light of her hardships, laughingly carrying buckets of water for all household use, no mean feat. In the evening all she had was a tiny oil-lamp, but none of this dampened her spirits. She had already registered her name on the barristers' list to start practising. From her I gleaned all the latest news about our mutual friends who had managed by good fortune to survive the uprising.

I looked up Aniela and her son. Both had been through many harrowing experiences. Aniela, penniless and sick, had been living somewhere deep in the country but with the help of some kind people had made a full recovery. Now in excellent health once again she had regained her usual sunny disposition. Her marvellous capacity for organization, coupled with her vast store of long-suppressed energy, were now coming to the fore. She had started arranging her financial affairs and was already receiving rent from her properties. From poor Cinderella she once again changed to re-emerge as a well-groomed, smartly dressed woman. As always, she knew everything there was to know about everyone we knew. There was no end to her store of anecdotes and tales. She told me that the handful of our friends and acquaintances who had survived the uprising had somehow or other settled into a new life. Her stepsister Marysia, released from a prisoner-of-war camp, was now in France, about to marry an American officer. With great difficulty I tore myself away from my dear friend, for I had to settle into my new life as well.

I went to Kalisz, my parents' home town. The town was damaged but abounding in empty apartments left by German tenants who, under the new law, were allowed to live only in basements or attics. I found a large, comfortable, spacious apartment with great ease. As I had every hope of making a decent living, all that remained was for me to return to Zakopane to fetch Eva. It was hard for Granny to part with the child to whom she had grown so attached. Eva, for her part, had no desire to leave her in order to accompany me. 'I want to remain with Granny – won't go with Aunt Marysia', she sobbed repeatedly.

I drove to Poronin to take leave of Mrs Maria who was happily reunited with her husband, newly returned from the Stalag camp. All 'her' children and 'her' grown-ups, whom she had sheltered and protected, had survived the war. As I embraced this generous, great lady for the last time, I wanted to say something memorable to express my admiration and gratitude. I felt very silly as such phrases as 'thank you' or 'I am grateful' could not serve to convey in the smallest degree what I felt I owed her. Cursing the ineptitude of my powers of expression on such an occasion, I merely held her tightly in silent warm embrace. She understood without the words having to be spoken. I vowed that somehow, my future actions would speak louder than any words to express my everlasting gratitude to her.

I settled in Kalisz, rescuing my own identity once more. My name was placed on the barristers' list and I was open for business. When, for the first time in five years, I found myself in court, facing the judge, I felt as though all that horror had never occurred, as though I had stood on that dais just the day before.

Soon I was put in touch with my husband. I learned that he was now serving with the Polish Division of the British Army. I communicated with my parents who had luckily outlived the war in Palestine. From them I learned that my sister-in-law and niece, having by some miracle survived as well, were also living in Palestine. That story of the Polish railway guard who had seen the 'foreign' Jews led away by the Germans into the forest was true. Unfortunately our fears about their fate proved to be largely well founded. When ordered out of the train to march through the woods, some of them committed suicide by swallowing poison, while the fate of the rest turned out unexpectedly different. As 'foreign' citizens they were placed in Bergen-Belsen concentration camp where, though the conditions were horrible, they were treated better than the other inmates. They were neither beaten nor compelled to work.

At the Polish Hotel in Chmielna Street where my sister-in-law had applied and paid for her journey to Palestine, several Jews, considering United States papers to be safer, had registered applications for America against higher payment. After three months' stay in Bergen-Belsen those with American documents were sent off under the pretext of being exchanged for Germans in America, to the envy of all the rest. Later it turned out, however, that instead of America, they had been sent to Auschwitz where they had been murdered.

My sister-in-law went to Palestine from Bergen-Belsen but enquiries about my brother's disappearance proved fruitless. No evidence of his whereabouts could ever be found – he had vanished without trace. It seemed certain that he had been murdered by the Germans.

It was hard work persuading Eva that I was her mother. At last, when she started calling me 'Mamma', I felt she did so only to please me. In her heart she was not convinced at all. After about six months I was sent a photo of my husband. I told the child that this was her father, giving her the picture to hold in her little hands. She took the picture and kissed it, whispering 'I am so happy, I have a daddy now, but please, tell me the truth – where is my mamma?'

Endings

THUS THE JOURNAL ends. With the end of the war came the gradual piecing together of everyone's lives as connections were remade and families learned whether their loved ones had survived or perished in the European holocaust. Ruth learned what had happened to her husband George. Within days of the German invasion of Poland the Polish army was routed and in disarray and George, as Ruth mentions in the journal, escaped to Soviet-held Lithuania. Some months later he was arrested by Soviet soldiers and sent to a prisoner-of-war camp in Siberia. They were put to work in the nickel mines near Murmansk. For two years he was not allowed to wash or change his clothes and he and other prisoners helped each other remove lice from their bodies. No one told the hungry, frozen and often sick prisoners that the German–Soviet pact had ended, but some time thereafter it became clear that they were being left largely to their own devices. So George set out with a few of his fellow prisoners across the frozen Siberian wastes with no proper shoes and just felt pads to protect his severely frostbitten feet. They passed through Tashkent and Uzbekistan, where he contracted malaria, through Iran and Syria and gradually made their way across Europe until they reached Italy. There George joined General Wladyslaw Anders, the commander of the Polish forces in the Middle East and Italy, and in 1944 served as an officer during the capture of Monte Cassino, where the Polish forces distinguished themselves in a decisive victory in the Italian campaign of the war.

From May 1945 Ruth's name appeared on a list of advocates in Poznan noting that she was practising in Kalisz. She also registered herself with the Jewish Central Committee in Poland in the hope that family overseas would be looking for her. Ruth's sister Esther, who had lived in Palestine since the 1930s – and who lives there still – learned that her sister and niece had survived, not from any list but through a letter from her brother Isadore in South Africa. 'I fainted', Esther relates 'and Izhak [her husband] poured water over me. I calmed down and went to tell our parents who wanted to thank God for their salvation. Father went to synagogue to pray and mother gave all her savings – about £500 sterling – towards a commemorative stained-glass window.'

Isadore's letter to Esther followed his emotional meeting with the South African soldier who immediately on his return to South Africa came to tell his story to Isadore. He had been taken prisoner by the Germans in Italy and sent to a prisoner-of-war camp in Upper Silesia. From there he had escaped and made his way to the Russian lines. As he and a number of other rescued prisoners were journeying along, they came to a small Polish station, Sokova, where the train stopped for a short time. Among the voluntary helpers there giving food to the rescued prisoners was a woman who asked whether any of the prisoners came from South Africa. When the soldier replied that he came from Johannesburg she was overjoyed. She had a loaf of bread with her and seeing how emaciated he looked, she insisted that he have it. She gave the soldier a photograph of Eva and wrote a message on the back:

Beloved Brother
I'm taking this opportunity to send the photograph of Eva. I trust that this soldier will arrive before I could get a letter to you. Get in touch with father. Please send the papers for our departure at once. Don't think of the cost because I haven't any strength left to fight on. The date of my birth is 29 May 1910. Eva's is 4 March 1940. Send it to the poste restante, central Warsaw because I haven't got an address as yet. Joseph is no longer alive. Nor Eda nor Tusia. We have no family at all. Nor any

acquaintances. Hurry with those papers. Where is George? I kiss
you and your family.

The photograph showed Eva wearing a crucifix around her neck,
which had helped to camouflage her true identity in the years of
living as a Polish Catholic child. In 1944 Isadore's wife had given
birth to a daughter whom they named Ruth in memory of the sister
they thought dead in the holocaust.

As Ruth recorded in her journal, once the war was over and she
had settled in Kalisz, she again began practising as a barrister and
regaining her self-respect and position in society. When two Polish
soldiers arrived with a letter from George, the husband she had not
seen for many years, urging her to join him in Italy, she was most
unsure of what to do. Eva explains that: 'To leave with one suitcase
and go into the unknown was really daunting for her. She had been
away from him more than she had been with him and with the
experiences each had had, she knew they would both have
changed.' A convoy was leaving the day after the letter arrived and
with borders closing down all around her she grasped the urgency
of the situation. With the single suitcase she was permitted and
with no papers, Ruth and Eva set off. Eva, who was then six years
old, remembers going across thick snow and getting stuck and that
her mother wanted to jettison the suitcase. 'But I said no, I wanted
my dress.'

When after considerable delay and many weeks of travelling,
Ruth and Eva arrived at Bari in southern Italy where they expected
to be reunited with George, he was not there. They had taken so
long to come to him that he had gone to look for his wife and
daughter and it was more than a week before he returned. Eva
remembers thinking 'This is a strange man. But it was about my
mother that I had nightmares. In fact for very many years I had
these nightmares about my mother not being my mother. I don't
think I was convinced for a very long time that she was indeed my
mother.' It was at Bari that Eva, the child of the Warsaw ghetto
and of war, saw her first fried eggs. 'I thought it was a fantastic
luxury and a treat.' And her father taught her to ride a bicycle.

Ruth's driving need was to see her parents and to take Eva to
meet them. Thus she made plans to travel to Palestine with Eva,
again leaving George, who had not yet been demobilized. It was a

time when the British, who held Palestine as a Protectorate, were not allowing those without papers to disembark from the boats bringing the war damaged of Europe to the country. Thus the journey to Israel proved to be yet another harrowing experience, as those without accreditation threw themselves off the boat in their desperation to reach a safe haven or simply because they could no longer bear the sight of guns trained at them after their long journey away from Nazi Europe. Eva recalls that when her mother lay dying she had recurring and terrible visions of people jumping overboard.

The first thing Ruth did on arriving in Israel was to rent a typewriter. During the year that she was there, 1946, she did little else than sit at the typewriter, working on this journal. On its completion and before she left Israel it was translated into English and then hidden away. Eva was sent to school where she joined the first class at Carmel college in Tel Aviv, opposite her grandparents' apartment. One of Eva's earliest memories is that she was not allowed to go out because the English soldiers enforced a curfew. All in all Israel was not to be an entirely happy experience for Eva. The settler community of Palestine, as it then was, was in every way informal and without pretension. All the refinements of a middle-class European life had been shed in the brasher more ideological climes of the Middle East. Despite the holocaust and the war, Ruth remained primly bourgeois in her values and style. Eva was dressed like a doll, with ribbons and bows, and sent exquisitely attired to school where the young Israelis romped casually in shorts and scruffy shirts. According to Eva's aunt Esther, this created problems for Eva and one day during playtime, she was chased by some of the children. She fell, hit her head and lost consciousness. She was rushed to the Hadassah Hospital in Jerusalem where she lay in a coma for several days. Esther remembers that Ruth never left her side, and kept crying 'I saved her from the Nazis, could it be possible that I lose her in Palestine?'

Independence was about to be declared in Israel and with it unrest and war were brewing. Ruth's father determined that it would be best for Ruth and Eva to leave: they had had enough of war. His insistence that they go on their way led to an extraordinary family feud. Esther, the younger sister and an ardent Zionist, was equally adamant that Ruth and Eva should stay. 'I absolutely could not understand how she could leave our homeland and how could she leave her parents', Esther explains, and argued her case most forcibly. 'It made my father so angry that he slapped me for the first time in my life. I cried, kissed his hand and begged for forgiveness.' But it took Esther another three years to forgive Ruth. She did not go to see them off and for three years she did not communicate with the sister whom she had once thought dead.

George, still with General Anders' army, was about to be demobilized in England where Ruth and George would meet. Eva was sent to boarding-school in Sevenoaks in rural Kent because it was felt that she needed to learn English, while her mother took a room in St John's Wood in north-west London. Finally in 1947 the small family of George, Ruth and Eva were reunited and together they boarded a ship for South Africa, where Ruth's brother Isadore waited to welcome them to a new life.

'It was a good place to lick your wounds', Eva observes; 'whatever discomfort they had was of my mother's making.' Ruth had changed dramatically. Before the war she had been an ardent and observant Jew while George had been Jewish in a more nominal sense. Their reactions to their wartime experiences had wholly reversed this balance. 'Father had become much more Jewish and mother much less so. In fact mother was positively phobic about being recognized as Jewish. She did not want us to mention to anyone that we were Jewish, never to use any words of Yiddish or to do or say anything which might reveal Jewishness.' And yet on Friday nights they would go to Ruth's brother Isadore, who had remained orthodox, for the sabbath and would celebrate other Jewish festivals too. 'It was like treading on eggshells. It did not work to any logical pattern, she had become irrational. Admitting to being Jewish was like choosing to be persecuted, choosing death.' George felt that declaring his Jewishness was a defiant affirmation of life, a difference of opinion which was the source of great friction between them.

Everyone who knew Ruth agreed that she was a quite remarkable survivor, that she was brave, dramatic and clever, with great spirit and foresight. But those very qualities and her life experiences made her enormously demanding in everyday life. Eva says of her mother: 'She was totally unsuited to a life without crisis. She found it very difficult to adjust to the mundane. Everything had to be a crisis, had to lead to something. You could not relax, she was impatient with ordinary social intercourse, you had to do something. She had no time for trivial talk.' For both parents the immediate post-war years were tough. Eva thought they experienced difficulty in adjusting to an ordinary life together, having struggled so long alone. Each felt somewhat left out of the other's experiences which had been so out of the ordinary, so filled with horror and fear, and each had fought so hard to survive in such different circumstances. It was inevitable with two equally dominant and powerful person-alities that life inside the family was often explosive but there was a great love between them. Eighteen months after George's death in 1977, Ruth died and they were buried side by side with the epitaph on their joint headstone 'Together in death as in Life'.

In September 1949 Ruth and George had a second child, Annabelle. Annabelle was the only member of the Altbeker-Cyprys family not to have lived through the holocaust but this very fact meant that she has spent her life feeling like an outsider in her own family. 'I always felt excluded', she explains. 'The fact that I could not speak Polish added to the problem. Every time people from the past appeared in their lives I could not participate.' The question Eva always poses is 'Would you really have wanted to share what we experienced?' In other ways too their lives diverged as Ruth's attitude to each of her daughters was very different. After Eva's fall in Israel she was never allowed to play any sport or indeed to do anything in a very independent way. Annabelle by contrast was positively encouraged to take up sport and to reach out into the world.

Annabelle's birth had other consequences for Ruth. She had been given an exemption for her legal training in Poland and had obtained a grant to study Roman Dutch law which she needed to practise law in South Africa. The birth of her second daughter and the realization that she would need to master Afrikaans if she were again to succeed as an advocate finally brought an end to her days as a lawyer. George had set up in business selling scarves and jewellery and needed Ruth's help. She became very actively involved and went on frequent buying trips to Italy and France.

The strict obedience which had been expected of Ruth and her siblings by their parents was also expected by Ruth of her children although she often flouted other conventions of motherhood.

According to Eva and Annabelle their mother never understood the needs of children: to her the big issues related to survival; all else mattered little. Thus birthdays were largely ignored. Eva explains, 'You might wait until midday for a present on your birthday and even then it was quite likely to be something that was already in the house and had simply been wrapped up as a gift.' Ruth would say to Eva, 'I would have killed myself for you, what do birthdays matter?' She frequently forgot to collect Annabelle from the crèche where she had placed her. Both sisters attest to Ruth's half hour of 'kissing time', the only time allocated to hugs and kisses regardless of how the children might feel.

Eva completed her schooling in South Africa and was sent off to finishing-school in Switzerland for a year. Thereafter Ruth told Eva she had to study medicine and thus she enrolled at the University of the Witwatersrand in Johannesburg. She endured it for a year before switching to what she really wanted to do, which was languages. In her last year there she met Alex Panas, a half-Italian, half-Greek refugee from the Congo who arrived in South Africa with his grand piano and little else. According to Eva her parents 'could not stand the sight of him. His crime was that he was not Polish.' After completing her degree and to escape the oppression of parental disapproval, Eva went to Austria and then to Italy, where she and Alex married. She then enrolled at the University of Turin, where she obtained a PhD in languages.

The killings at Sharpeville and the growing feeling of instability and unrest in South Africa decided Ruth and George to move on again. The family had never really fitted into South Africa. 'We were too strange,' Eva recalls, 'too European, with such different life experiences from those around us. Everyone had so much, swimming-pools and possessions and the children expected to be given everything.' Part of the problem lay with Ruth herself, unwilling or unable to make concessions to different life styles. Ruth ignored the lesson Israel might have taught about the import-ance of a dress code for a schoolchild and insisted on making Eva's school uniform. The only resemblance it bore to the official uniform was a shared colour, otherwise it ensured that Eva would again stand out as markedly different from the other children. Ruth had also insisted that Eva develop the upper-class English accent which she had begun to acquire in Sevenoaks, sending her to elocution lessons to reinforce it. Thus it was no surprise that Eva should remember that 'I was always considered a bit strange. There was indeed nobody like me.' It was only when Eva went to Switzerland, to the finishing-school, that she felt herself fitting in for the first time in her life. 'Everyone was different there, they came from all over the world and being worldly wise and exotic was suddenly valued,' Eva remembers.

Today Eva is a tranquil, easy-going person with, in her own words, 'an enormous capacity to be very, very still', a quality which helped ensure her survival in the ghetto. She has no first-hand memories of her youth and Ruth's journal constitutes the only memory Eva will ever have of those dark and terrible years. That is the daytime Eva. For on countless sleepless nights Eva is plagued by unformed terrors when, shivering and sweating, she is doubled over with pain, as a high-pitched whine whistles through her head. 'In the morning I remember nothing of my dreams except the unremitting terror. I can feel things but I can't remember. My poor memory has probably been my salvation. Unlike my mother I have no recall of dreadful past events. Her recall was almost frightening and she could recite whole passages of Goethe and Schiller in German as well as lengthy tracts in Latin, which she spoke fluently.' Eva's conviction that her inability to remember has saved her from a more traumatic life is reinforced by what she knows of the life of Jasio, who lived in the prostitute's flat in Gentile Warsaw with his mother Aniela. After the war Jasio and Aniela went to live in Canada, where he became an outstanding scholar and now works as a successful psychiatrist. Eva observes that 'Sadly most of his own life is tempered by what he remembers of those six years. He has vivid and debilitating recall of that dreadful time. Even now on seeing me he evokes endless experiences shared but not remembered by me. He still shakes his head in alternating wonder and disapproval at my blank stares when he asks "Don't you remember . . .?" He deeply believes that we are the sum of our memories, our past. I realize that I am, if not the wiser for my deficiency, definitely happier than he will ever be.'

According to Eva, her mother wanted to live in London and have an account at Harrods, the two things which symbolized stability and class for her. In 1963 she fulfilled her ambition. Annabelle, who had been at Roedean, one of the top private girls' schools in

South Africa, was moved to Roedean in England. The Altbeker-Cypryses bought a large house in Heath Drive, Hampstead, and invited Eva and Alex to come from Italy to live with them. Annabelle did well at school and then read law at the London School of Economics. She now practises as a solicitor in London. Neither sister married Jewish husbands and neither Eva's three children nor Annabelle's two have been brought up as Jews.